A-Z BOURNEMOUTH

CONTENTS

REFERENCE

A Road — A35

B Road — B3064

Dual Carriageway

One-way Street
Traffic flow on A Roads is also indicated by a heavy line on the driver's left.

Road Under Construction
Opening dates are correct at the time of publication

Proposed Road

Restricted Access

Pedestrianized Road

Track & Footpath

Residential Walkway

Railway — Station — Tunnel — Level Crossing

Built-up Area — ST. IVES — PARK

Beach

Local Authority Boundary

National Park Boundary

Posttown Boundary

Postcode Boundary (within Posttown)

Map Continuation — 24 — Large Scale City Centre — 4

Airport

Car Park (selected) — P

Church or Chapel — †

Cycleway (selected)

Fire Station — ■

Hospital — H

House Numbers (A & B Roads Only) — 83 96

Information Centre — i

National Grid Reference — ⁴10

Park & Ride — Marshes End — P+R

Police Station — ▲

Post Office — ★

Safety Camera with Speed Limit
Fixed cameras and long term road work cameras. Symbols do not indicate camera direction. — 30

Toilet:
without facilities for the Disabled
with facilities for the Disabled

Viewpoint

Educational Establishment

Hospital or Healthcare Building

Industrial Building

Leisure or Recreational Facility

Place of Interest

Public Building

Shopping Centre or Market

Other Selected Buildings

SCALE

Map Pages 6-73
1:15,840 4 inches (10.16cm) to 1 mile 6.31cm to 1km

0   ¼   ½ Mile

0   250   500   750 Metres

Map Pages 4-5
1:7,920 8 inches (20.32cm) to 1 mile 12.63cm to 1km

0   ⅛   ¼ Mile

0   100   200   300   400 Metres

Copyright of Geographers' A-Z Map Company Limited

Fairfield Road, Borough Green, Sevenoaks, Kent TN15 8PP
Telephone: 01732 781000 (Enquiries & Trade Sales)
01732 783422 (Retail Sales)
www.az.co.uk
Copyright © Geographers' A-Z Map Co. Ltd.
Edition 7 2012

2 **KEY TO MAP PAGES**

Ibsley

B3081

Romford **Verwood** *Ringwood Forest*

6 **7** Ebblake

River Allen

B3078

Stanbridge

Blashford

Inset Page 10 **Three Legged Cross**

Woolsbridge

Ashley Heath

Moortown

B3082

Hillbutts

Furzehill

Colehill

Pilford

10 **11** **12** **13**

West Moors

St. Leonards

Kingston

River Avon

Sturminster Marshall

Little Canford

14 **15** **16** **Stapehill**

Trickett's Cross

River Stout

Wimborne Minster

17 **18** **19**

Ferndown

A338

A31

East End

Lambs Green

Merley

Canford Magna

Longham

West Parley

Bournemouth Airport ✈

20 **21** **22** **23** **24** **25** **26** **27**

Corfe Mullen

Bearwood

Kinson

Ensbury

Hurn

A350

Hillbourne

Broadstone

West Howe

East Howe

Moordown

Charminster

Jumpers Common

Lytchett Minster

B3067

36 **37** **38** **39** **40** **41** **42** **43** **44**

Upton P+R

Canford Heath

Newtown

Wallisdown

Winton

Littledown

Iford

A35

A351

Turlin Moor

Oakdale

Branksome

Pokesdown

Boscombe

Tuckton

54 **55** **56** **57** **58** **59** **60** **61** **62**

Hamworthy

POOLE

Parkstone

Westbourne

BOURNEMOUTH

Southbourne

LARGE SCALE 4 POOLE TOWN CENTRE

Poole Harbour

68 **69** **70**

Canford Cliffs

Poole Bay

LARGE SCALE 5 BOURNEMOUTH TOWN CENTRE

Brownsea Island

Sandbanks

ISLE OF PURBECK

A351

B3351

Corfe Castle

Studland

Studland Bay

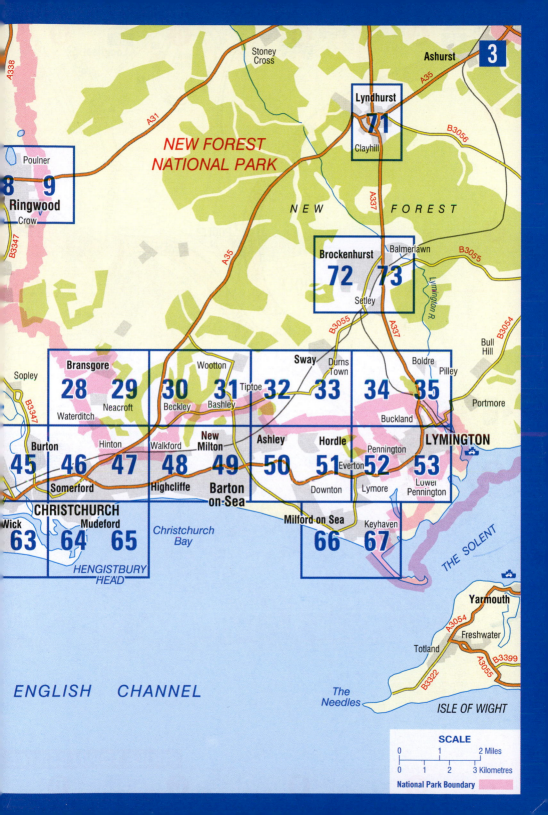

POOLE TOWN CENTRE

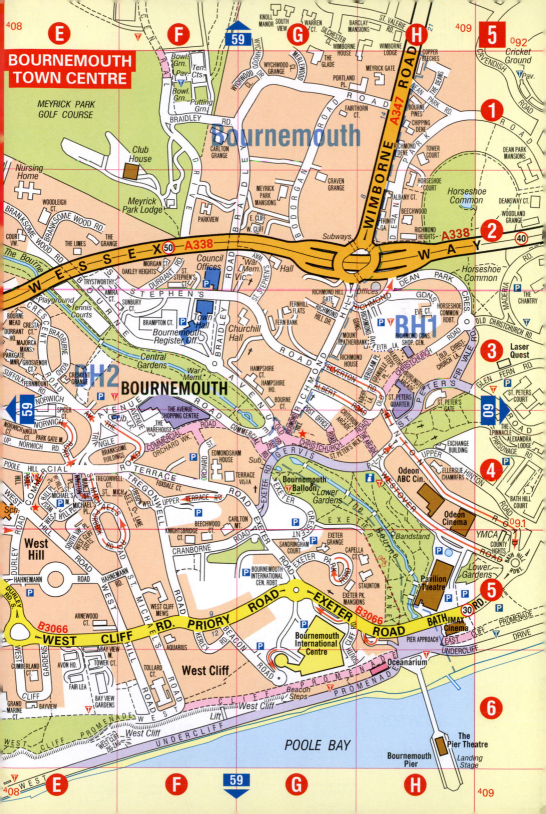

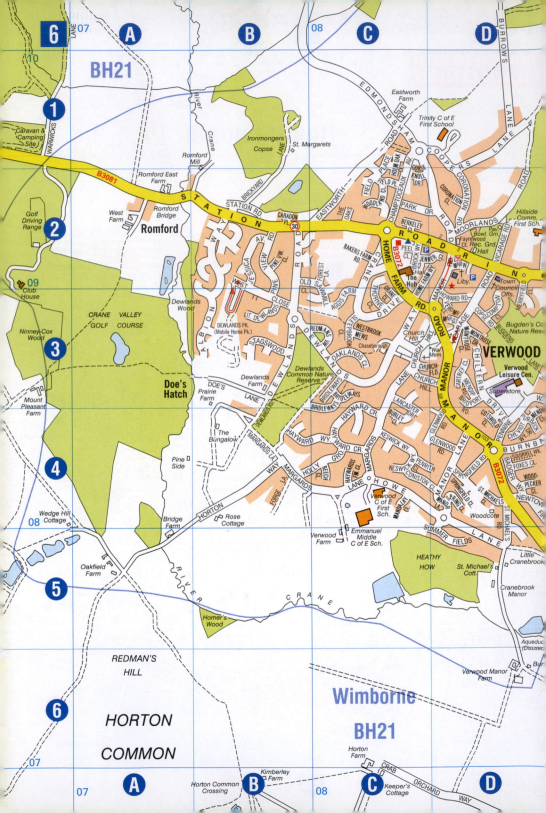

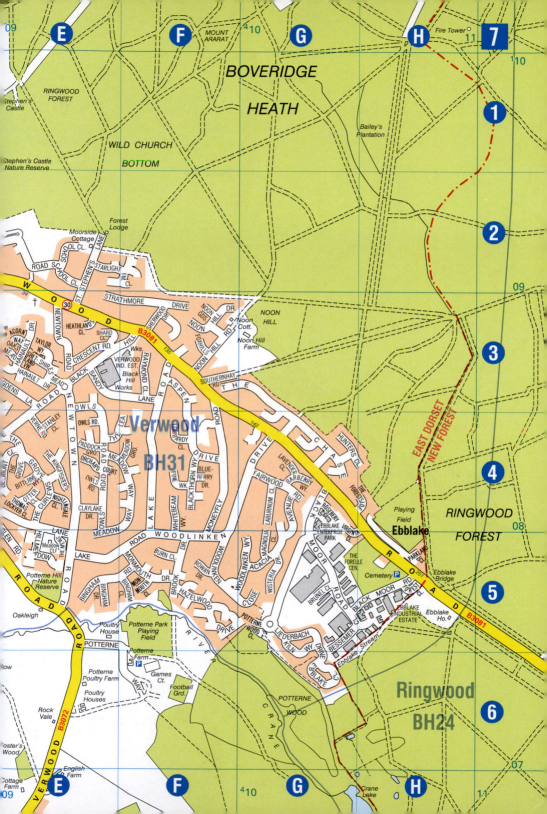

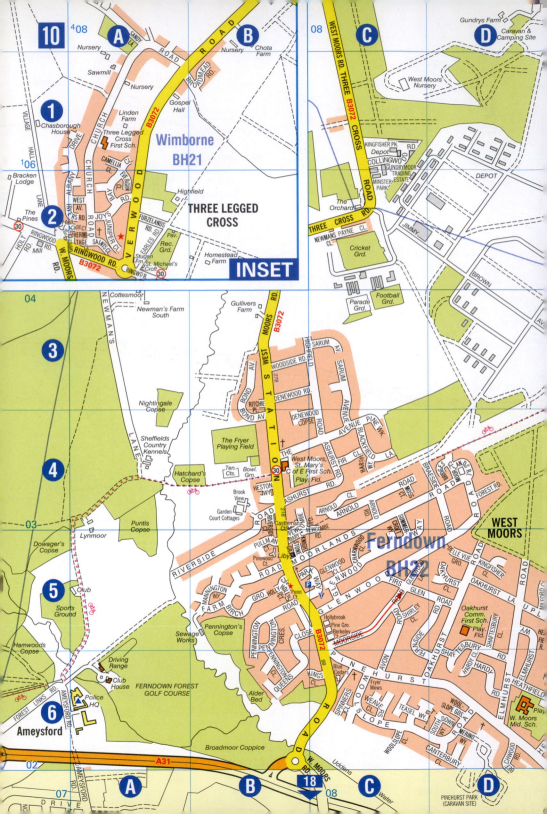

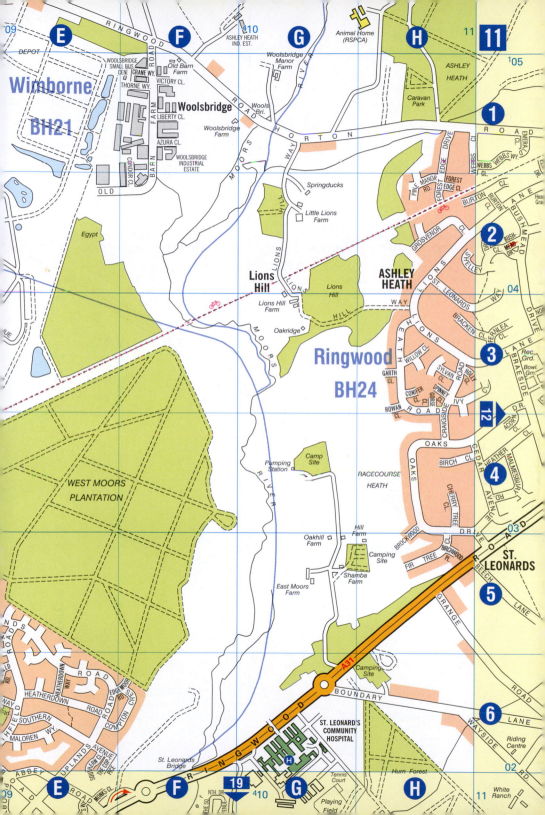

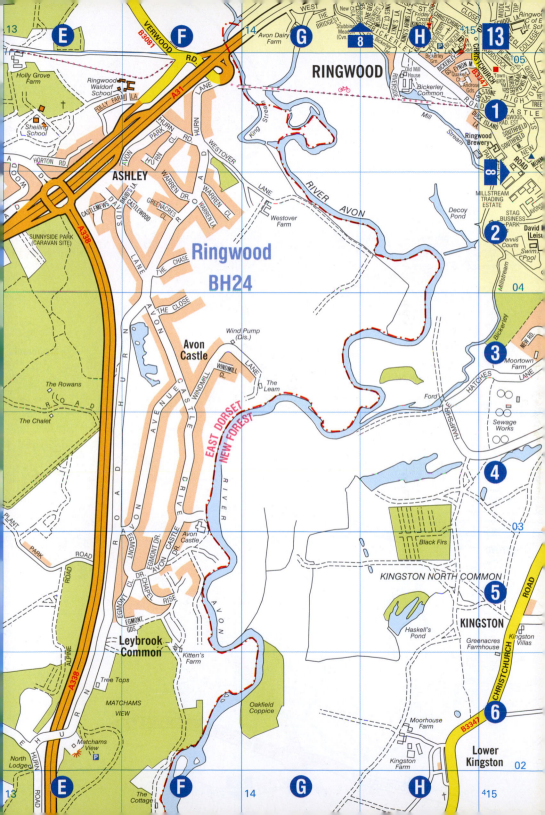

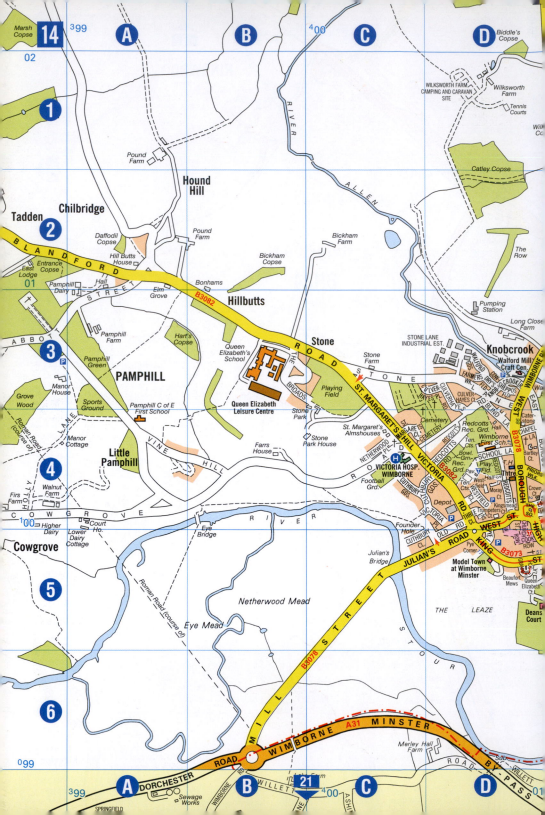

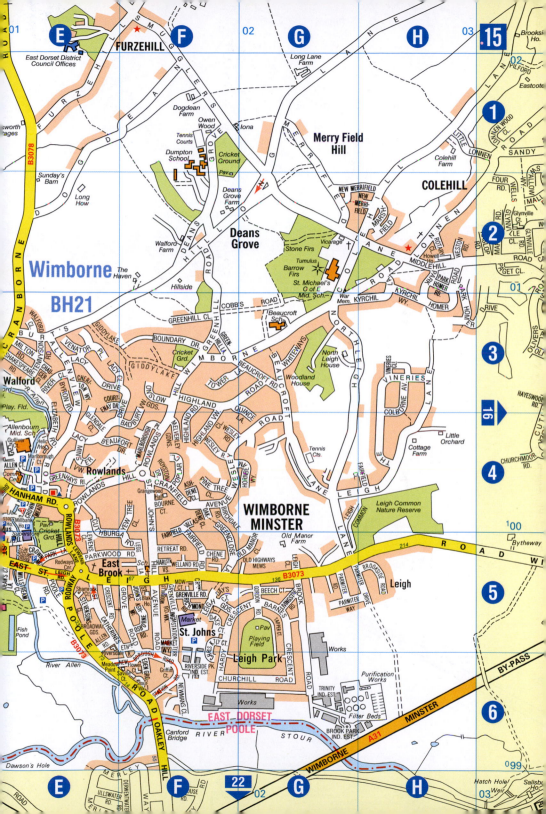

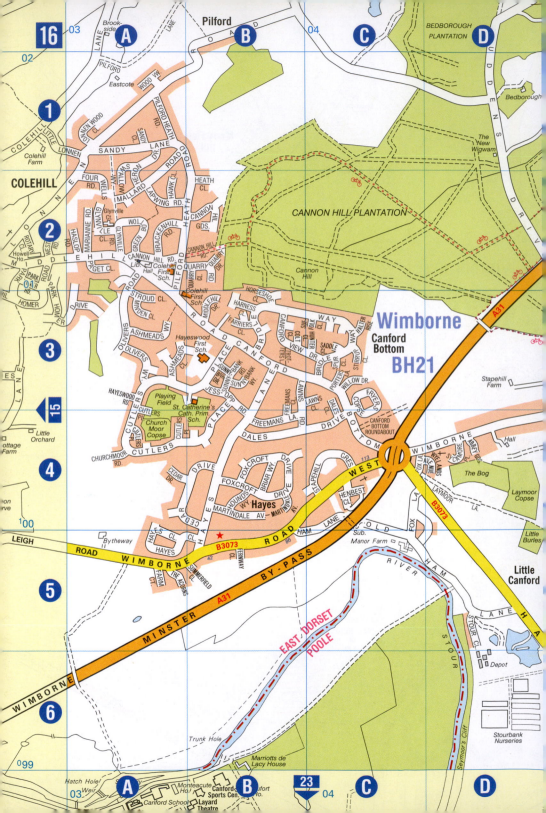

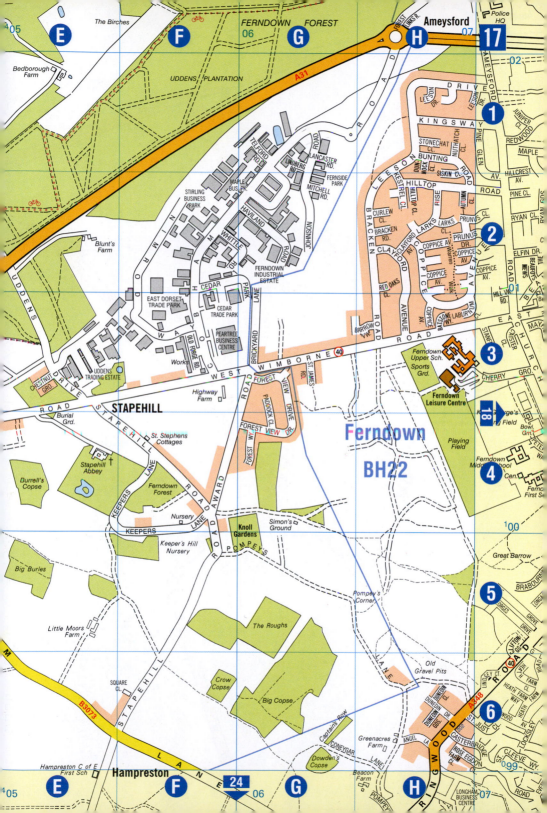

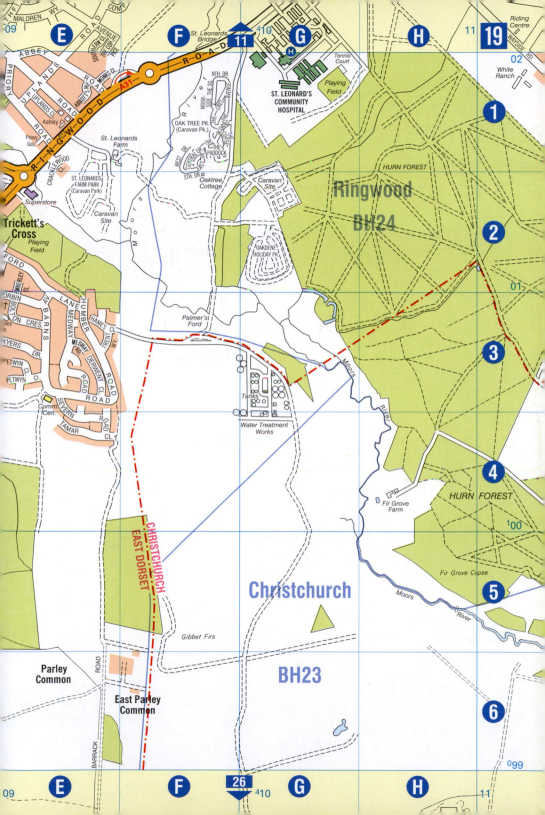

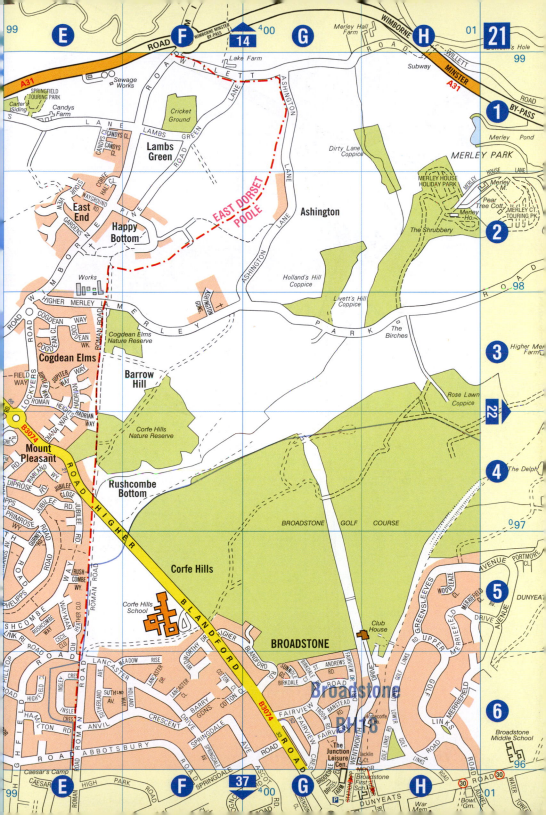

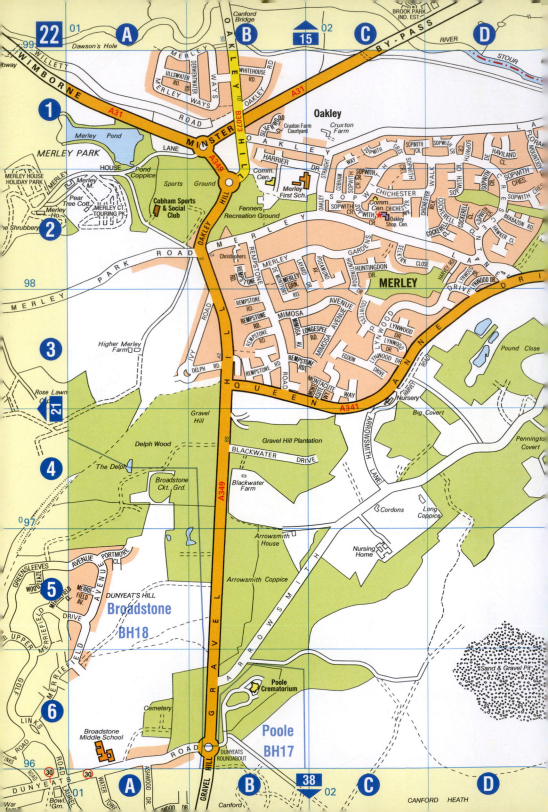

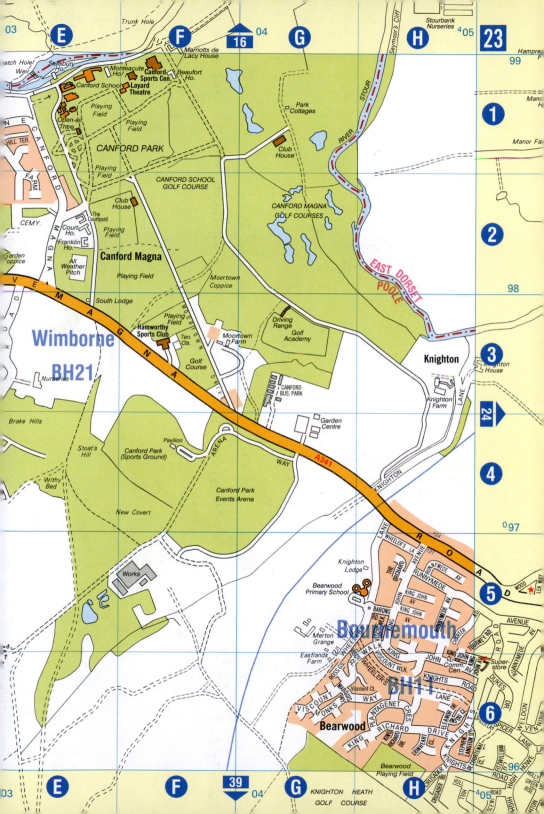

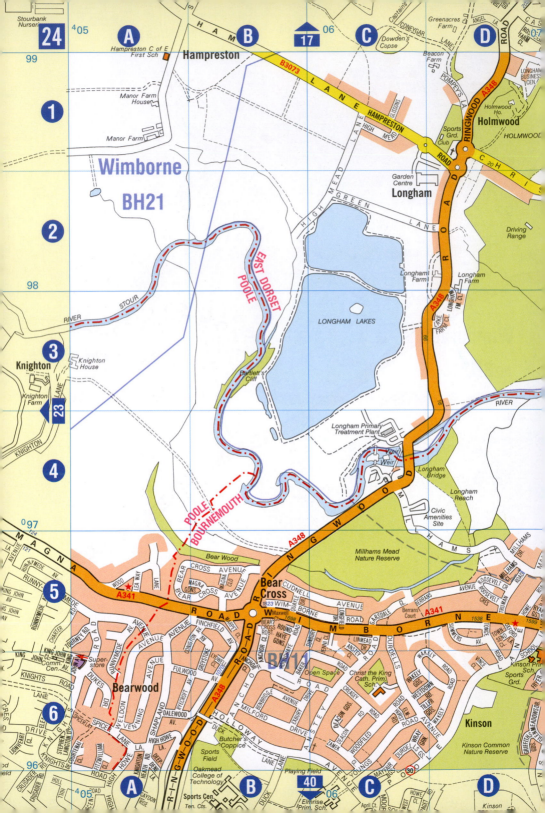

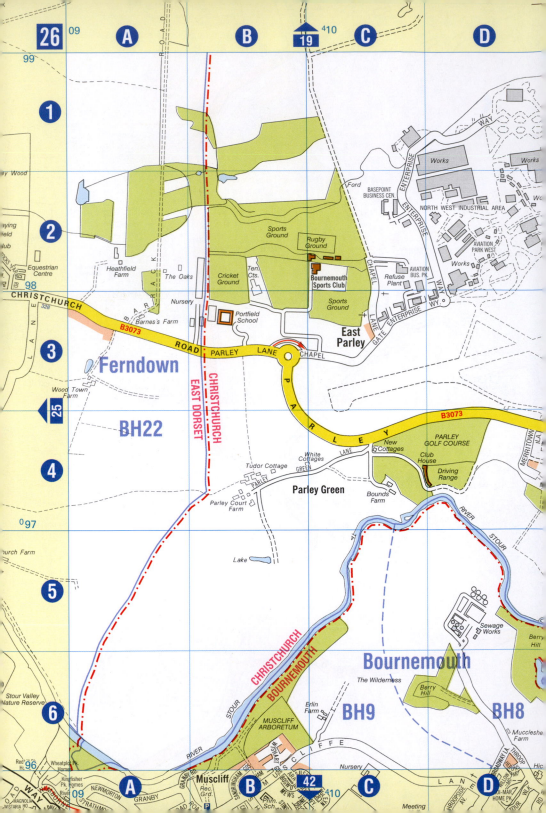

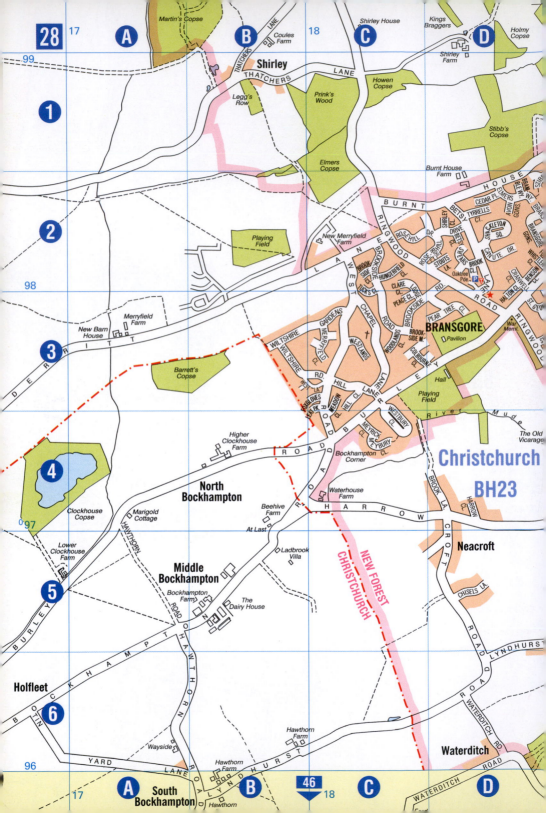

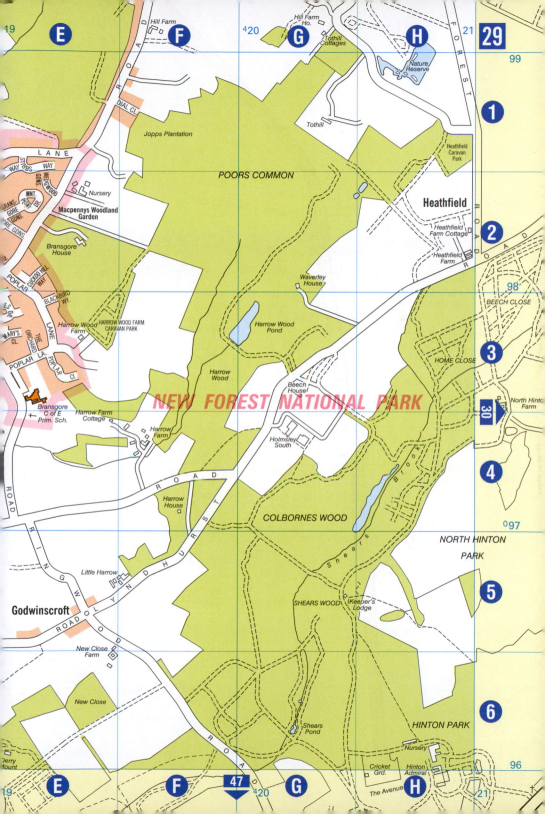

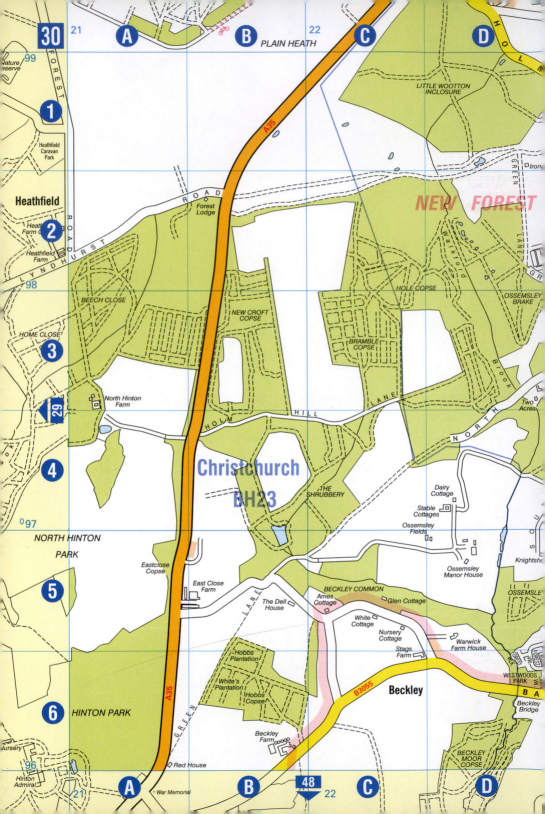

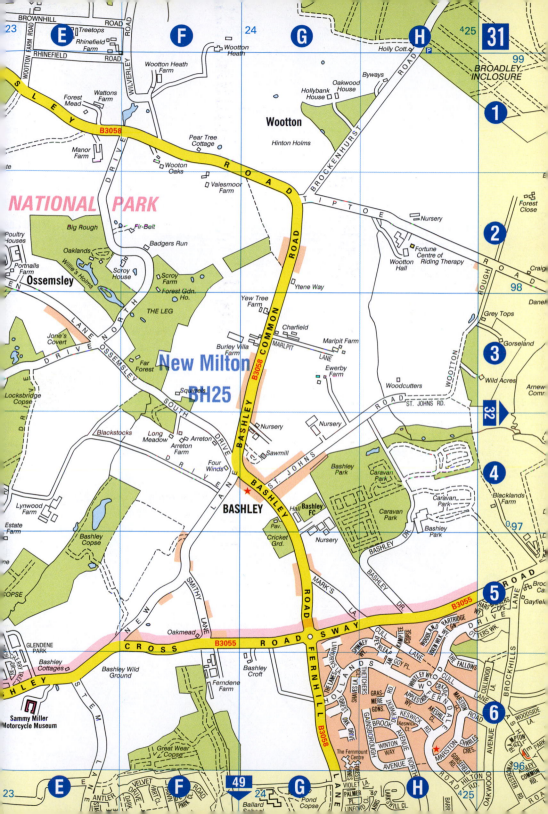

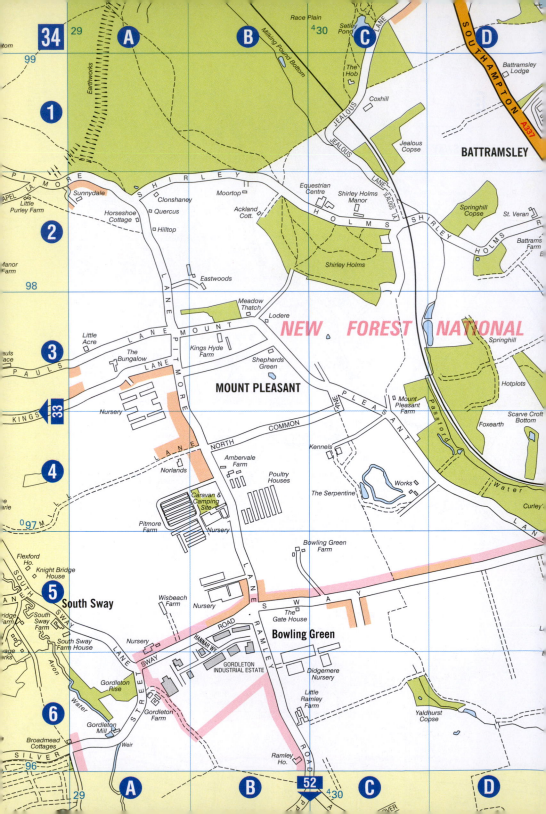

99

A **B** **C** **D**

Race Plain

Milking Pound Bottom

Setley Pond

SOUTHAMPTON

A337

1

Earthworks

The Hob

Coxhill

Battramsley Lodge

Jealous Copse

JEALOUS LANE

JEALOUS LANE

BATTRAMSLEY

PITMORE LA

CHAPEL LA

Sunnydale

SHIRLEY

Moortop

Clonshaney

Quercus

Hilltop

Ackland Cott.

Equestrian Centre

Shirley Holms Manor

HOLMS

SHIRLEY HOLMS LA

SHIRLEY HOLMS

Springhill Copse

St. Veran

Battrams Farm

2

Little Purley Farm

Horseshoe Cottage

LANE

Manor Farm

98

Eastwoods

Meadow Thatch

Lodere

NEW FOREST NATIONAL

Springhill

LANE MOUNT

3

Little Acre

The Bungalow

PAULS

Pauls Place

LANE PITMORE

Kings Hyde Farm

Shepherds Green

MOUNT PLEASANT

PLEASANT

Mount Pleasant Farm

Hotplots

Scarve Croft Bottom

Foxearth

Passford

KINGS

33

Nursery

LANE

COMMON

NORTH

Kennels

Water

Curley

4

Norlands

Ambervale Farm

Poultry Houses

The Serpentine

Works

0 97

Pitmore Farm

Caravan & Camping Site

Nursery

Bowling Green Farm

Flexford Ho.

Knight Bridge House

SOUTH

5

South Sway

Wisbeach Farm

Nursery

LANE

S W A Y

The Gate House

Bowling Green

SWAY

South Sway Farm

Bridge Farm

ridge Farm

vage arks

South Sway Farm House

Nursery

STREET SWAY

ROAD

Hannah Wy.

GORDLETON INDUSTRIAL ESTATE

RAMLEY LANE

Didgemere Nursery

Yaldhurst Copse

6

Avon Water

Gordleton Rise

Gordleton Farm

Gordleton Mill

Little Ramley Farm

Broadmead Cottages

SILVER

Weir

ROAD

Ramley Ho.

96

29

A **B** 52 **C** **D**

4 30

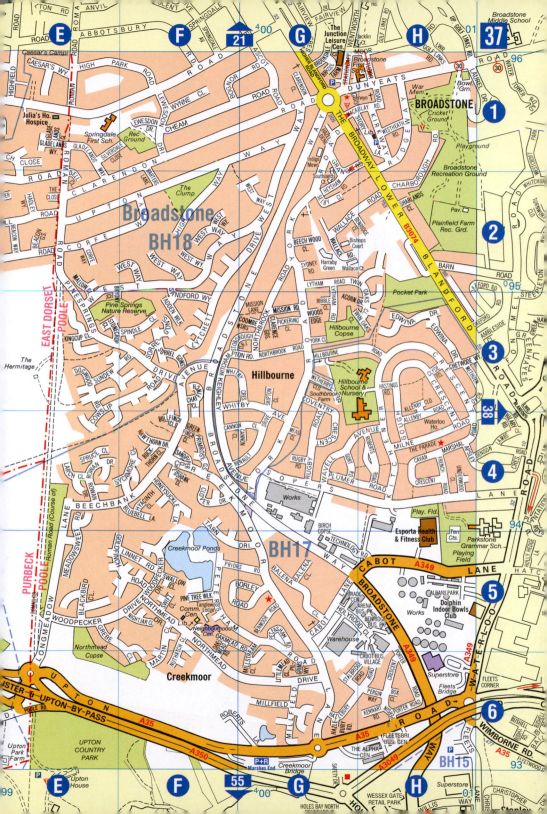

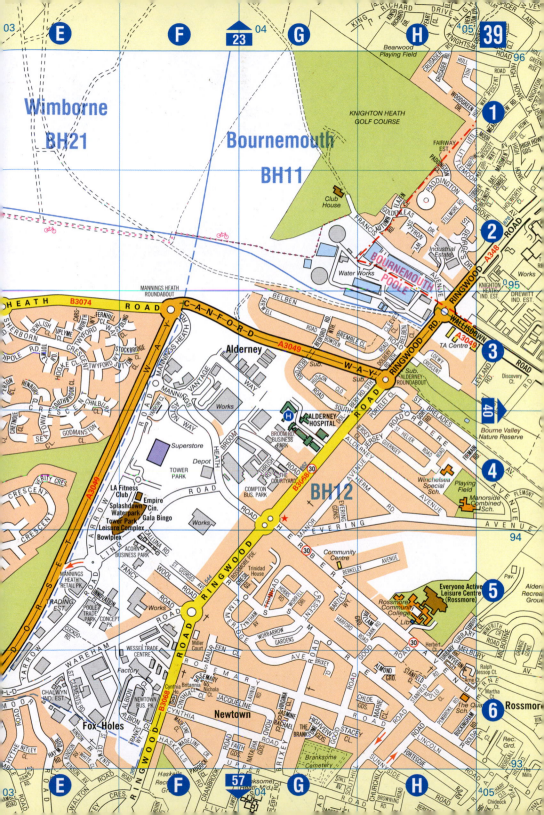

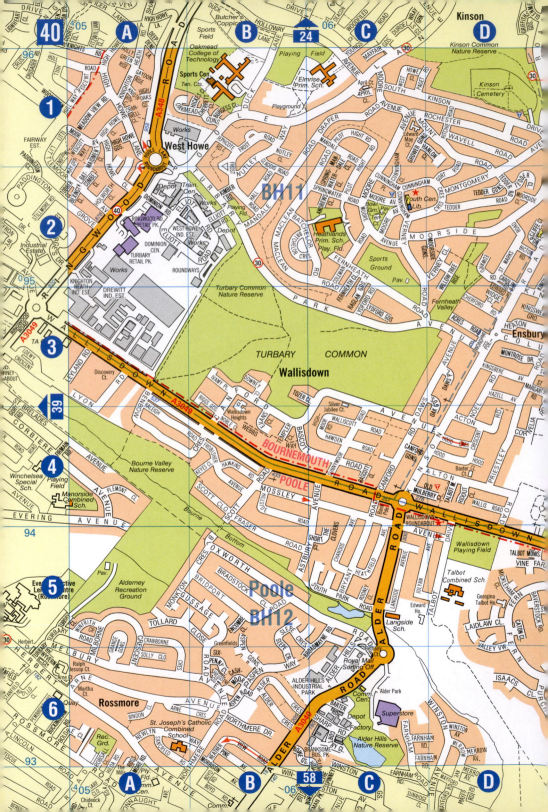

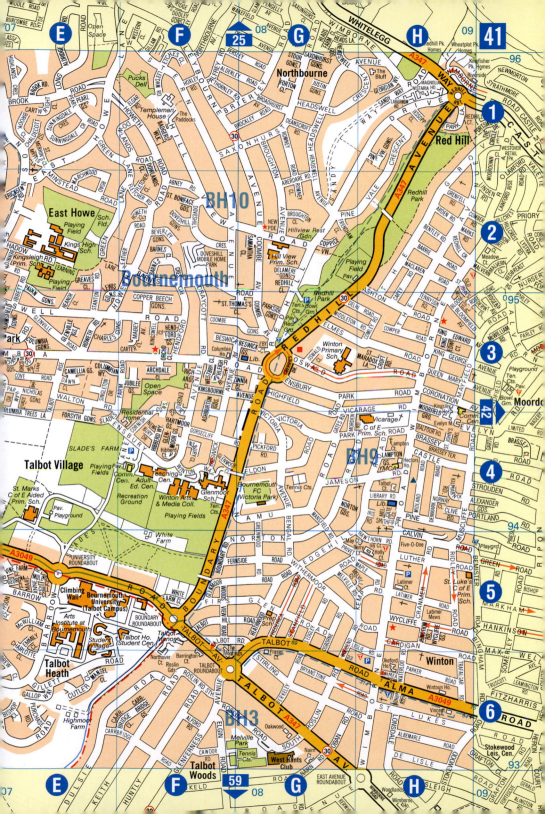

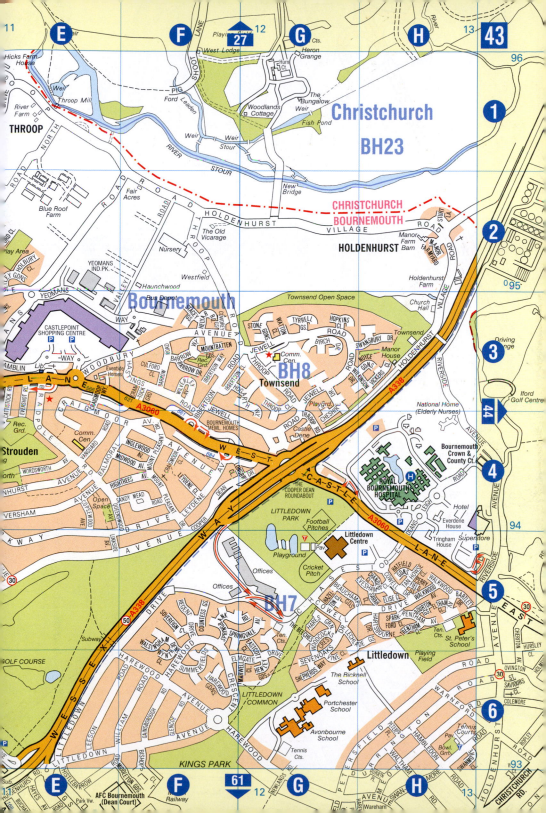

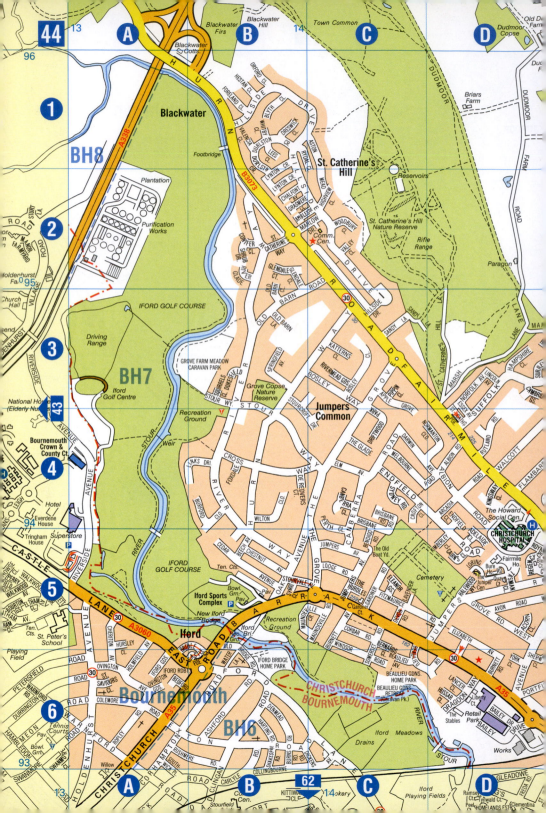

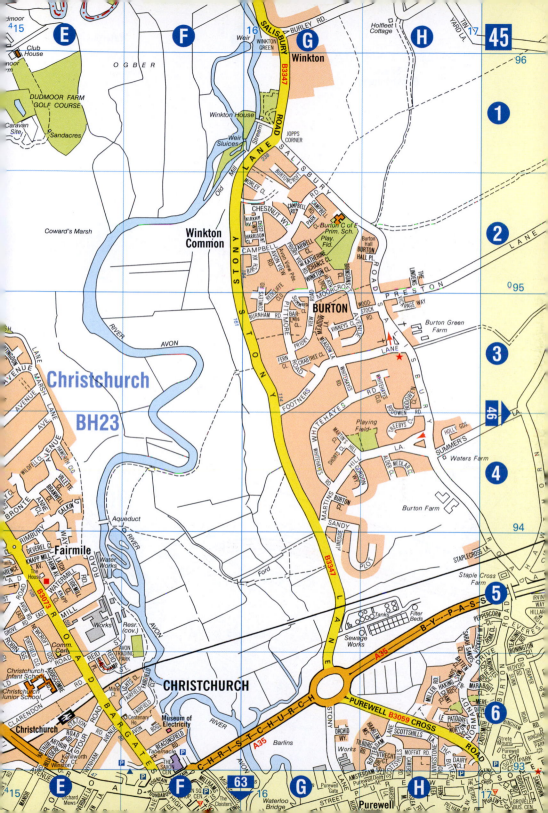

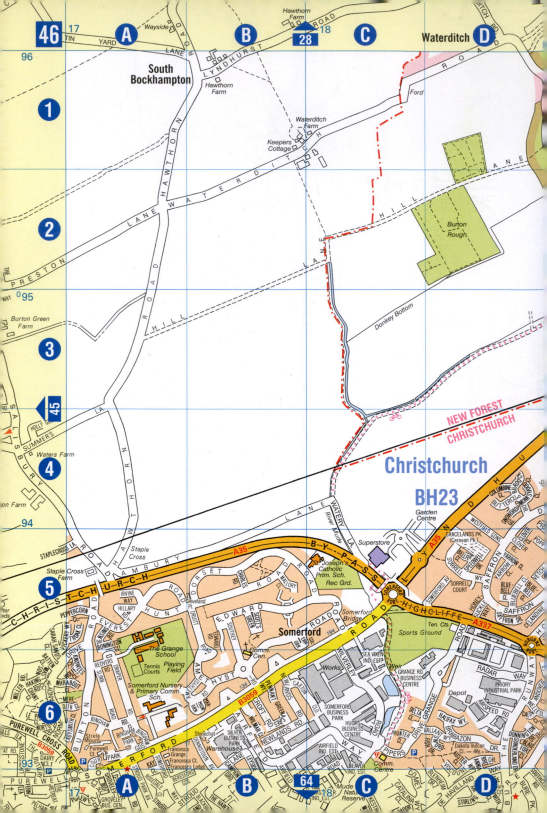

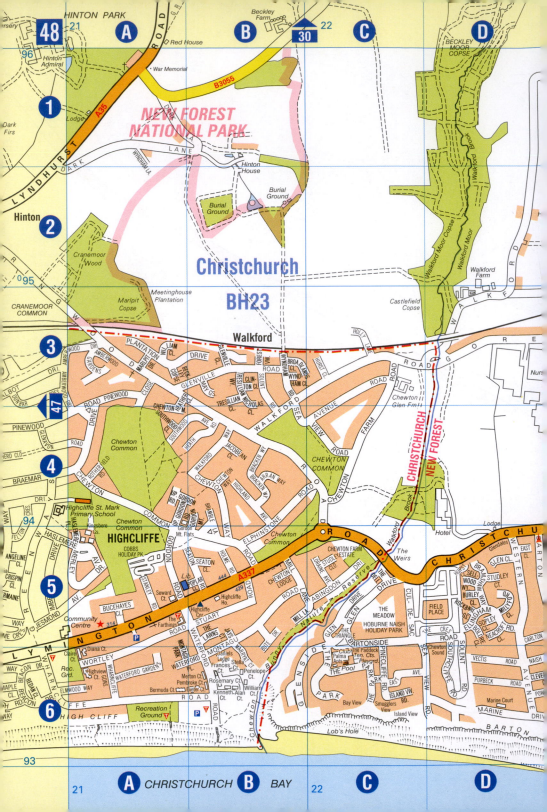

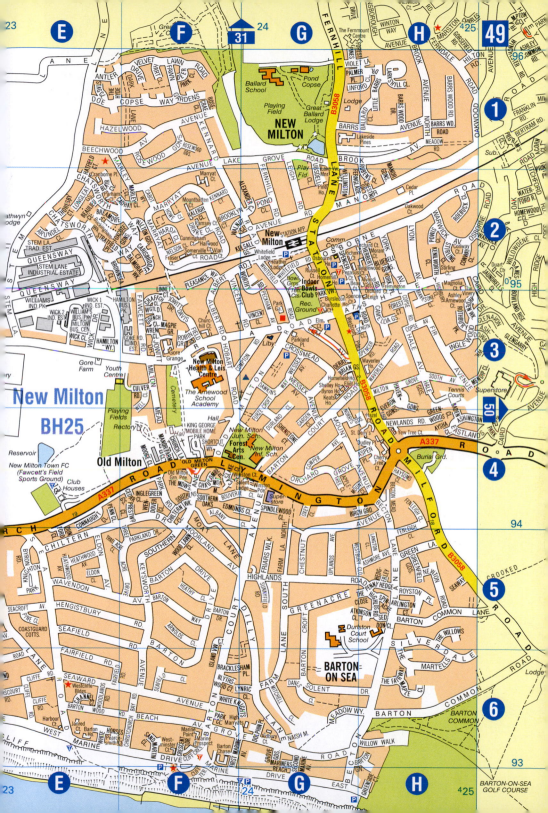

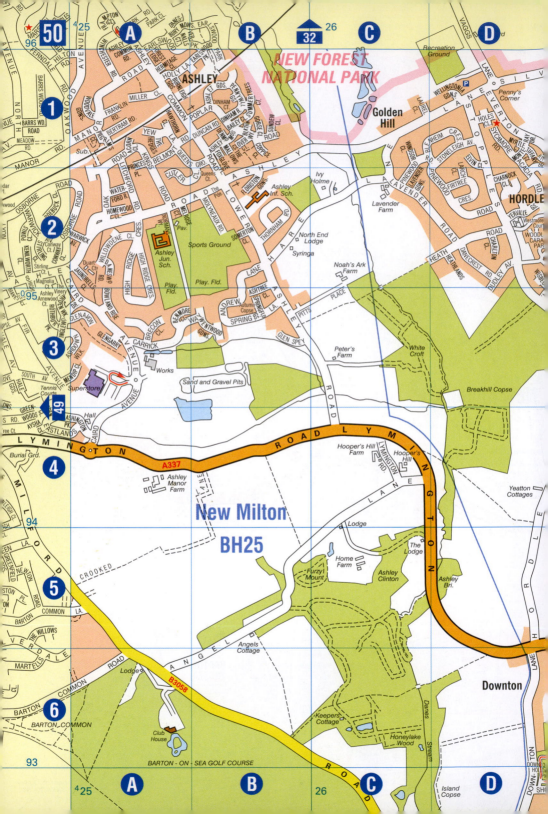

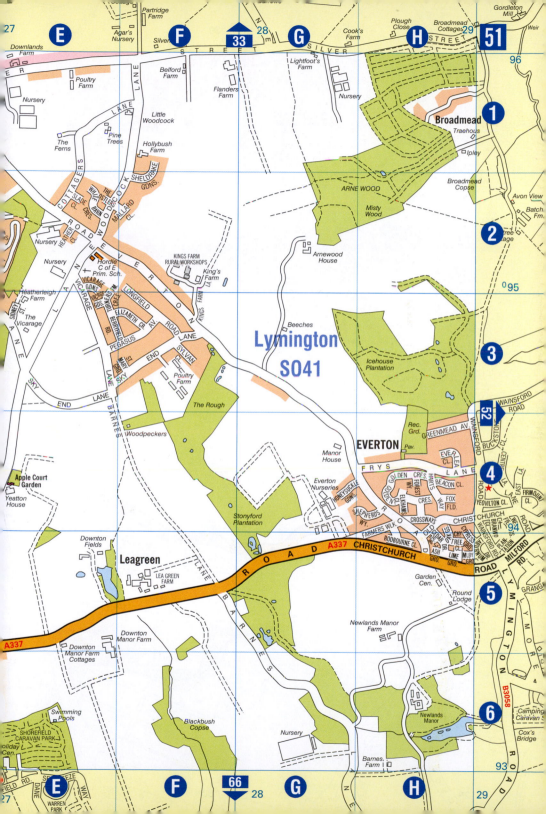

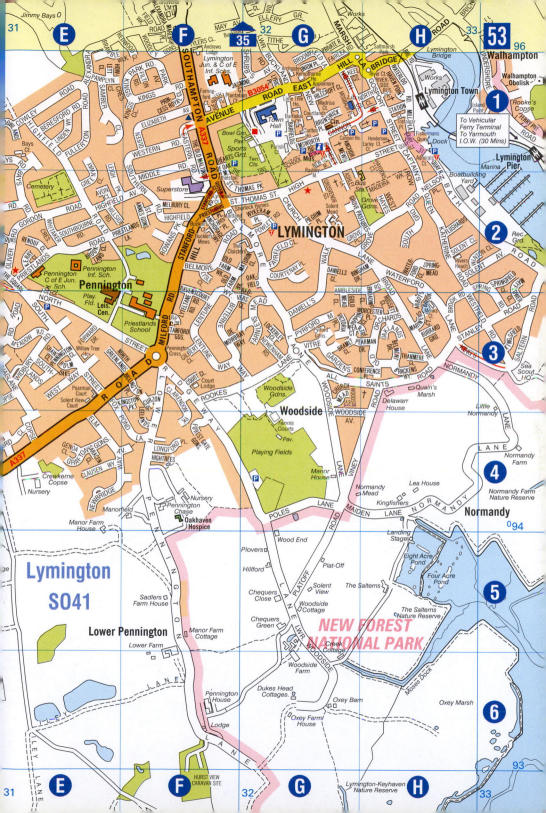

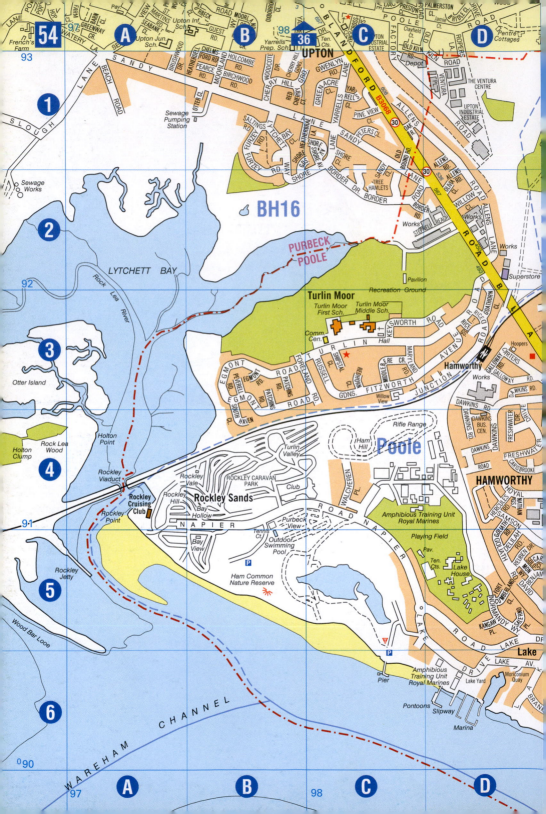

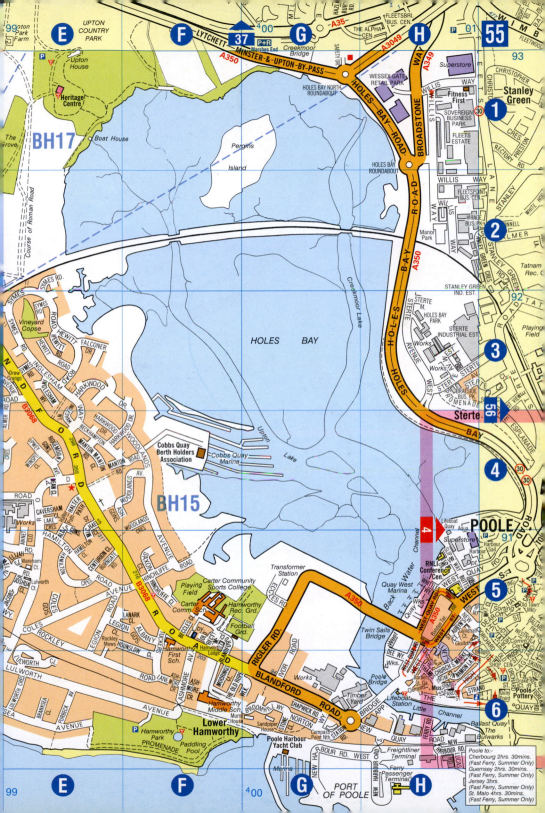

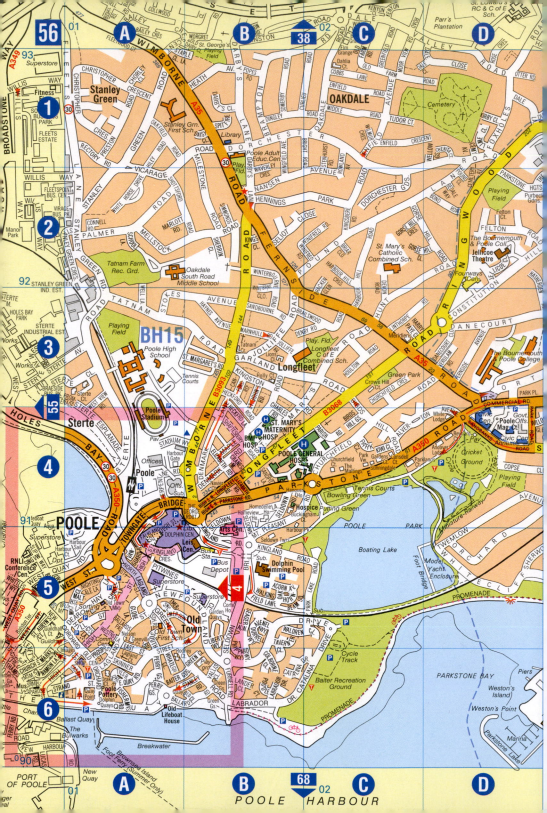

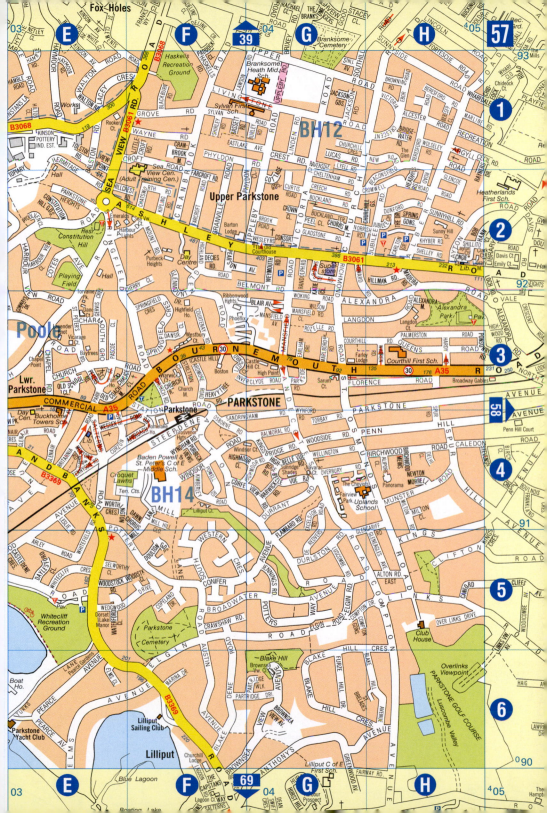

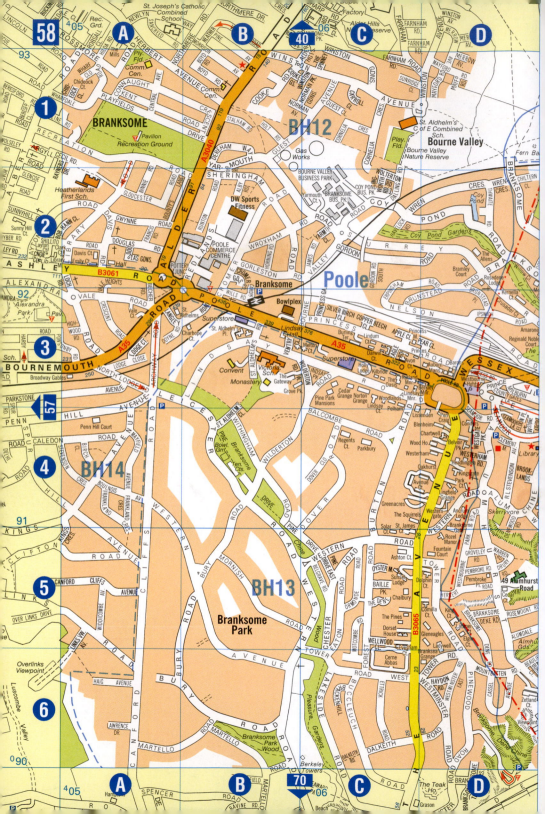

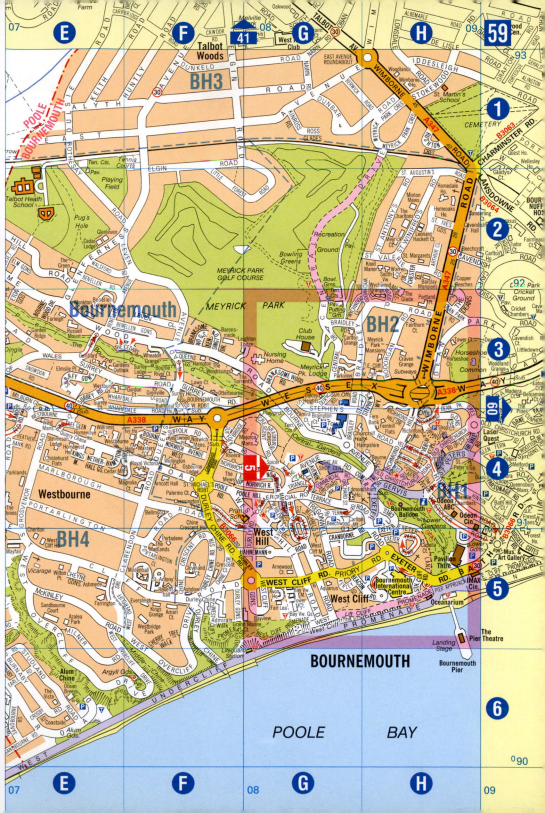

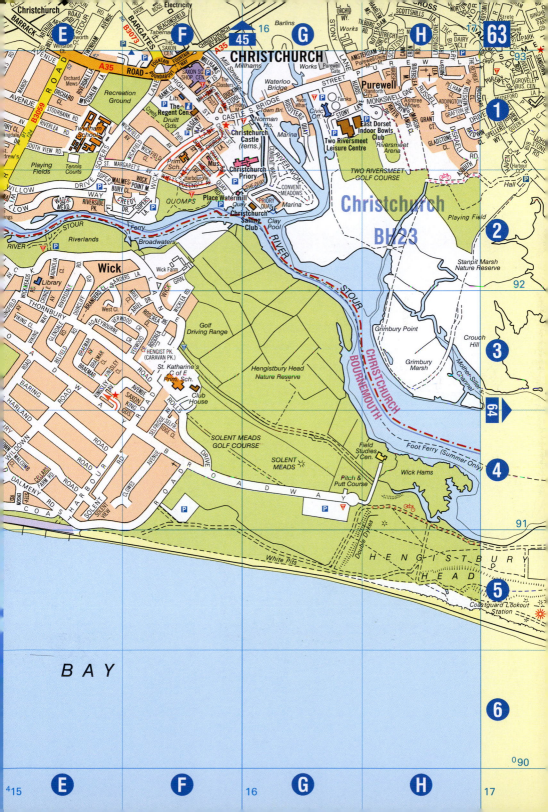

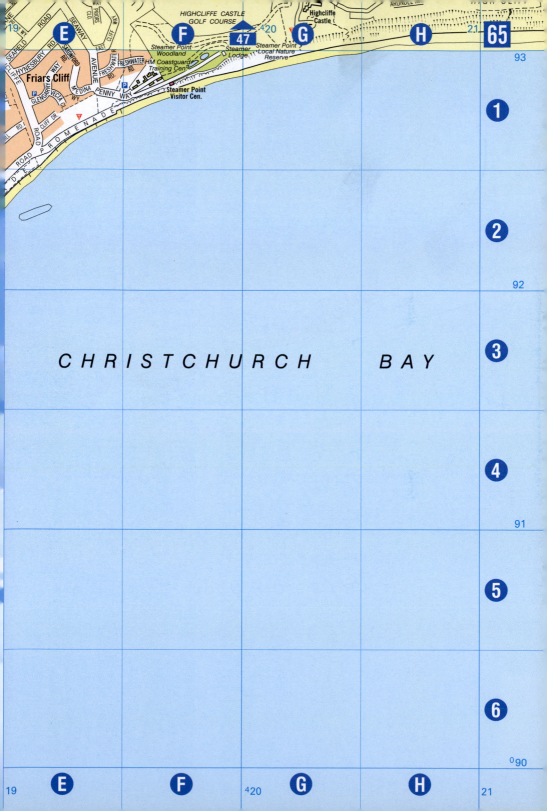

HIGHCLIFFE CASTLE
GOLF COURSE

Highcliffe
Castle

ARUNDELL

Steamer Point
Woodland

Steamer
Lodge

Steamer Point
Local Nature
Reserve

HM Coastguard
Training Cen.

Steamer Point
Visitor Cen.

SEAWAY
ROAD
SEAFIELD

HYNESBURY

AVENUE
SALKFORD

MEDINA

FRESHWATER
RD.

FRESHWATER

CLIFF
WAY

PRIORS

Friars Cliff

GLENGARRY
VECTA CL.
WAY

ROAD
CLIFF DR.

PENNY WAY

PROMENADE

ROAD

1

2

93

92

C H R I S T C H U R C H   B A Y

3

4

91

5

6

90

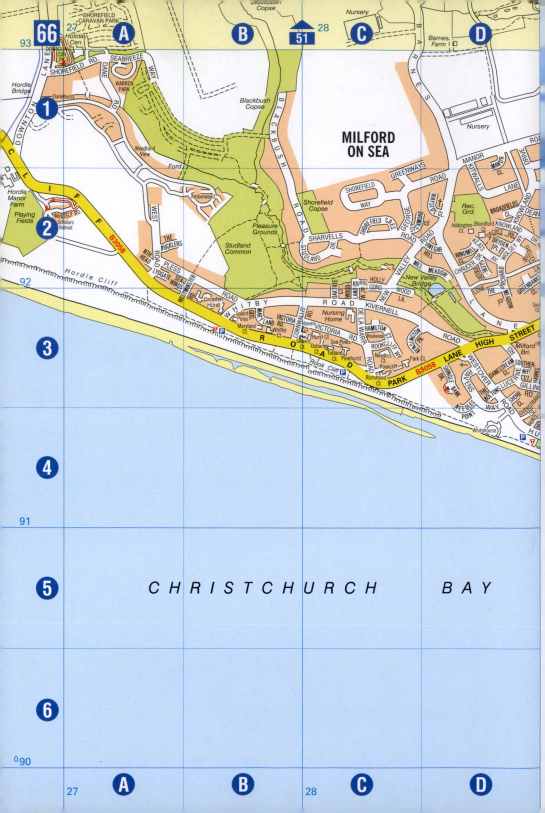

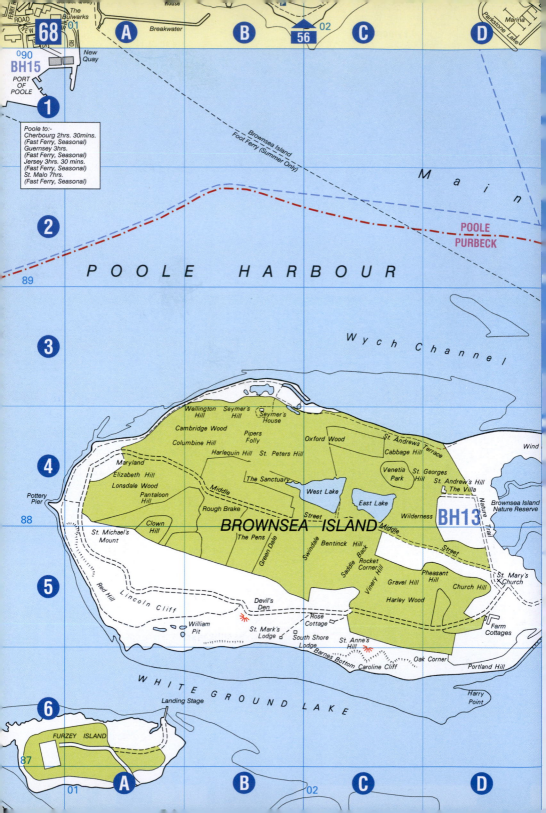

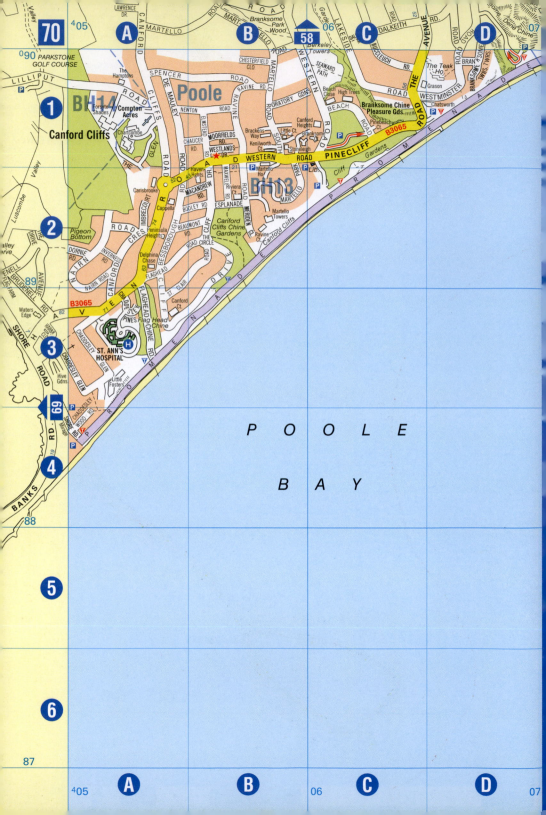

POOLE BAY

Poole

BH14

Canford Cliffs

BH13

PARKSTONE GOLF COURSE

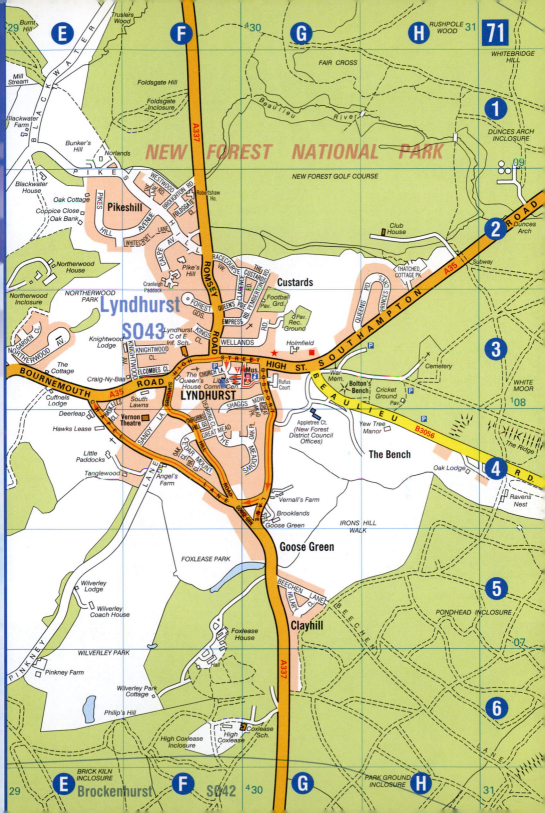

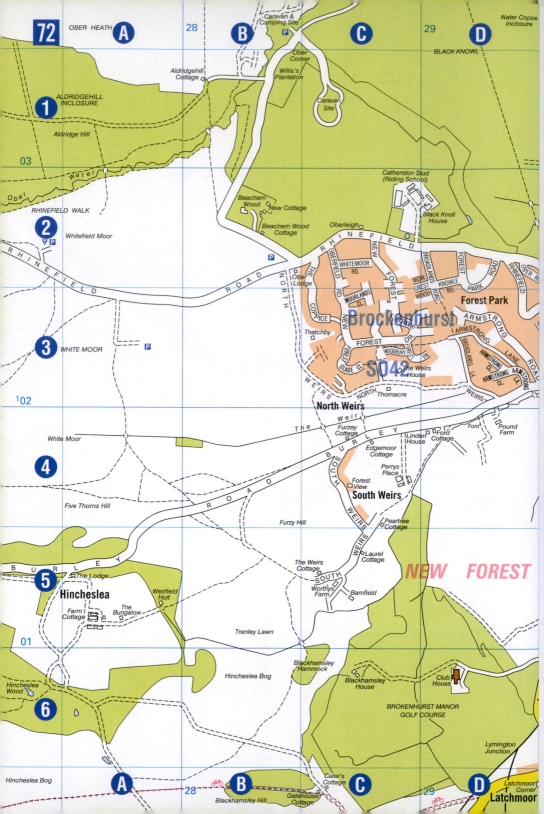

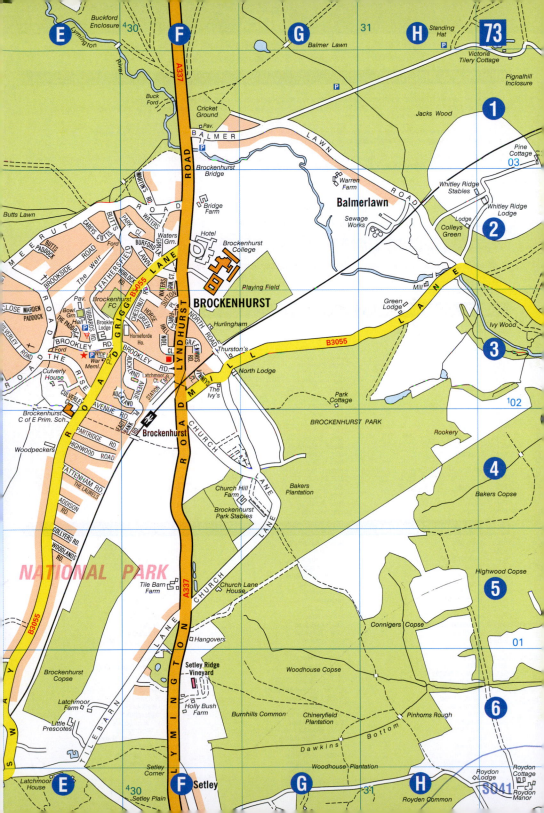

INDEX

Including Streets, Places & Areas, Hospitals etc., Industrial Estates,
Selected Flats & Walkways, Stations and Selected Places of Interest.

HOW TO USE THIS INDEX

1. Each street name is followed by its Postcode District, then by its Locality abbreviation(s) and then by its map reference;
   e.g. **Abbotsbury Rd.** BH18: Broad . . . .6E **21** is in the BH18 Postcode District and the Broadstone Locality and is to be found in square 6E on page **21**. The page number is shown in bold type.

2. A strict alphabetical order is followed in which Av., Rd., St., etc. (though abbreviated) are read in full and as part of the street name;
   e.g. **Avoncliffe Rd.** appears after **Avon Causeway** but before **Avon Cl.**

3. Streets and a selection of flats and walkways that cannot be shown on the mapping, appear in the index with the thoroughfare to which they are connected shown in brackets; e.g. **Adams Ct.** BH5: Bour . . . .3F **61** (off Hawkwood Rd.)

4. Addresses that are in more than one part are referred to as not continuous.

5. Places and areas are shown in the index in BLUE TYPE and the map reference is to the actual map square in which the town centre or area is located and not to the place name shown on the map; e.g. ALDERNEY 4G **39**

6. An example of a selected place of interest is Bournemouth Aviation Mus. 4E **27**

7. An example of a station is Bournemouth Station (Rail) . . . .3B **60**, also included is Park & Ride.
   e.g. Marshes End (Park & Ride) 6G **37**

8. An example of a Hospital, Hospice or selected Healthcare Facility is ALDERNEY HOSPITAL 4G **39**

9. Map references for entries that appear on large scale pages **4** & **5** are shown first, with small scale map references shown in brackets;
   e.g. **Adelaide La.** BH1: Bour 3H **5** (4H **59**)

GENERAL ABBREVIATIONS

All. : Alley	**Gdns.** : Gardens	**Pk.** : Park
App. : Approach	**Gth.** : Garth	**Pas.** : Passage
Arc. : Arcade	**Ga.** : Gate	**Pl.** : Place
Av. : Avenue	**Grn.** : Green	**Prom.** : Promenade
Bri. : Bridge	**Gro.** : Grove	**Ri.** : Rise
Bldg. : Building	**Hgts.** : Heights	**Rd.** : Road
Bldgs. : Buildings	**Ho.** : House	**Rdbt.** : Roundabout
Bus. : Business	**Ind.** : Industrial	**Shop.** : Shopping
Cvn. : Caravan	**Info.** : Information	**Sth.** : South
Cen. : Centre	**Intl.** : International	**Sq.** : Square
Cl. : Close	**Junc.** : Junction	**Sta.** : Station
Comn. : Common	**La.** : Lane	**St.** : Street
Cnr. : Corner	**Lit.** : Little	**Ter.** : Terrace
Cott. : Cottage	**Lwr.** : Lower	**Twr.** : Tower
Cotts. : Cottages	**Mnr.** : Manor	**Trad.** : Trading
Ct. : Court	**Mans.** : Mansions	**Up.** : Upper
Cres. : Crescent	**Mkt.** : Market	**Va.** : Vale
Cft. : Croft	**Mdw.** : Meadow	**Vw.** : View
Dr. : Drive	**Mdws.** : Meadows	**Vs.** : Villas
E. : East	**M.** : Mews	**Vis.** : Visitors
Ent. : Enterprise	**Mt.** : Mount	**Wlk.** : Walk
Est. : Estate	**Mus.** : Museum	**W.** : West
Fld. : Field	**Nth.** : North	**Yd.** : Yard
Flds. : Fields	**Pde.** : Parade	

LOCALITY ABBREVIATIONS

A'ton : **Ashington**	Hang : **Hangersley**	Pil : **Pilley**
A'ley : **Ashley**	Hay : **Hayes**	Poole : **Poole**
Ashl H : **Ashley Heath**	Highc : **Highcliffe**	Portm : **Portmore**
B Sea : **Barton on Sea**	Hight : **Hightown**	Poul : **Poulner**
Bash : **Bashley**	Highw : **Highwood**	Ring : **Ringwood**
Bea H : **Beacon Hill**	Hill : **Hillbutts**	Rock : **Rockford**
Blas : **Blashford**	Hin : **Hinton**	St I : **St Ives**
Bock : **Bockhampton**	Holt : **Holt**	St L : **St Leonards**
Bold : **Boldre**	Hor : **Hordle**	S'bks : **Sandbanks**
Bour : **Bournemouth**	Hurn : **Hurn**	Shir : **Shirley**
Bour A : **Bournemouth International Airport**	Key : **Keyhaven**	Sop : **Sopley**
Bran : **Bransgore**	King : **Kingston**	Stap : **Staplehill**
Broad : **Broadstone**	Linf : **Linford**	Stu M : **Sturminster Marshall**
Broc : **Brockenhurst**	Lit C : **Little Canford**	Sut : **Sutton**
Bro H : **Broom Hill**	Long : **Longham**	Sway : **Sway**
Burt : **Burton**	Lymi : **Lymington**	Thr C : **Three Legged Cross**
Can M : **Canford Magna**	Lymo : **Lymore**	Tip : **Tiptoe**
Chri : **Christchurch**	Lyn : **Lyndhurst**	Upt : **Upton**
Cole : **Colehill**	Lyt M : **Lytchett Minster**	Ver : **Verwood**
Cor M : **Corfe Mullen**	Match : **Matchams**	Wal : **Walhampton**
Cowg : **Cowgrove**	Mer : **Merley**	Walk : **Walkford**
Crow : **Crow**	M Sea : **Milford on Sea**	Wat : **Waterditch**
Down : **Downton**	Mude : **Mudeford**	W Moo : **West Moors**
E Par : **East Parley**	Nea : **Neacroft**	W Par : **West Parley**
Ever : **Everton**	New M : **New Milton**	W Min : **Wimborne Minster**
Fern : **Ferndown**	Oss : **Ossemsley**	Wink : **Winkton**
Fri C : **Friars Cliff**	Pamp : **Pamphill**	Wool : **Woolsbridge**
Hamp : **Hampreston**	Penn : **Pennington**	Woot : **Wootton**
Hamw : **Hamworthy**	Pic H : **Picket Hill**	

Bartonside Rd. BH25: New M 5C 48
Barton Way BH25: B Sea 5F 49
Barton Wood Rd. BH25: B Sea 6E 49
Bascott Cl. BH11: Bour 4C 40
Bascott Rd. BH11: Bour 4B 40
Basepoint Bus. Cen. BH23: Bour A 2C 26
BASHLEY 4G 31
Bashley Comn. Rd. BH25: Bash 4G 31
Bashley Cross Rd. BH25: Bash 6D 30
Bashley Dr. BH25: Bash 5H 31
Bashley FC 4G 31
Bashley Rd. BH25: Bash 4G 31
Bassett Ho. BH1: Bour 3D 60
  (off Knyveton Rd.)
Bassett Rd. BH12: Poole 1F 57
Batchelor Cres. BH11: Bour 2B 40
Batchelor Rd. BH11: Bour 2B 40
Batcombe Cl. BH11: Bour 2A 40
Bath Hill Ct. BH1: Bour 4H 5 (4A 60)
Bath Hill Rdbt. BH1: Bour 5H 5 (5A 60)
Bath Rd. BH1: Bour 5H 5 (5H 59)
  SO41: Lymi 2H 53
Batstone Way BH22: Fern 3H 17
Batten Cl. BH23: Chri 6H 45
BATTRAMSLEY 1D 34
BATTRAMSLEY CROSS 2E 35
Baverstock Rd. BH12: Poole 5D 40
Baxter Ct. BH10: Bour 4D 40
Bay Cl. BH16: Upt 1B 54
  BH21: Thr C 2A 10
Bay Hog La. BH15: Poole 4A 4 (5H 55)
Bays Ct. SO41: Penn 1E 53
Bays Rd. SO41: Penn 1E 53
Baytrees BH14: Poole 3E 57
Bay Tree Way BH23: Chri 4F 47
Bay Vw. BH25: New M 6C 48
Bayview BH2: Bour 6E 5 (5G 59)
Bay Vw. Gdns. BH2: Bour 6E 5 (5G 59)
Bay View M. BH2: Bour 5E 5 (5G 59)
Beach Av. BH25: B Sea 6F 49
Beach Cl. BH13: Poole 1C 70
Beach Rd. BH13: Poole 1C 70
  BH16: Upt 1A 54
Beacon Cl. SO41: Ever 4H 51
Beacon Dr. BH23: Highc 6H 47
Beacon Gdns. BH18: Broad 2E 37
BEACON HILL 3A 36
Beacon Hill La. BH21: Cor M 2B 36
Beacon Hill Touring Pk. BH16: Bea H 4B 36
Beacon Pk. Cres. BH16: Upt 5A 36
Beacon Pk. Rd. BH16: Upt 6A 36
Beacon Rd. BH2: Bour 5F 5 (5G 59)
  BH18: Broad 2D 36
Beaconsfield Rd. BH12: Poole 1H 57
  BH23: Chri 6F 45
Beacon Way BH10: Broad 2E 37
Beamish Rd. BH17: Poole 5D 38
BEAR CROSS 5B 24
Bear Cross Av. BH11: Bour 5A 24
Bear Cross Rdbt. BH11: Bour 5B 24
BEARWOOD 6A 24
Beatty Cl. BH24: Poul 3E 9
Beatty Rd. BH9: Bour 4B 42
Beauchamp Pl. BH23: Chri 6E 45
Beauchamps Gdns. BH7: Bour 5G 43
Beau Ct. BH4: Bour 4E 59
  (off Portarlington Rd.)
  BH25: New M 2G 49
Beaucroft La. BH21: Cole 3G 15
Beaucroft Rd. BH21: Cole 3G 15
Beaufort Cl. BH23: Chri 6D 46
Beaufort Dr. BH21: W Min 4E 15
Beaufort Ho. BH4: Bour 5E 59
  (off West Cliff Rd.)
Beaufort M. BH21: W Min 5D 14
Beaufort Rd. BH6: Bour 2A 62
Beaufoys Av. BH22: Fern 2A 18
  (not continuous)
Beaufoys Cl. BH22: Fern 2A 18
Beaufoys Ct. BH22: Fern 3A 18
Beaulieu Av. BH23: Chri 6C 44
Beaulieu Cl. BH25: New M 2E 49
Beaulieu Gdns. Home Pk. BH23: Chri 6C 44
Beaulieu Gdns. Retreat (Caravan Pk.)
  BH23: Chri 6C 44
Beaulieu Rd. BH4: Bour 6D 58
  BH23: Chri 6C 44
  SO43: Lyn 3G 71
Beaumont Ct. BH5: Bour 3D 60
Beaumont Rd. BH13: Poole 1C 64
Beaver Ind. Est. BH23: Chri 1C 64
Beccles Cl. BH15: Hamw 5F 55
Becher Rd. BH14: Poole 3A 58

Beckhampton Rd. BH15: Hamw 4E 55
BECKLEY 6C 30
Beckley Copse BH23: Walk 3A 48
Becton La. BH25: B Sea 4H 49
Becton Mead BH25: B Sea 4H 49
Bedale Way BH15: Poole 2D 56
Bedford Cres. BH7: Bour 6A 44
Bedford Rd. Nth. BH12: Poole 3G 39
Bedford Rd. Sth. BH12: Poole 3G 39
Beech Av. BH6: Bour 3A 62
  BH23: Chri 5B 44
Beechbank Av. BH17: Broad, Poole 4E 37
Beech Cl. BH18: Broad 1E 37
  BH31: Ver 4C 6
  SO41: Ever 5H 51
Beech Ct. BH21: W Min 5G 15
Beechcroft BH1: Bour 2H 59
  BH23: Highc 5H 47
Beechcroft La. BH24: Ring 3D 8
Beechcroft M. BH24: Ring 3D 8
  (off Beechcroft La.)
Beechen La. SO43: Lyn 5G 71
Beeches, The BH7: Bour 5G 43
Beechey Rd. BH8: Bour 2A 60
Beechfield BH4: Bour 4E 59
  (off Portarlington Rd.)
Beech La. BH24: St L 5A 12
Beechleigh Pl. BH24: Ring 3C 8
  (off Southampton Rd.)
Beechwood BH1: Bour 2H 5
Beechwood Av. BH5: Bour 3F 61
  BH25: New M 1E 49
Beech Wood Cl. BH18: Broad 2G 37
Beechwood Cl. BH2: Bour 4F 5 (4G 59)
Beechwood Gdns. BH5: Bour 3G 61
Beechwood Lodge BH4: Bour 5E 59
  (off Portarlington Rd.)
Beechwood Rd. BH22: W Moo 6D 10
Belben Cl. BH12: Poole 3H 39
Belben Rd. BH12: Poole 3G 39
Belfield Rd. BH6: Bour 3E 63
Belgrave Ct. BH1: Bour 4C 60
Belgrave Rd. BH13: Poole 5C 58
Belle Vue BH15: Poole 4B 56
  (off Mt. Pleasant Rd.)
Belle Vue Cl. BH6: Bour 3B 62
Belle Vue Cres. BH6: Bour 3D 62
Belle Vue Gdns. BH6: Bour 3D 62
Belle Vue Gro. BH22: W Moo 5D 10
Belle Vue Mans. BH6: Bour 4C 62
Belle Vue Rd. BH6: Bour 3B 62
  BH14: Poole 4G 57
Belle Vue Wlk. BH22: W Par 1G 25
Bellflower Cl. BH23: Chri 5D 46
Bell Heather Cl. BH16: Upt 5B 36
Bell La. BH15: Poole 4B 56
  (off High St.)
Bellmoor BH4: Bour 4F 59
Belmont Av. BH8: Bour 3C 42
Belmont Cl. BH31: Ver 4E 7
Belmont Dr. SO41: Lymi 3H 53
Belmont Rd. BH14: Poole 2G 57
  BH25: A'ley 1A 50
Belmore La. SO41: Lymi 2F 53
Belmore Rd. SO41: Lymi 2F 53
Belmour Lodge BH4: Bour 4E 59
  (off Marlborough Rd.)
Belvedere Rd. BH3: Bour 1A 60
  BH23: Chri 6E 45
Belvoir Pk. BH13: Poole 4D 58
Bemister Rd. BH9: Bour 5A 42
Benbow Cres. BH12: Poole 3A 40
Benbridge Av. BH11: Bour 6B 24
BENCH, THE 4H 71
Bendigo Rd. BH23: Chri 5C 44
Benellen Av. BH4: Bour 3E 59
Benellen Gdns. BH4: Bour 3E 59
Benellen Rd. BH4: Bour 2E 59
Benellen Towers BH4: Bour 3E 59
Bengal Rd. BH9: Bour 4G 41
Benjamin Cl. BH1: Bour 3A 60
Benjamin Rd. BH15: Hamw 5D 54
Benmoor Rd. BH17: Poole 5G 37
Benmore Cl. BH25: New M 3A 50
Benmore Rd. BH9: Bour 4A 42
Bennett Ho. BH4: Bour 4E 59
  (off Westbourne Cl.)
Bennett Rd. BH8: Bour 1B 60
Bennett's All. BH15: Poole 5A 4
Bennion Rd. BH10: Bour 2E 41
Benridge Bus. Pk. BH17: Poole 5H 37
Benridge Cl. BH18: Broad 2G 37
Benson Cl. BH23: Bran 2D 28

Benson Rd. BH17: Poole 6B 38
Bentley Rd. BH9: Bour 2H 41
Bentley Way SO41: Bold 5F 35
Benton Ct. BH23: Chri 1D 62
Bere Cl. BH17: Poole 3B 38
Beresford Cl. BH12: Poole 1H 57
Beresford Gdns. BH23: Chri 1A 64
Beresford Rd. BH6: Bour 3H 61
  BH12: Poole 1H 57
  SO41: Lymi 1E 53
Berkeley Av. BH12: Poole 5G 39
Berkeley Cl. BH31: Ver 2C 6
Berkeley Ct. BH1: Bour 3A 60
  (off Cavendish Rd.)
  BH22: W Moo 5C 10
Berkeley Mans. BH1: Bour 4C 60
  (off Christchurch Rd.)
Berkeley Rd. BH3: Bour 6G 41
Berkley Av. BH22: W Par 6B 18
Berkley Mnr. BH12: Poole 3D 58
Bermuda Ct. BH23: Highc 6A 48
Bernards Cl. BH23: Chri 5C 44
Berne Ct. BH1: Bour 5A 60
Berrans Av. BH11: Bour 5C 24
Berrans Ct. BH11: Bour 5C 24
Berry Cl. BH9: Bour 5H 41
Berryfield Rd. SO41: Hor 3E 51
Berthia Gate BH8: Bour 1D 60
  (off Holdenhurst Rd.)
Bertram Rd. BH25: A'ley 1A 50
Berwick Rd. BH3: Bour 1G 59
Berwyn Ct. BH5: Broad 1G 37
Bessborough Rd. BH13: Poole 2A 70
Bessemer Ct. BH31: Ver 5G 7
Beswick Av. BH10: Bour 3F 41
Beswick Gdns. BH10: Bour 3G 41
Bethany Ct. BH12: Poole 6C 40
Bethany Ho. BH1: Bour 2D 60
Bethia Cl. BH8: Bour 1D 60
Bethia Rd. BH8: Bour 6D 42
Betsy Cl. BH23: Bran 2D 28
Bettiscombe Cl. BH17: Poole 3C 38
Beverley Gdns. BH10: Bour 2F 41
Beverley Grange BH4: Bour 4E 59
  (off Portarlington Rd.)
Beverley Hall BH1: Bour 4C 60
Bexington Cl. BH11: Bour 2A 40
Bianco BH1: Bour 4H 59
Bickerley Gdns. BH24: Ring 5B 8
Bickerley Grn. BH24: Ring 5B 8
Bickerley Rd. BH24: Ring 4B 8
Bickerley Ter. BH24: Ring 4B 8
Bickley, The BH24: Ring 4B 8
  (off Strides La.)
Bicknell Ct. BH4: Bour 4E 59
  (off Westbourne Cl.)
Bicton Rd. BH11: Bour 2D 40
Billington Pl. SO41: Penn 3F 53
Bindon Cl. BH12: Poole 6A 40
Bingham Av. BH14: Poole 2G 69
Bingham Cl. BH23: Chri 6A 46
  BH31: Ver 5F 7
Bingham Dr. BH31: Ver 5E 7
  SO41: Lymi 2G 53
Bingham Rd. BH9: Bour 5A 42
  BH23: Chri 6A 46
  BH31: Ver 5E 7
Binnie Rd. BH12: Poole 2A 58
Birch Av. BH22: W Par 2H 25
  BH23: Burt 2G 45
  BH25: Bash 5E 31
Birch Cl. BH14: Poole 4A 58
  BH21: Cor M 5D 20
  BH24: St L 4H 11
Birch Copse BH17: Poole 4G 37
Birchdale Rd. BH21: W Min 4F 15
Birch Dr. BH8: Bour 3G 43
Birch Grange BH15: Poole 6C 38
Birch Gro. BH22: W Moo 5B 10
  BH25: New M 4G 49
Birch Rd. BH24: St I 3D 12
Birch Wlk. BH22: Fern 6D 18
Birchwood Cl. BH23: Chri 5G 47
Birchwood M. BH14: Poole 4H 57
Birchwood Pl. BH24: St L 5H 11
Birchwood Rd. BH14: Poole 4H 57
  BH16: Upt 1B 54
Birchy Hill SO41: Sway 2G 33
Birds Hill Gdns. BH15: Poole 4C 56
Birds Hill Rd. BH15: Poole 3C 56
Birkdale Ct. BH18: Broad 6G 21
Birkdale Rd. BH18: Broad 6G 21

Bishop Cl.—Brierley Cl.

Bishop Cl. BH12: Poole 6E **41**
Bishop Ct. BH24: Ring 4C **8**
Bishop Rd. BH9: Bour 5A **42**
Bishops Cl. BH7: Bour 6F **43**
Bishops Ct. BH18: Broad 2G **37**
Bitterne Way BH31: Ver 4E **7**
SO41: Lymi 3F **53**
Blackberry La. BH23: Chri 1B **64**
Blackbird Cl. BH17: Poole 5E **37**
Blackbird Way BH23: Bran 3E **29**
Blackburn Rd. BH12: Poole 1F **57**
Blackbush Rd. SO41: M Sea 1B **66**
Blackfield La. BH22: W Moo 4C **10**
Blackfield Rd. BH8: Bour 2D **42**
Black Hill BH31: Ver 3E **7**
Black Moor Rd. BH31: Ver 4G **7**
Blacksmith Cl. BH21: Cor M 6D **20**
Blackthorn Cl. SO41: Penn 3D **52**
Blackthorn Way BH25: A'ley 1B **50**
BH31: Ver 4F **7**
BLACKWATER 1A **44**
Blackwater SO43: Lyn 1E **71**
Blackwater Dr. BH21: Mer 4B **22**
Blair Av. BH14: Poole 3G **57**
Blair Cl. BH25: New M 2E **49**
Blake Dene Rd. BH14: Poole 6F **57**
Blake Hill Av. BH14: Poole 6H **57**
Blake Hill Cres. BH14: Poole 6G **57**
Blake Ho. BH21: W Min 5F **15**
Blandford Cl. BH15: Hamw 6F **55**
Blandford Ct. SO41: M Sea 2D **66**
Blandford Rd. BH15: Hamw 6G **55**
BH16: Hamw, Upt 6C **36**
BH21: Cor M 2B **20**
BH21: Hill, Pamp 2A **14**
Blandford Rd. Nth. BH16: Bea H, Upt 3A **36**
Blaney Way BH21: Cor M 5C **20**
BLASHFORD 1C **8**
Blenheim BH13: Poole 4C **58**
Blenheim Ct. *BH4: Bour* *4E **59***
(off Marlborough Rd.)
BH23: Chri 5D **44**
Blenheim Cres. SO41: Hor 1C **50**
Blenheim Dr. BH23: Mude 1D **64**
Blind La. BH21: W Min 3D **14**
Bloomfield Av. BH9: Bour 3H **41**
Bloomfield Pl. BH9: Bour 3H **41**
Bloxworth Rd. BH12: Poole 5B **40**
Bluebell Cl. BH23: Chri 5D **46**
Bluebell Gdns. BH25: New M 2H **49**
Bluebell La. BH17: Poole 4F **37**
Blue Cedars BH22: W Moo 6C **10**
Bluff, The BH10: Bour 1H **41**
Blyth Cl. BH23: Chri 1B **44**
Blythe Rd. BH21: Cor M 5D **20**
Blythswood Ct. BH25: B Sea 6F **49**
BMI THE HARBOUR HOSPITAL 4B **56**
Bob Hann Cl. BH12: Poole 2H **57**
Bockhampton Rd. BH23: Bock, Wink 6A **28**
Bodley Rd. BH13: Poole 2B **70**
Bodorgan Rd. BH2: Bour 2G **5** (3H **59**)
Bodowen Cl. BH23: Burt 3H **45**
Bodowen Rd. BH23: Burt 3H **45**
Bognor Rd. BH18: Broad 1F **37**
BOLDRE 2F **35**
Boldre Cl. BH12: Poole 6H **39**
BH25: New M 5D **48**
Boldre La. SO41: Bold 4F **35**
Boleyn Cres. BH9: Bour 1C **42**
Bolton Cl. BH6: Bour 4C **62**
Bolton Cres. BH22: Fern 3E **19**
Bolton Rd. BH6: Bour 4C **62**
Boltons, The SO41: M Sea 3D **66**
Bolton's Bench 3G **71**
Bond Av. BH22: W Moo 3B **10**
Bond Cl. SO41: Sway 1F **33**
Bond Rd. BH15: Poole 2D **56**
Bonham Rd. BH9: Bour 6H **41**
Bonington Cl. BH23: Chri 5A **46**
Bonita Ct. BH1: Bour 2E **61**
Border Dr. BH16: Upt 2C **54**
Border Rd. BH16: Upt 2C **54**
Boreham Rd. BH6: Bour 2B **62**
Borley Rd. BH17: Poole 5G **37**
Borthwick La. BH1: Bour 2D **60**
Borthwick Rd. BH1: Bour 2E **61**
BOSCOMBE 3E **61**
Boscombe Beach BH5: Bour 4E **61**
Boscombe Cliff Rd. BH5: Bour 4E **61**
Boscombe Gro. Rd. BH1: Bour 2D **60**
(not continuous)
Boscombe Overcliff Dr. BH5: Bour 4F **61**
Boscombe Prom. BH5: Bour 4E **61**
Boscombe Spa Grange BH5: Bour 3E **61**
Boscombe Spa Rd. BH5: Bour 3D **60**
Boscombe Surf Reef 4E **61**
Bosley Cl. BH23: Chri 3C **44**
Bosley Way BH23: Chri 3C **44**
Boston BH14: Poole 3F **57**
Boston Lodge *BH4: Bour* *4E **59***
(off Marlborough Rd.)
Bosworth M. BH9: Bour 1B **42**
Boulnois Av. BH14: Poole 4A **58**
Boundary Dr. BH21: Cole 3F **15**
Boundary La. BH24: Match, St L 6G **11**
Boundary Rd. BH9: Bour 5F **41**
BH10: Bour 5F **41**
Boundary Rdbt. BH12: Poole 5F **41**
Boundway SO41: Sway 2C **32**
Bounty's La. BH12: Poole 2A **58**
Bourne, The *BH4: Bour* *3F **59***
(off Surrey Rd.)
Bourne Av. BH2: Bour 2E **5** (4G **59**)
Bourne Cl. BH2: Bour 4F **59**
Bourne Ct. BH2: Bour 3G **5** (4H **59**)
BH21: W Min 4F **15**
Bourne Mead BH2: Bour 3E **5**
BOURNEMOUTH 4G **5** (4H **59**)
BOURNEMOUTH AIRPORT 3F **27**
Bournemouth Aviation Mus. 4E **27**
Bournemouth Balloon 4G **5** (4H **59**)
Bournemouth BMX Track 1D **62**
Bournemouth Central Bus. Pk. BH1: Bour 3C **60**
Bournemouth Crematorium BH8: Bour 4C **42**
Bournemouth Indoor Bowls Cen. 2F **61**
Bournemouth International Cen. 5G **5** (5H **59**)
Bournemouth Intl. Cen. Rdbt. BH2: Bour 5G **5**
Bournemouth Memorial Homes BH8: Bour 4F **43**
Bournemouth Pier 6H **5** (6H **59**)
Bournemouth Rd. BH14: Poole 3F **57**
SO43: Lyn 3E **71**
Bournemouth Sports Club 2C **26**
Bournemouth Station (Rail) 3B **60**
Bournemouth Sta. Rdbt. BH8: Bour 3B **60**
Bournemouth University
Christchurch Rd. 4B **60**
Talbot Campus 5E **41**
Bournemouth W. Rdbt. BH2: Bour 3F **59**
Bourne Pines BH1: Bour 1H **5**
(Dean Pk. Rd.)
BH1: Bour 3C **60**
(Christchurch Rd.)
Bourne River Ct. BH4: Bour 3F **59**
Bourneside Mnr. *BH2: Bour* *4F **59***
(off Cambridge Rd.)
BOURNE VALLEY 1C **58**
Bourne Valley Bus. Pk. BH12: Poole 2C **58**
Bourne Valley Nature Reserve
Bourne Valley 1C **58**
Poole 4A **40**
Bourne Valley Rd. BH12: Poole 3C **58**
Bournewood Dr. BH4: Bour 3E **59**
Bourton Gdns. BH7: Bour 5H **43**
Bouverie Cl. BH25: B Sea 4F **49**
Boveridge Gdns. BH9: Bour 1B **42**
Bovington Cl. BH17: Poole 4D **38**
Bowden Rd. BH12: Poole 3G **39**
Bower Rd. BH8: Bour 5D **42**
Bowland Ri. BH25: New M 3A **50**
BOWLING GREEN 5B **34**
Bowling Grn. All. BH15: Poole 4B **4**
Bowlplex
Branksome 3B **58**
Poole 5E **39**
Box Cl. BH17: Poole 6H **37**
Boyd Rd. BH12: Poole 1B **58**
Brabazon Dr. BH23: Chri 6D **46**
Brabazon Rd. BH21: Mer 2D **22**
Brabourne Av. BH22: Fern 5A **18**
Bracken Cl. BH24: Ashl H 3H **11**
Brackendale Ct. BH21: Thr C 2A **10**
Brackendale Rd. BH8: Bour 5C **42**
Bracken Glen BH15: Poole 3C **56**
Brackenhill BH13: Poole 6C **58**
Brackenhill Rd. BH21: Cole 2A **16**
Bracken Rd. BH6: Bour 3A **62**
BH22: Fern 2H **17**
Brackens Way BH13: Poole 1B **70**
SO41: Lymi 3H **53**
Bracken Way BH23: Walk 4B **48**
Bracklesham Pl. BH25: B Sea 6F **49**
Brackley Cl. BH23: Bour A 3G **27**
Bradburne Rd. BH2: Bour 3E **5** (4G **59**)
Bradford Rd. BH9: Bour 1C **42**
Bradpole Rd. BH8: Bour 3E **43**
Bradstock Cl. BH12: Poole 5B **40**
Braemar Av. BH6: Bour 3E **63**
Braemar Cl. BH6: Bour 3E **63**
Braemar Dr. BH23: Highc 4H **47**
Braeside Bus. Pk. BH15: Poole 3H **55**
Braeside Rd. BH22: W Moo 4C **10**
BH24: St L 3A **12**
Braidley Rd. BH2: Bour 3F **5** (4G **59**)
Brailswood Rd. BH15: Poole 3B **56**
Braishfield Gdns. BH8: Bour 3D **42**
Bramble La. BH23: Highc 4B **48**
Bramble Wlk. SO41: Lymi 6E **35**
Bramble Way BH23: Bran 2D **28**
Bramley Cl. SO41: Lymi 3G **53**
Bramley Ct. BH12: Poole 2D **58**
BH22: Fern 3B **18**
Bramley Rd. BH10: Bour 6E **25**
BH22: Fern 3A **18**
Brampton Ct. BH2: Bour 3F **5** (4G **59**)
Brampton Rd. BH15: Poole 1B **56**
Bramshaw Gdns. BH8: Bour 2D **42**
Bramshaw Way BH25: New M 5D **48**
Branders Cl. BH6: Bour 3E **63**
Branders La. BH6: Bour 2E **63**
Brandon Ct. *BH12: Poole* *3D **58***
(off Poole Rd.)
Branksea Av. BH15: Hamw 6D **54**
Branksea Castle 5E **69**
Branksea Cl. BH15: Hamw 6E **55**
Branksea Grange BH13: Poole 6D **58**
BRANKSOME 1A **58**
Branksome Bldgs. BH2: Bour 4E **5**
Branksome Bus. Pk. BH12: Poole 2C **58**
(Bourne Valley Bus. Pk.)
BH12: Poole 6C **40**
(Cortry Cl.)
Branksome Chine Pleasure Gdns. 1C **70**
Branksome Cl. BH25: New M 3H **49**
Branksome Ct. BH13: Poole 1C **70**
Branksome Dene Chine 6D **58**
Branksome Dene Rd. BH4: Bour 5D **58**
Branksome Dorset Provincial Masonic Mus. 2E **61**
Branksome Ga. BH13: Poole 4D **58**
Branksome Hill Rd. BH4: Bour 1D **58**
BRANKSOME PARK 5C **58**
Branksome Station (Rail) 3B **58**
Branksome Towers BH13: Poole 1D **70**
Branksome Wood Gdns. BH2: Bour 3F **59**
Branksome Wood Rd. BH2: Bour 2E **5** (3G **59**)
BH4: Bour 2D **58**
BH12: Poole 2D **58**
BRANSGORE 3C **28**
Bransgore Gdns. BH23: Bran 2D **28**
Branwell Cl. BH23: Chri 4E **45**
Branwood Cl. SO41: Ever 4A **52**
Brassey Cl. BH9: Bour 4A **42**
Brassey Rd. BH9: Bour 4H **41**
Brassey Ter. BH9: Bour 4H **41**
Braxton Courtyard SO41: Lymo 6A **52**
Braxton Gdns. 5A **52**
Breach La. BH24: Hight, Poul 3G **9**
Breamore Cl. BH25: New M 2E **49**
Brecon Cl. BH10: Bour 5G **25**
BH25: New M 3A **50**
Bredy Cl. BH17: Poole 4B **38**
Breeze BH5: Bour 3E **61**
Bremble Cl. BH12: Poole 3G **39**
Briar Cl. BH15: Poole 2C **56**
BH23: Chri 1B **64**
Briarfield *BH4: Bour* *4E **59***
(off Portarlington Rd.)
Briarswood Rd. BH16: Upt 6C **36**
Briar Way BH21: Hay 4B **16**
Brickfield La. SO41: Wal 6H **35**
Brickyard La. BH21: Cor M 3A **20**
BH22: Fern 3G **17**
BH31: Ver 2B **6**
Bridge App. BH15: Hamw, Poole 5A **4** (6H **55**)
Bridge Pl. BH10: Bour 4F **25**
Bridge Rd. SO41: Lymi 1H **53**
Bridges, The BH24: Ring 4A **8**
Bridges Cl. BH22: W Moo 4D **10**
Bridge St. BH23: Chri 1G **63**
Bridgewater Rd. BH12: Poole 1H **57**
Bridge Yd. SO41: Lymi 1H **53**
Bridle Cl. BH16: Upt 6D **36**
Bridle Cres. BH7: Bour 5A **44**
Bridle Way BH21: Cole 3B **16**
Bridleways BH31: Ver 3C **6**
Bridport Rd. BH12: Poole 5B **40**
BH31: Ver 3D **6**
Brierley Av. BH22: W Par 2G **25**
Brierley Cl. BH10: Bour 6G **25**

78 A-Z Bournemouth

Brierley Rd. BH10: Bour 1F 41
Brightlands Av. BH6: Bour 3D 62
Brighton Rd. SO41: Sway 1E 33
Bright Rd. BH15: Poole 1C 56
Brinsons Cl. BH23: Burt 2G 45
Brisbane Rd. BH23: Chri 4C 44
Britannia Ct. BH12: Poole 6F 39
Britannia Rd. BH14: Poole 4E 57
Britannia Way BH23: Mude 6D 46
Brixey Cl. BH12: Poole 6G 39
Brixey Rd. BH12: Poole 6G 39
Broad Av. BH8: Bour 4D 42
Broadfields Cl. SO41: M Sea 2D 66
Broadhurst Av. BH10: Bour 1G 41
Broadlands *BH4: Bour* *4E 59*
(off Marlborough Rd.)
Broadlands Av. BH6: Bour 3D 62
Broadlands Cl. BH8: Bour 2D 42
BH23: Walk 3B 48
Broadlands La. SO42: Broc 3D 72
Broadlands Rd. SO42: Broc 2D 72
Broad La. SO41: Lymi 2H 53
Broadleas BH22: Fern 5A 18
Broadly Cl. SO41: Penn 3D 52
Broadmayne Rd. BH12: Poole 6B 40
BROADMEAD 1H 51
Broadmead Cl. SO41: Lymi 3H 53
Broadmead Rd. BH21: Thr C 1B 10
Broadmoor Rd. BH21: Cor M 5B 20
Broads, The BH21: W Min 3B 14
Broadshard Ct. BH24: Ring 2C 8
Broadshard La. BH24: Ring 2C 8
BROADSTONE 1G 37
Broadstone Golf Course 5H 21
Broadstone Way BH15: Poole 1H 55
BH17: Broad, Poole 3F 37
BH18: Broad 3F 37
Broadwater Av. BH14: Poole 5F 57
Broadway BH6: Bour 3D 62
Broadway, The BH10: Bour 5F 25
BH18: Broad 1G 37
Broadway Gables BH14: Poole 3H 57
Broadway Gdns. BH10: Bour 5F 25
BH21: W Min 5E 15
Broadway La. BH8: Bour 2C 42
Broadway M. *BH14: Poole* *4D 56*
(off Park Rd.)
BROCKENHURST 3E 73
Brockenhurst Rd. BH9: Bour 3B 42
BH25: Woot 2G 31
Brockenhurst Station (Rail) 4F 73
Brockhills La. BH25: New M 6A 32
Brockley Rd. BH10: Bour 1G 41
Brocks Pine BH24: St L 4B 12
Brock Way BH31: Ver 2C 6
Brockwood BH24: St L 5H 11
BROG STREET 1D 20
Brog St. BH21: Cor M 2C 20
Brokenhurst Manor Golf Course 6D 72
Brombys, The BH15: Poole 4C 4
Bronte Av. BH23: Chri 4E 45
Brook Av. BH25: New M 1G 49
Brook Av. Nth. BH25: New M 6H 31
Brook Cl. BH10: Bour 1E 41
Brookdale Cl. BH18: Broad 1G 37
Brookdale Farm BH18: Broad 1G 37
Brook Dr. BH31: Ver 5F 7
Brooke Ho. *BH8: Bour* *2C 60*
(off Lowther Rd.)
Brookland Cl. SO41: Penn 2E 53
Brooklands BH4: Bour 4D 58
Brook La. BH21: Cor M 5C 20
BH23: Nea 4D 28
Brookley Ct. *BH8: Bour* *6C 42*
(off Richmond Pk. Rd.)
Brookley Lodge SO42: Broc 3E 73
Brookley Rd. SO42: Broc 3E 73
Brooklyn BH14: Poole 2H 69
Brooklyn Ct. BH25: New M 2F 49
Brook Pk. Ind. Est. BH21: W Min 6G 15
Brook Rd. BH10: Bour 1E 41
BH12: Poole 2G 57
BH21: W Min 5G 15
SO41: Lymi 3H 53
Brooks Cl. BH24: Ring 5D 8
Brookside Cl. BH23: Bran 2C 28
Brookside Pk. Homes BH21: Cor M 1B 36
Brookside Rd. BH21: W Min 5H 15
BH23: Bran 2C 28
SO42: Broc 2E 73
Brookside Way BH23: Highc 4G 47
Brook Vw. BH22: W Moo 4B 10
Brook Way BH23: Fri C 6E 47
Broomfield Ct. BH22: Fern 3C 18
Broomfield La. SO41: Lymi 1G 53
Broomhill Cl. SO41: Penn 3D 52
Broomhill Way BH15: Hamw 6G 55
Broom La. *BH6: Bour* *3H 61*
(off Pine Av.)
Broom Rd. BH12: Poole 4F 39
Broom Rd. Bus. Pk. BH12: Poole 4G 39
Broughton Av. BH10: Bour 1G 41
Broughton Cl. BH10: Bour 2G 41
Broughton Rd. SO43: Lyn 2F 71
Brownen Rd. BH9: Bour 5B 42
Brownhill Rd. BH25: Woot 1E 31
Browning Av. BH5: Bour 3F 61
Browning Rd. BH12: Poole 1H 57
Brownings Cl. SO41: Penn 1C 52
Brownlow Ct. *BH4: Bour* *4E 59*
(off Marlborough Rd.)
Brownsea Av. BH21: Cor M 5D 20
Brownsea Cl. BH25: New M 2E 49
Brownsea Ct. BH14: Poole 1F 69
BROWNSEA ISLAND 4B 68
Brownsea Island Nature Reserve 4D 68
Brownsea Rd. BH13: S'bks 6F 69
Brownsea Vw. Av. BH14: Poole 1F 69
Brownsea Vw. Cl. BH14: Poole 6G 57
Brudenell Av. BH13: S'bks 2H 69
Brudenell Rd. BH13: S'bks 2H 69
Brunel Cl. BH31: Ver 5G 7
Brune Way BH22: W Par 6B 18
Brunstead Pl. BH12: Poole 3D 58
Brunstead Rd. BH12: Poole 3C 58
Brunswick Pl. SO41: Lymi 1G 53
Brushwood Dr. BH16: Upt 1A 54
Bryanstone Rd. BH3: Bour 6G 41
Bryant Rd. BH12: Poole 5C 40
Bryony Cl. BH18: Broad 3E 37
Bryony Gdns. BH6: Bour 1A 62
Bub La. BH23: Chri 1A 64
Buccaneers Cl. BH23: Chri 1H 63
Buccleuch Rd. BH13: Poole 6C 58
Bucehayes Cl. BH23: Highc 5A 48
Buchanan Av. BH7: Bour 1E 61
Buckingham Ct. BH15: Poole 4B 56
Buckingham Mans. BH1: Bour 4A 60
Buckingham Rd. BH12: Poole 6H 39
Buckingham Wlk. BH25: New M 2E 49
BUCKLAND 6F 35
Buckland Dene SO41: Lymi 6F 35
Buckland Gdns. SO41: Lymi 5F 35
Buckland Gro. BH23: Chri 3G 47
Buckland Rd. BH12: Poole 2G 57
Buckland Ter. BH12: Poole 2G 57
Buckland Vw. SO41: Lymi 6F 35
Bucklers, The SO41: M Sea 2A 66
Bucklers Ct. SO41: Lymi 2F 53
Bucklers M. SO41: Lymi 2F 53
Bucklers Way BH8: Bour 2D 42
Buckstone Cl. SO41: Ever 4A 52
Buckthorn Cl. BH17: Poole 4F 37
Buddens Mdw. BH21: Cor M 1C 36
Buffalo M. BH15: Poole 4A 4 (5H 55)
Bugden's Copse Nature Reserve 3D 6
Bugdens La. BH31: Ver 3D 6
Buldowne Wlk. SO41: Sway 1F 33
Bullfinch Cl. BH17: Poole 4F 37
Bull La. BH15: Poole 5B 4
Bunting Rd. BH22: Fern 1H 17
Burbridge Cl. BH17: Poole 5C 38
Burcombe La. BH24: Hang 2G 9
Burcombe Rd. BH10: Bour 6E 25
Burdock Cl. BH23: Chri 4D 46
Bure Cl. BH23: Fri C 1D 64
Bure Ct. BH23: Mude 1D 64
Bure Haven Dr. BH23: Mude 1C 64
(not continuous)
Bure Homage Gdns. BH23: Mude 1D 64
Bure Homage La. BH23: Mude 1C 64
Bure Ho. BH23: Chri 5D 44
Bure La. BH23: Fri C, Mude 2D 64
Bure Pk. BH23: Fri C 1D 64
Bure Rd. BH23: Fri C 1D 64
Burford Cl. BH23: Chri 4B 44
Burford Ct. BH1: Bour 4B 60
Burford La. SO42: Broc 2F 73
Burgess Cl. BH11: Bour 1B 40
Burleigh Rd. BH6: Bour 1B 62
Burley Cl. BH25: New M 5D 48
BH31: Ver 4C 6
Burley Rd. BH12: Poole 1G 57
BH23: Bock, Bran, Wink 1G 45 & 5A 28
SO42: Broc 5A 72
Burling Ter. BH12: Poole 3C 58
Burlington Arc. BH1: Bour 3H 5
Burnaby Ct. BH4: Bour 6D 58
Burnaby Rd. BH4: Bour 6E 59
Burnbake Rd. BH31: Ver 4D 6
Burnbrae Rd. BH22: W Par 2F 25
Burn Cl. BH31: Ver 5F 7
Burnett Av. BH23: Chri 5C 44
Burnett Rd. BH23: Chri 6D 44
Burngate Rd. BH15: Hamw 5E 55
Burnham Dr. BH8: Bour 6C 42
Burnham Rd. BH23: Burt 3G 45
Burnleigh Gdns. BH25: A'ley 1A 50
Burnside BH23: Chri 5F 47
Burns Rd. BH6: Bour 6B 44
Burnt Ho. La. BH23: Bran 2C 28
SO41: Pil 2H 35
Burrard Gro. SO41: Lymi 3H 53
Burrows La. BH31: Ver 1D 6
Bursledon Ho. BH25: New M 3G 49
Burtley Rd. BH6: Bour 4C 62
BURTON 2G 45
Burton Cl. BH23: Burt 4G 45
BH24: Ashl H 2H 11
Burtoncroft BH23: Burt 2G 45
Burton Hall BH23: Burt 2H 45
Burton Hall Pl. BH23: Burt 2H 45
Burton Rd. BH13: Poole 4C 58
BH23: Chri 6A 46
Burt's Hill BH21: Cole, W Min 3E 15
Bury Rd. BH13: Poole 6A 58
Bushell Rd. BH15: Poole 6A 38
Bushey Rd. BH8: Bour 4C 42
Bushmead Dr. BH24: Ashl H 2A 12
Bute Dr. BH23: Highc 5B 48
Butlers La. BH24: Poul 2E 9
Buttercup Dr. BH23: Chri 4D 46
Buttery, The BH23: Chri 6H 45
Button's La. BH15: Poole 5B 4
Butts Lawn SO42: Broc 2E 73
Butts Paddock SO42: Broc 2E 73
Byron Ct. BH22: Fern 4B 18
Byron Ho. BH25: New M 3G 49
Byron Rd. BH5: Bour 3F 61
BH21: W Min 3E 15
BH25: B Sea 5E 49

C

Cabot Bus. Village BH17: Poole 6H 37
Cabot La. BH17: Poole 5G 37
Cabot Way BH25: New M 2F 49
Cadhay Cl. BH25: New M 2F 49
Cadnam Way BH8: Bour 2D 42
Cadogan Rd. BH24: Ring 4D 8
Caernarvon Ho. *BH2: Bour* *4G 59*
(off Norwich Av.)
Caesar's Way BH18: Broad 1E 37
Caird Av. BH25: New M 3A 50
Cairns Cl. BH23: Chri 5D 44
Caister Cl. BH22: Fern 3A 18
Calder Rd. BH17: Poole 5D 38
Caledonian Cl. BH23: Chri 6D 46
Caledonian Ct. BH1: Bour 3D 60
Caledon Rd. BH14: Poole 4H 57
Calkin Cl. BH23: Chri 4E 45
Calluna Rd. BH12: Poole 5F 39
Calmore Cl. BH8: Bour 2D 42
Calpe Av. SO43: Lyn 2F 71
Calvin Rd. BH9: Bour 5H 41
Cambridge Gdns. BH23: Chri 3D 44
Cambridge Rd. BH2: Bour 4F 59
Camden Cl. BH9: Bour 4B 42
Camden Hurst SO41: M Sea 3B 66
Camelford Ct. *BH4: Bour* *4F 59*
(off Marlborough Rd.)
Camelia BH23: Highc 5H 47
Camellia Cl. BH21: Thr C 1A 10
Camellia Gdns. BH10: Bour 3E 41
BH25: New M 3H 49
Cameron Rd. BH23: Chri 6H 45
Cammel Rd. BH22: W Par 1F 25
Campbell Rd. BH1: Bour 2E 61
BH23: Burt 2G 45
Campion Gro. BH23: Chri 1B 64
Campion Way SO41: Lymi 6G 35
Canberra Cl. BH23: Chri 4C 44
Canberra Rd. BH23: Chri 5C 44
Candys Cl. BH21: Cor M 1E 21
Candy's La. BH21: Cor M 1D 20
Canford Av. BH11: Bour 4B 40
CANFORD BOTTOM 3B 16
Canford Bottom BH21: Cole, Lit C 3B 16

Canford Bottom Rdbt.—Cherrett Cl.

Canford Bottom Rdbt. BH21: Cole 4C 16
Canford Bus. Pk. BH21: Mer 3G 23
CANFORD CLIFFS 1B 70
Canford Cliffs Av. BH14: Poole 5H 57
Canford Cliffs Chine Gdns. 2B 70
Canford Cliffs Rd. BH13: Poole 6A 58
Canford Ct. BH13: Poole 3A 70
Canford Cres. BH13: Poole 2A 70
Canford Gdns. BH11: Bour 4C 40
CANFORD HEATH 3C 38
Canford Heath Nature Reserve 1B 38
Canford Heath Rd. BH17: Poole 3A 38
Canford Hgts. BH13: Poole 1B 70
CANFORD MAGNA 2E 23
Canford Magna BH21: Can M 1E 23
Canford Magna Golf Courses 1G 23
Canford Pk. Events Arena 4F 23
Canford Rd. BH11: Bour 4C 40
BH15: Poole 1D 4 (3B 56)
Canford School Golf Course 2F 23
Canford Sports Cen. 1F 23
Canford Vw. Dr. BH21: Cole 3B 16
Canford Way BH12: Poole 3F 39
Cannon Cl. BH18: Broad 4F 37
Cannon Hill Gdns. BH21: Cole 2B 16
Cannon Hill Rd. BH21: Cole 2A 16
Cannon Ho. SO41: Lymi 1G 53
Cannon St. SO41: Lymi 1G 53
Canons Wlk. SO41: M Sea 2E 67
Canterbury Cl. BH22: W Moo 6D 10
Canute Dr. BH23: Bran 2D 28
Canute Ho. BH15: Poole 5B 4
Capella Ct. BH2: Bour 5G 5 (5H 59)
Capesthorne BH23: Mude 2D 64
Cappella BH13: Poole 2A 70
Capstans, The BH14: Poole 1F 69
Capstone Gdns. BH8: Bour 1D 60
Capstone Pl. BH8: Bour 1D 60
Capstone Rd. BH8: Bour 1B 60
Captain's Row SO41: Lymi 1H 53
Caradon Pl. BH31: Ver 2B 6
Carbery Av. BH6: Bour 3B 62
Carbery Gdns. BH6: Bour 2C 62
Carbery La. BH6: Bour 3A 62
Carbery Mt. *BH6: Bour* *3B 62*
(off Carbery Av.)
Carbery Row *BH6: Bour* *3A 62*
(off Southbourne Rd.)
Cardigan Rd. BH9: Bour 5H 41
BH12: Poole 2B 58
Carey Rd. BH9: Bour 3H 41
Careys Cotts. SO42: Broc 2E 73
Careys Rd. BH8: Bour 1D 42
Carina Ct. BH13: S'bks 6G 69
Carisbrooke BH13: Poole 2A 70
Carisbrooke Ct. BH25: New M 2F 49
Carisbrooke Cres. BH15: Hamw 4D 54
Carisbrooke Way BH23: Chri 4G 47
Carlinford BH5: Bour 4F 61
Carlton Av. BH25: B Sea 5D 48
Carlton Ct. BH1: Bour 3D 60
Carlton Dene BH6: Bour 4A 62
Carlton Grange BH2: Bour 1F 5 (3G 59)
Carlton Gro. BH12: Poole 2H 57
Carlton Ho. BH1: Bour 2A 60
SO41: Lymi 1G 53
Carlton Mt. BH2: Bour 4F 5 (4G 59)
Carlton Rd. BH1: Bour 3C 60
Carlyle Rd. BH6: Bour 1B 62
Carmel Cl. BH15: Hamw 5D 54
Carnarvon Rd. BH1: Bour 3E 61
Carnegie Cl. BH12: Poole 2H 57
Caroline Av. BH23: Mude 1A 64
Caroline Rd. BH11: Bour 2D 40
Carpenter Cl. SO41: Lymi 6F 35
Carrbridge Cl. BH3: Bour 6F 41
Carrbridge Gdns. BH3: Bour 6F 41
Carrbridge Rd. BH3: Bour 6E 41
Carrick Way BH25: New M 3A 50
Carrington Caravan Pk. SO41: M Sea 4F 67
Carrington Cl. SO41: M Sea 2E 67
Carrington La. SO41: M Sea 2E 67
Carroll Av. BH22: Fern 4C 18
Carroll Cl. BH12: Poole 1C 58
Carsworth Way BH17: Poole 3E 39
Carter Cl. BH10: Bour 3F 41
Carters Av. BH15: Hamw 3D 54
Carters La. BH15: Poole 4B 4 (5A 56)
Cartref Cl. BH31: Ver 3D 6
Cartwright Cl. BH10: Bour 1E 41
Carvers Ind. Est. BH24: Ring 4B 8
Carvers La. BH24: Ring 4C 8
Carysfort Rd. BH1: Bour 3D 60
Cashmoor Cl. BH12: Poole 6B 40
Caslake Cl. BH25: New M 4F 49
Cassel Av. BH4: Bour 6D 58
BH13: Poole 6D 58
Casterbridge Rd. BH22: Fern 6H 17
Castle Av. BH23: Highc 5G 47
Castle Cl. SO41: M Sea 4E 67
Castlecourt BH6: Bour 2A 62
Castledene Cres. BH14: Poole 5E 57
Castle Gate Cl. BH8: Bour 3C 42
Castle Hill BH14: Poole 3F 57
Castle Hill Ct. BH14: Poole 3G 57
Castle La. E. BH7: Bour 4G 43
Castle La. W. BH8: Bour 3C 42
BH9: Bour 1A 42
Castlemain Av. BH6: Bour 2H 61
Castleman Ct. BH22: W Moo 4B 10
Castleman Gdns. BH24: Ashl H 1B 12
Castleman Way BH24: Ring 5C 8
Castlemews BH24: A'ley 2E 13
Castle Pde. BH7: Bour 6B 44
Castlepoint Shop. Cen. BH8: Bour 3E 43
Castle Rd. BH9: Bour 4H 41
Castle St. BH15: Poole 5B 4 (6A 56)
BH23: Chri 1F 63
Castleton Av. BH10: Bour 5F 25
Castle Way BH8: Bour 3D 42
Castlewood BH24: A'ley 2F 13
Catalina Cl. BH23: Mude 1C 64
Catalina Dr. BH15: Poole 6B 56
Caterstone BH21: W Min 4D 14
Catherine Wheel Gdns. *BH23: Chri* *2C 44*
(off Marlow Dr.)
Caton Cl. BH12: Poole 5D 40
Cattistock Rd. BH8: Bour 4E 43
Cavan Cres. BH17: Poole 4H 37
Cavendish Cnr. Mobile Home Pk.
BH24: Poul 3D 8
Cavendish Ct. BH1: Bour 3A 60
Cavendish Hall BH1: Bour 2A 60
Cavendish Mnr. BH1: Bour 3A 60
Cavendish Pl. BH1: Bour 2A 60
SO41: Lymi 1F 53
Cavendish Rd. BH1: Bour 1H 5 (2H 59)
Caversham Cl. BH15: Hamw 4E 55
Cawdor Rd. BH3: Bour 6F 41
Caxton Cl. BH23: Chri 6B 46
Cecil Av. BH8: Bour 6B 42
Cecil Cl. BH21: Cor M 5E 21
Cecil Ct. BH8: Bour 5B 42
Cecil Hill BH8: Bour 5B 42
Cecil Rd. BH5: Bour 3E 61
BH12: Poole 1H 57
Cedar Av. BH10: Bour 5F 25
BH23: Chri 5B 44
BH24: St L 4A 12
Cedar Cl. BH16: Upt 5B 36
Cedar Ct. BH4: Bour 5D 58
Cedar Dr. BH21: Hay 4B 16
SO41: Ever 5H 51
Cedar Gdns. BH25: New M 4F 49
Cedar Gate BH24: Ring 4D 8
Cedar Grange BH13: Poole 3C 58
Cedar Lodge BH4: Bour 2E 59
Cedar Mnr. BH4: Bour 4E 59
Cedar Mt. SO43: Lyn 4F 71
Cedar Pk. BH21: Stap 2F 17
Cedar Pl. BH23: Bran 2D 28
BH25: New M 2H 49
Cedars, The BH4: Bour 3E 59
Cedar Trade Pk. BH21: Stap 3F 17
Cedar Way BH22: Fern 1A 18
Celandine Cl. BH23: Chri 5D 46
Cellars Farm Rd. BH6: Bour 4E 63
Cemetery Av. BH15: Poole 1D 56
Cemetery Rd. BH21: W Min 4D 14
Centenary Cl. SO41: Sway 1G 33
Centenary Ho. BH23: Chri 6F 45
Centenary Way BH1: Bour 2E 61
Central Av. BH12: Poole 1A 58
BH21: Cor M 4D 20
Central Dr. BH2: Bour 1F 5 (3G 59)
BH24: St L 1F 19
Centre Cinema
Lymington 1G 53
Centre for Community Arts
Boscombe 2F 61
Centre La. SO41: Ever 4A 52
Centre Pl. BH24: Ring 4B 8
Centurion Cl. BH15: Hamw 5E 55
Cerne Abbas BH13: Poole 6C 58
Cerne Cl. BH9: Bour 1B 42
Chaddesley Glen BH13: S'bks 3H 69
Chaddesley Pines BH13: Poole 3A 70
Chaddesley Wood Rd. BH13: S'bks 4A 70
Chaffey Cl. BH24: Poul 3E 9
Chaffinch Cl. BH17: Poole 3F 37
BH25: New M 3F 49
Chalbury BH13: Poole 5C 58
Chalbury Cl. BH17: Poole 3E 39
Chaldecott Gdns. BH10: Bour 1E 41
Chaldon Rd. BH17: Poole 3D 38
Chalfont Av. BH23: Chri 2B 44
Chalice Cl. BH14: Poole 3E 57
Chalwyn Ind. Est. BH12: Poole 6E 39
Champion Cl. SO41: M Sea 3F 67
Champtoceaux Av. BH31: Ver 2C 6
Chancerygate Trade Cen. BH17: Poole 5G 37
Chander Cl. BH22: Fern 5B 18
Chandlers Cl. BH7: Bour 5H 43
Chandos Av. BH12: Poole 5C 40
Channel Ct. BH25: B Sea 6E 49
Chant Cl. BH23: Chri 6H 45
Chantry, The BH1: Bour 3H 5 (3A 60)
Chantry Cl. BH23: Highc 4H 47
Chapel Cl. BH21: Cor M 5C 20
Chapel Ga. BH23: E Par 3C 26
Chapel La. BH15: Poole 3B 4 (5A 56)
BH21: Cor M 6C 20
BH21: W Min 4D 14
BH23: Bran 3C 28
BH23: E Par 2C 26
SO41: Sway 2H 33
SO43: Lyn 3E 71
Chapel Point BH14: Poole 3E 57
Chapel Ri. BH24: A'ley 5F 13
Chapel Rd. BH14: Poole 3E 57
Chapter House, The *BH5: Bour* *3F 61*
(off Hawkwood Rd.)
Charborough Rd. BH18: Broad 2H 37
Charhope Ct. BH14: Poole 3B 58
Charing Cl. BH24: Ring 5C 8
Charles Cres. BH25: New M 6H 31
Charles Gdns. BH10: Bour 3E 41
Charles Keightley Ct. BH21: W Min 6F 15
Charles Rd. BH15: Poole 3B 56
BH23: Chri 5B 46
Charlotte Cl. BH12: Poole 5E 41
BH23: Mude 1C 64
Charlotte Ct. BH25: New M 3G 49
Charlton Cl. BH9: Bour 1C 42
SO41: Hor 2D 50
Charltons, The BH2: Bour 2H 59
CHARMINSTER 3B 42
Charminster Av. BH9: Bour 4B 42
Charminster Cl. BH8: Bour 3B 42
Charminster Pl. BH8: Bour 3B 42
Charminster Rd. BH8: Bour 1A 60
Charmouth Gro. BH14: Poole 3E 57
Charnock Cl. SO41: Hor 2D 50
Charnwood Av. BH9: Bour 2B 42
Charnwood Cl. BH22: W Moo 5C 10
Charnwood Ho. BH6: Bour 4D 62
Charris Camping & Caravan Pk.
BH21: Cor M 1D 20
Chartcombe BH13: Poole 1A 70
Charter Rd. BH11: Bour 5H 23
Chartwell BH13: Poole 4D 58
Chase, The *BH8: Bour* *6D 42*
(off Queens Pk. Sth. Dr.)
BH24: A'ley 2F 13
BH31: Ver 3F 7
Chaseborough BH31: Ver 3C 6
Chaseside BH7: Bour 5G 43
Chatsworth BH13: Poole 1D 70
Chatsworth Rd. BH8: Bour 1B 60
BH14: Poole 2F 57
Chatsworth Way BH25: New M 2E 49
Chaucer Cl. BH21: W Min 3E 15
Chaucer Dr. SO41: M Sea 2D 66
Chaucer Rd. BH13: Poole 1B 70
Chaucombe Pl. BH25: New M 4F 49
Cheam Rd. BH18: Broad 1F 37
Cheddington Rd. BH9: Bour 1A 42
Chedington Cl. BH17: Poole 3C 38
Chelmsford Rd. BH16: Upt 6B 36
Chelsea Gdns. BH8: Bour 1C 60
Cheltenham Rd. BH12: Poole 2G 57
Chene Rd. BH21: W Min 5F 15
Chequers Cl. SO41: Penn 2D 52
Cherford Rd. BH11: Bour 3D 40
Cherita Ct. BH15: Poole 1D 56
Cheriton BH4: Bour 5E 59
Cheriton Av. BH7: Bour 5A 44
Cheriton Way BH21: W Min 3E 15
Cherrett Cl. BH11: Bour 1B 40

80 A-Z Bournemouth

Compton Lodge BH4: Bour 4F 59
    (off Marlborough Rd.)
Compton Rd. BH25: New M 3G 49
Concept Pk. BH12: Poole 5E 39
Condor Cl. BH21: Wool 1F 11
Conel Ct. BH9: Bour 5G 41
    (off Talbot Rd.)
Coneygar La. BH22: Long 6G 17
Conference Pl. SO41: Lymi 3H 53
Conifer Av. BH14: Poole 5F 57
Conifer Cl. BH22: W Par 2H 25
  BH23: Chri 2B 44
  BH24: St L 3H 11
Conifer Cres. SO41: Penn 2D 52
Conifers BH13: Poole 4D 58
Coniston Av. BH11: Bour 5A 24
Coniston Cl. BH31: Ver 4C 6
Coniston Rd. BH24: Ring 5D 8
Connaught Cl. BH25: New M 4E 49
Connaught Cres. BH12: Poole 1A 58
Connaught Rd. BH7: Bour 2H 61
Connell Rd. BH15: Poole 2A 56
Consort Cl. BH12: Poole 2G 57
Consort Ho. BH22: Fern 3B 18
Constable Cl. BH22: Fern 5A 18
Constitution Hill Gdns.
  BH14: Poole 2E 57
Constitution Hill Rd. BH14: Poole ..5D 56
Convent Mdws. BH23: Chri 2G 63
Convent Wlk. BH23: Chri 1G 63
Conway Cl. BH25: New M 2H 49
Conway Ct. BH25: New M 2H 49
Conways Dr. BH14: Poole 3E 57
Cook Cl. BH24: Poul 3E 9
Cooke Gdns. BH12: Poole 1B 58
Cooke Rd. BH12: Poole 1B 58
Cook Row BH21: W Min 5D 14
Coombe Av. BH10: Bour 2G 41
Coombe Gdns. BH10: Bour 3F 41
Coombe La. SO41: Sway 2H 33
Coombe Nurseries BH18: Broad 3G 37
Cooper Dean Dr. BH8: Bour 4F 43
Cooper Dean Roundabout, The BH7: Bour ..4G 43
Coopers La. BH31: Ver 1D 6
Copeland Dr. BH14: Poole 5F 57
Copper Beech Cl. BH12: Poole 3C 58
Copper Beeches BH2: Bour ..1H 5 (2H 59)
Copper Beech Gdns. BH10: Bour ...3F 41
Coppercourt Leaze BH21: W Min ...5E 15
    (off Poole Rd.)
Coppice, The BH22: W Moo 6E 11
  BH23: Mude 1D 64
  SO42: Broc 2C 72
Coppice Av. BH22: Fern 2H 17
Coppice Cl. BH24: St I 3B 12
  BH25: A'ley 1B 50
Coppice Vw. BH10: Bour 2G 41
Copse, The BH24: St L 1F 19
Copse Av. BH25: New M 3H 49
Copse Cl. BH14: Poole 4D 56
Copse Rd. BH25: New M 3H 49
  BH31: Ver 3D 6
Copse Way BH23: Chri 5G 47
Copsewood Av. BH8: Bour 4E 43
Copythorne Cl. BH8: Bour 3D 42
Corbar Rd. BH23: Chri 5C 44
Corbiere Av. BH12: Poole 4H 39
Corbin Av. BH22: Fern 3E 19
Corbin Ct. SO41: Penn 3D 52
Corbin Rd. SO41: Penn 2D 52
Corfe Halt Cl. BH21: Cor M 2E 21
CORFE HILLS 5F 21
Corfe Hills Nature Reserve 4F 21
Corfe Ho. BH15: Poole 4D 4 (5B 56)
Corfe Lodge Rd. BH18: Broad 1C 36
CORFE MULLEN 5D 20
Corfe Vw. Rd. BH14: Poole 4F 57
  BH21: Cor M 6C 20
Corfe Way BH18: Broad 2E 37
Corhampton Rd. BH6: Bour 1H 61
Cormorant Ho. BH15: Hamw 6G 55
    (off Norton Way)
Cornelia Cres. BH12: Poole 1C 58
Cornelia Rd. BH10: Bour 4D 40
Corner Point BH6: Bour 2B 62
Cornflower Dr. BH23: Chri 4E 47
Cornford Way BH23: Chri 5F 47
Cornish Gdns. BH10: Bour 4F 41
Corn Mkt. BH21: W Min 5D 14
    (off West Row)
Cornmarket Ct. BH21: W Min 4D 14
    (off West St.)
Cornwallis Rd. SO41: M Sea 3B 66

Coronation Av. BH9: Bour 3H 41
  BH16: Upt 6B 36
Coronation Cl. BH31: Ver 2D 6
Coronation Rd. BH31: Ver 2D 6
Corporation Rd. BH1: Bour 2B 60
Corscombe Cl. BH17: Poole 3C 38
Cortmerron BH4: Bour 5E 59
    (off West Cliff Rd.)
Cortry Cl. BH12: Poole 6C 40
Cotes Av. BH14: Poole 2E 57
Cotlands Rd. BH1: Bour 3B 60
Cotswold Cl. BH31: Ver 4D 6
Cotswold Ct. BH23: Chri 5B 46
    (off Hunt Rd.)
Cottage Gdns. BH12: Poole 2G 57
Cottagers La. SO41: Hor 2E 51
Cotton Cl. BH18: Broad 6F 21
Countess Cl. BH21: Mer 3C 22
Countess Gdns. BH7: Bour 5F 43
County Court
  Bournemouth 4H 43
County Gates La. BH4: Bour 3D 58
County Hgts. BH1: Bour 5H 5
Court Cl. BH23: Chri 6A 46
  SO41: Lymi 3F 53
Courtenay Dr. BH21: W Min 3E 15
Courtenay Pl. SO41: Lymi 2G 53
Courtenay Rd. BH14: Poole 3F 57
Courthill Rd. BH14: Poole 3G 57
Courtlands SO41: Lymi 1G 53
Courtleigh Mnr. BH5: Bour 3D 60
Court Lodge SO41: Lymi 3F 53
Courtney Pl. BH21: Cor M 6C 20
Court Rd. BH9: Bour 4B 42
Court Vw. BH7: Bour 2E 5
Courtyard, The BH1: Bour 3B 60
  BH4: Bour 3F 59
    (off Wharfdale Rd.)
  BH12: Poole 4G 39
  BH15: Poole 4B 4
  BH21: Can M 2E 23
Covena Rd. BH6: Bour 1B 62
Coventry Cl. BH21: Cor M 1C 36
Coventry Cres. BH17: Poole 3G 37
Cove Rd. BH10: Bour 3E 41
Cowdrey Gdns. BH8: Bour 3F 43
Cowdry's Fld. BH21: W Min 3D 14
Cowell Dr. BH7: Bour 5G 43
COWGROVE 4A 14
Cowgrove Rd. BH21: Cowg 4A 14
Cowley Rd. BH17: Poole 5B 38
  SO41: Lymi 1E 53
Cowleys Rd. BH23: Burt 3G 45
Cowper Av. BH25: New M 4G 49
Cowper Rd. BH9: Bour 3H 41
Cowpitts La. BH24: Hang, Poul 1E 9
Cowslip Cl. BH23: Chri 4E 47
Cowslip Rd. BH18: Broad 4E 37
Cox Av. BH9: Bour 1B 42
Cox Cl. BH9: Bour 1B 42
Cox Gdns. BH22: Fern 3B 18
Coxstone La. BH24: Ring 5C 8
Coy Pond Bus. Pk. BH12: Poole ...2C 58
Coy Pond Rd. BH12: Poole 2C 58
Crabbswood La. SO41: Sway 3C 32
Crab Orchard Way BH21: Thr C 6C 6
Crabton Cl. Rd. BH5: Bour 3F 61
Crabtree Cl. BH23: Burt 3G 45
Cracklewood Cl. BH22: W Moo 2E 19
Craghead BH1: Bour 4D 60
Craigleith BH1: Bour 3C 60
Craigmoor Av. BH8: Bour 3E 43
Craigmoor Cl. BH8: Bour 4F 43
Craigmoor Way BH8: Bour 3E 43
Craigside BH24: St L 4H 11
Craigwood Dr. BH22: Fern 4E 19
Cranborne Cres. BH12: Poole 5A 40
Cranborne Ho. BH8: Bour 3A 60
Cranborne Pl. BH25: New M 2E 49
Cranborne Rd. BH2: Bour 5F 5 (5G 59)
  BH21: W Min 3E 15
Cranbourne Ct. BH9: Bour 5B 42
    (off Rutland Rd.)
  BH17: Poole 3E 39
    (off Twyford Way)
Cranbrook M. BH12: Poole 1F 57
Cranbrook Rd. BH12: Poole 2F 57
Crane Cl. BH31: Ver 3C 6
Crane Dr. BH31: Ver 2C 6
Crane Ho. BH31: Ver 2C 6
    (off Peel Cl.)
Cranemoor Av. BH23: Chri 3G 47
Cranemoor Cl. BH23: Chri 3G 47

Cranemoor Gdns. BH23: Chri 3H 47
Cranes M. BH15: Poole 1D 4 (4B 56)
Crane Valley Golf Course 2A 6
Crane Way BH21: Wool 1F 11
Cranfield Av. BH21: W Min 4F 15
Cranleigh Cl. BH6: Bour 2C 62
Cranleigh Ct. BH6: Bour 2C 62
Cranleigh Gdns. BH6: Bour 2C 62
Cranleigh Paddock SO43: Lyn 2F 71
Cranleigh Rd. BH6: Bour 1B 62
Cranmer Rd. BH9: Bour 5H 41
Cransley Ct. BH4: Bour 5E 59
    (off Portarlington Rd.)
Crantock Grn. BH6: Bour 3F 43
Cranwell Cl. BH11: Bour 1A 40
  BH23: Bran 2D 28
Craven Cl. BH7: Bour 3B 60
    (off Knyveton Rd.)
Craven Grange BH2: Bour 2G 5 (3H 59)
Crawshaw Rd. BH14: Poole 5F 57
Creasey Rd. BH11: Bour 6C 24
Creech Rd. BH12: Poole 2G 57
Creedy Dr. BH23: Chri 2F 63
Creedy Path BH23: Chri 1F 63
CREEKMOOR 5G 37
Creekmoor La. BH17: Poole 4F 37
Crescent, The BH1: Bour 3E 61
  BH24: St L 1F 19
  BH25: New M 5D 48
Crescent Ct. BH2: Bour 5F 59
  BH25: B Sea 6F 49
    (off Marine Dr.)
Crescent Dr. BH25: B Sea 6F 49
Crescent Grange BH2: Bour 3E 5
Crescent Rd. BH2: Bour 3E 5 (4G 59)
  BH14: Poole 3A 58
  BH21: W Min 5E 15
  BH31: Ver 3E 7
Crescent Wlk. BH22: W Par 2G 25
Cresta Cl. BH2: Bour 3E 5
Cresta Gdns. BH22: W Par 1G 25
Crest Rd. BH12: Poole 1G 57
Cribb Cl. BH17: Poole 6C 38
Crichel Mt. Rd. BH14: Poole 2G 69
Crichel Rd. BH9: Bour 5A 42
Cricket Chambers BH1: Bour 3A 60
Cricket Cl. BH23: Mude 2B 64
Crimea Rd. BH9: Bour 6H 41
Cringle Av. BH6: Bour 3E 63
Crispin Cl. BH23: Highc 5H 47
Criterion Arc. BH1: Bour 4G 5 (4H 59)
Crittall Cl. SO41: Sway 1G 33
Crockford Cl. BH25: New M 6H 31
Croft Cl. BH21: Cor M 4D 20
Crofton Cl. BH23: Chri 4C 44
Croft Rd. BH9: Bour 3H 41
  BH12: Poole 1F 57
  BH23: Chri 6B 46
  BH23: Nea 5D 28
  BH24: Poul 2E 9
Cromer Gdns. BH12: Poole 2B 58
Cromer Rd. BH8: Bour 6D 42
  BH12: Poole 3B 58
Cromwell Pl. BH5: Bour 2H 61
Cromwell Rd. BH5: Bour 2H 61
  BH12: Poole 2H 57
  BH21: W Min 5F 15
Crooked La. BH25: New M 5A 50
Crosby Rd. BH4: Bour 6E 59
Crossmead Av. BH25: New M 3G 49
Cross Way BH23: Chri 4B 44
Crossways SO41: Ever 4H 51
Crossways, The BH16: Upt 6C 36
CROW 6E 9
Crow Arch La. BH24: Crow, Ring ...5D 8
Crow Arch La. Ind. Est. BH24: Ring ..6D 8
Crowe Hill Ct. BH15: Poole 3C 56
CROW HILL 6H 9
Crow La. BH24: Crow, Hight 5E 9
Crown Cl. BH12: Poole 2G 57
Crown Court
  Bournemouth 4H 43
Crown Ct. BH21: W Min 4D 14
Crown Mead BH21: W Min 4E 15
    (Hanham Rd.)
  BH21: W Min 5E 15
    (Park La.)
Crown Wlk. BH1: Bour 3E 61
Crusader Ct. BH4: Bour 3D 58
Crusader Rd. BH11: Bour 1H 39
Cruse Cl. SO41: Sway 1F 33
Cruxton Farm Courtyard BH21: Mer ..1B 22
Cucklington Gdns. BH9: Bour 1B 42

Dorset Rd.—Elm Ct.

Dorset Rd. BH4: Bour 2E **59**
BH23: Chri 5B **46**
Dorset Way BH17: Poole 6A **38**
Douglas Av. BH23: Chri 1D **62**
Douglas Cl. BH16: Upt 5C **36**
Douglas Ct. BH23: Chri 1D **62**
Douglas Gdns. BH12: Poole 2A **58**
Douglas M. BH6: Bour 2A **62**
BH16: Upt 5B **36**
Douglas Rd. BH6: Bour 3C **62**
BH12: Poole 2A **58**
Doulton Gdns. BH14: Poole 5F **57**
Doussie Cl. BH16: Upt 5A **36**
Dover Cl. BH13: Poole 4C **58**
Dover Rd. BH13: Poole 4C **58**
Doveshill Cres. BH10: Bour 2F **41**
Doveshill Gdns. BH10: Bour 2F **41**
Doveshill Mobile Home Pk. BH10: Bour 2F **41**
Dowden Ct. BH23: Chri 1D **62**
Dowlands Cl. BH10: Bour 1F **41**
Dowlands Rd. BH10: Bour 1F **41**
Downey Cl. BH11: Bour 3B **40**
Downland Pl. BH17: Poole 5C **38**
DOWNTON 1A **66**
Downton Cl. BH8: Bour 2C **42**
Downton Holiday Pk. SO41: Down 6D **50**
Downton La. SO41: Down 1A **66** & 6D **50**
Downy Ct. *BH14: Poole* *3H 57*
(off Bournemouth Rd.)
Doyne Rd. BH14: Poole 3A **58**
Dragoon Way BH23: Chri 6D **44**
Drake Cl. BH23: Mude 1B **64**
BH24: Poul 2F **9**
BH25: New M 2F **49**
Drake Ct. BH15: Poole 5B **4** (6A **56**)
Drake Rd. BH15: Poole 5B **4** (6A **56**)
Drakes Rd. BH22: Fern 6D **18**
Draper Rd. BH11: Bour 1C **40**
BH23: Chri 6A **46**
Draycott Rd. BH10: Bour 3F **41**
Dreswick Cl. BH23: Chri 1B **44**
Drew Cl. BH12: Poole 6E **41**
Drew Grange BH15: Hamw 3E **55**
Drewitt Ind. Est. BH11: Bour 3A **40**
Driftwood BH5: Bour 4F **61**
Driftwood Pk. BH23: Chri 4C **44**
Drive, The BH12: Poole 2H **57**
BH13: S'bks 2H **69**
Droxford Rd. BH6: Bour 1H **61**
Druids Cl. BH22: W Par 1F **25**
Druitt Rd. BH23: Chri 5B **46**
Drummond Rd. BH1: Bour 3D **60**
Drury Rd. BH4: Bour 5D **58**
Dryden Cl. BH24: Ashl H 2A **12**
Dryden Pl. SO41: M Sea 2D **66**
Duart Ct. BH25: New M 2A **50**
Ducking Stool La. BH23: Chri 1F **63**
Ducking Stool Wlk. *BH23: Chri* *1F 63*
(off Ducking Stool La.)
Duck Island La. BH24: Ring 5B **8**
Duck La. BH11: Bour 6B **24**
Dudley Av. SO41: Hor 2D **50**
Dudley Gdns. BH10: Bour 6F **25**
Dudley Pl. BH25: New M 4H **49**
Dudley Rd. BH10: Bour 6F **25**
Dudmoor Farm Golf Course 1E **45**
Dudmoor Farm Rd. BH23: Chri 1D **44**
Dudmoor La. BH23: Chri 1D **44**
DUDSBURY 2F **25**
Dudsbury Av. BH22: Fern 5B **18**
Dudsbury Cres. BH22: Fern 5B **18**
Dudsbury Gdns. BH22: W Par 3G **25**
Dudsbury Golf Course 2E **25**
Dudsbury Hillfort 3F **25**
Dudsbury Rd. BH22: W Par 2F **25**
Dudsway Ct. BH22: Fern 5B **18**
Dugdell Cl. BH22: Fern 3D **18**
Dukes Cl. BH6: Bour 1B **62**
Dukes Ct. *BH31: Ver* *2D 6*
(off Jenner Cl.)
Dukes Dr. BH11: Bour 6A **24**
Dukesfield BH23: Chri 3B **44**
Dulsie Rd. BH3: Bour 1E **59**
Dunbar Cres. BH23: Chri 3H **47**
Dunbar Rd. BH3: Bour 1G **59**
Duncan Rd. BH25: A'ley 1B **50**
Duncliff Rd. BH6: Bour 3E **63**
Dundas Rd. BH17: Poole 5C **38**
Dune Crest BH13: S'bks 6G **69**
Dunedin Cl. BH22: Fern 6H **17**
Dunedin Dr. BH22: Fern 6H **17**
Dunedin Gdns. BH22: Fern 6H **17**
Dunedin Gro. BH23: Chri 6E **47**
Dunford Cl. BH25: New M 5E **49**
Dunford Rd. BH12: Poole 2H **57**
Dunholme Mnr. BH1: Bour 4C **60**
Dunkeld Rd. BH3: Bour 1F **59**
Dunlin Cl. BH23: Mude 2D **64**
Dunnock Cl. BH22: Fern 1H **17**
Dunstans La. BH15: Poole 1E **57**
Dunyeats Rd. BH18: Broad 1H **37**
Dunyeats Rdbt. BH17: Poole 6B **22**
Durdells Av. BH11: Bour 5C **24**
Durdells Gdns. BH11: Bour 6C **24**
Durland Cl. BH25: New M 4G **49**
Durley Chine BH2: Bour 5F **59**
Durley Chine Ct. BH2: Bour 5F **59**
Durley Chine Rd. BH2: Bour 4F **59**
Durley Chine Rd. Sth.
BH2: Bour 5F **59**
Durley Gdns. BH2: Bour 5F **59**
Durley Rd. BH2: Bour 5E **5** (5G **59**)
Durley Rd. Sth. BH2: Bour 5E **5** (5F **59**)
Durlston Cres. BH23: Chri 1B **44**
Durlston Rd. BH14: Poole 5G **57**
DURNS TOWN 1G **33**
Durnstown SO41: Sway 1G **33**
Durrant Ho. BH2: Bour 3E **5**
Durrant Rd. BH2: Bour 2F **5** (3G **59**)
BH14: Poole 4G **57**
Durrant Way SO41: Sway 1F **33**
Durrell Way BH15: Poole 5B **56**
Durrington Pl. BH7: Bour 1H **61**
Durrington Rd. BH7: Bour 6H **43**
Durweston Cl. BH9: Bour 2B **42**
DW Sports Fitness
Branksome 2B **58**

E

Eaglehurst *BH12: Poole* *3C 58*
(off Eagle Rd.)
Eagle Rd. BH12: Poole 3C **58**
Earle Rd. BH4: Bour 6E **59**
Earles Rd. BH21: Thr C 2A **10**
Earley Ct. SO41: Lymi 1H **53**
Earlham Dr. BH14: Poole 3G **57**
Earlsdon Lodge *BH2: Bour* *3F 59*
(off Surrey Rd.)
Earlsdon Way BH23: Highc 5G **47**
Earlswood *BH4: Bour* *5E 59*
(off Clarendon Rd.)
Earlswood Pk. BH25: A'ley 6A **32**
East Av. BH3: Bour 1E **59**
BH25: New M 6C **48**
East Av. Rdbt. BH3: Bour 1G **59**
East Bank Rd. SO42: Broc 4F **73**
East Borough BH21: W Min 3D **14**
(not continuous)
EAST BROOK 5E **15**
Eastbrook Row BH21: W Min 5E **15**
EAST CLIFF 4A **60**
East Cliff BH2: Bour 2G **5** (3H **59**)
East Cliff Grange *BH1: Bour* *3D 60*
(off Knyveton Rd.)
East Cliff Prom. BH1: Bour 5H **5** (5A **60**)
East Cliff Way BH23: Fri C 6E **47**
East Cl. BH25: B Sea 5D **48**
Eastcott Cl. BH7: Bour 5G **43**
East Dorset Indoor Bowls Club 1H **63**
East Dorset Sailing Club 2G **69**
E. Dorset Trade Pk. BH21: Stap 3F **17**
East Dr. BH24: St L 1F **19**
EAST END 2E **21**
Easter Ct. BH5: Bour 3E **61**
Eastern Rd. SO41: Lymi 1F **53**
Eastern Way SO41: M Sea 3F **67**
Easter Rd. BH9: Bour 3A **42**
Eastfield Ct. BH24: Ring 4E **9**
Eastfield La. BH24: Poul, Ring 4E **9**
(not continuous)
East Hill SO41: Lymi 1G **53**
EAST HOWE 1E **41**
E. Howe La. BH10: Bour 2E **41**
Eastlake Av. BH12: Poole 1F **57**
Eastlands BH25: New M 4H **49**
East La. SO41: Ever 4A **52**
E. Overcliff Dr. BH1: Bour 5A **60**
EAST PARLEY 3C **26**
EAST PARLEY COMMON 6F **19**
East Quay BH15: Poole 5C **4** (6A **56**)
E. Quay Rd. BH15: Poole 5B **4** (6A **56**)
East St. BH15: Poole 4C **4** (5A **56**)
BH21: W Min 5E **15**
East Vw. Rd. BH24: Ring 4D **8**
East Way BH8: Bour 4B **42**
BH21: Cor M 6D **20**
Eastwood Av. BH22: Fern 3C **18**
Eastworth Rd. BH31: Ver 2C **6**
(not continuous)
Eaton Ct. BH1: Bour 3A **60**
Eaton Rd. BH13: Poole 5C **58**
EBBLAKE 4G **7**
Ebblake Cl. BH31: Ver 6G **7**
Ebblake Ent. Pk. BH31: Ver 4G **7**
Ebblake Ind. Est. BH31: Ver 5H **7**
Ebenezer La. BH24: Ring 4B **8**
Ebor Cl. BH22: W Par 1G **25**
Ebor Rd. BH12: Poole 1H **57**
Eccles Rd. BH15: Hamw 5G **55**
Eden Ct. BH1: Bour 4B **60**
BH4: Bour *5E 59*
(off West Cliff Rd.)
Eden Gro. BH21: W Min 6F **15**
Edgarton Rd. BH17: Poole 2B **38**
Edgehill Rd. BH9: Bour 5G **41**
Edgemoor Rd. BH22: W Moo 6E **11**
Edifred Rd. BH9: Bour 1A **42**
Edmondsham Ho. BH2: Bour 4F **5** (4G **59**)
Edmondsham Rd. BH31: Ver 1C **6**
Edmunds Cl. BH25: B Sea 4F **49**
Edward Ct. *BH8: Bour* *6B 42*
(off Richmond Pk. Rd.)
Edward Ho. BH12: Poole 5C **40**
Edward May Ct. BH11: Bour 1C **40**
Edward Rd. BH11: Bour 2D **40**
(not continuous)
BH14: Poole 2G **57**
BH23: Chri 5B **46**
Edwards Cl. SO41: Penn 2D **52**
Edwina Cl. BH24: Poul 2E **9**
Edwina Dr. BH17: Poole 3H **37**
Efford Ct. SO41: Penn 3D **52**
Efford Way SO41: Penn 3D **52**
Egdon Cl. BH22: Fern 6H **17**
Egdon Ct. BH16: Upt 6B **36**
Egdon Dr. BH21: Mer 3C **22**
Egerton Ct. *BH8: Bour* *1D 60*
(off Egerton Gdns.)
Egerton Gdns. BH8: Bour 1D **60**
Egerton Rd. BH8: Bour 1D **60**
Egmont Cl. BH24: A'ley 5E **13**
Egmont Dr. BH24: A'ley 5F **13**
Egmont Gdns. BH24: A'ley 5F **13**
Egmont Rd. BH16: Hamw 3B **54**
Elcombes Cl. SO43: Lyn 3F **71**
Elderberry La. BH23: Mude 1B **64**
Eldon Av. BH25: B Sea 5E **49**
Eldon Cl. BH25: B Sea 5E **49**
Eldon Pl. BH4: Bour 4D **58**
Eldon Rd. BH9: Bour 4G **41**
Eleanor Ct. *BH25: New M* *4F 49*
(off Caslake Cl.)
Eleanor Dr. BH11: Bour 6H **23**
Eleanor Gdns. BH23: Chri 5C **44**
Elfin Dr. BH22: Fern 2A **18**
Elgar Rd. BH10: Bour 1F **41**
Elgin Ct. BH13: Poole 5D **58**
Elgin Rd. BH3: Bour 6F **41**
BH4: Bour 1F **59**
BH14: Poole 6F **57**
Elijah Cl. BH15: Hamw 5E **55**
Eliot Ho. BH25: New M 3G **49**
Elise Cl. BH7: Bour 5H **43**
Elizabeth Av. BH23: Chri 5D **44**
Elizabeth Ct. BH1: Bour 4A **60**
BH15: Poole *4B 56*
(off Longfleet Rd.)
BH22: Fern *4B 18*
(off Victoria Rd.)
Elizabeth Cres. SO41: Hor 3F **51**
Elizabeth Gdns. BH23: Chri 5F **47**
Elizabeth Rd. BH15: Poole 1D **4** (4B **56**)
BH16: Upt *6C 36*
(off Douglas Cl.)
BH21: W Min 3E **15**
Eliza Ct. BH5: Bour 3F **61**
Elkhams Cl. SO41: Ever 4H **51**
Ellerslie Chambers BH1: Bour 4H **5** (4H **59**)
Ellery Gro. SO41: Lymi 6G **35**
Ellesfield Dr. BH22: W Par 6B **18**
Ellingham Rd. BH25: New M 5D **48**
Elliot Rd. BH11: Bour 2B **40**
Elliott Rd. BH11: Bour 2A **40**
Elm Av. BH23: Chri 4C **44**
BH25: New M 3G **49**
SO41: Penn 4E **53**
Elm Ct. BH25: New M 3G **49**

84 A-Z Bournemouth

Gundrymoor Trad. Est.—Heathlands Av.

Gundrymoor Trad. Est. BH21: W Moo 1C **10**
Gunville Cres. BH9: Bour 2B **42**
Gurjun Cl. BH16: Upt .5A **36**
Gurney Rd. BH21: Cor M 5E **21**
Gussage Rd. BH12: Poole 5A **40**
Guy's Cl. BH24: Ring .4D **8**
Gwenlyn Rd. BH16: Upt 1C **54**
Gwynne Rd. BH12: Poole 2A **58**
Gypsy La. BH24: Ring .3D **8**

H

Haarlem M. BH23: Chri 6H **45**
Hadden Rd. BH8: Bour 5D **42**
Hadley Way BH18: Broad 2E **37**
Hadow Rd. BH10: Bour 2E **41**
Hadrian Cl. BH22: W Par 1F **25**
Hadrian Way BH21: Cor M 3E **21**
Haglane Copse SO41: Penn 3E **53**
Hahnemann Rd. BH2: Bour 5E **5** (5G **59**)
Haig Av. BH13: Poole .6A **58**
Hainault Dr. BH31: Ver 3E **7**
Haking Rd. BH23: Chri 6H **45**
Hale Av. BH25: New M 3H **49**
Halebrose Ct. BH6: Bour 4C **62**
Hale Gdns. BH25: New M 3H **49**
Halewood Way BH23: Chri 5D **44**
Halifax Way BH23: Chri 6D **46**
Hall Rd. BH11: Bour 2B **40**
Halstock Cres. BH17: Poole 3B **38**
Halter Path BH15: Hamw 4E **55**
Halter Ri. BH21: Cole .3C **16**
Halton Cl. BH23: Bran 3D **28**
Hamble Ct. BH1: Bour 3D **60**
Hambledon Gdns. BH6: Bour 1A **62**
Hambledon Rd. BH6: Bour 1A **62**
BH7: Bour 6H **43**
Hamble Rd. BH15: Poole 6D **38**
Hamblin Way BH8: Bour 3E **43**
Ham Common Nature Reserve 5B **54**
Hamilton Bus. Pk. BH25: New M 3E **49**
Hamilton Cl. BH1: Bour 2D **60**
BH15: Hamw 5E **55**
BH23: Mude 3B **64**
Hamilton Ct. BH8: Bour 2B **60**
SO41: M Sea 3C **66**
Hamilton Cres. BH15: Hamw 5E **55**
Hamilton Pl. SO41: Lymi 2F **53**
Hamilton Rd. BH1: Bour 2D **60**
BH15: Hamw 5E **55**
BH21: Cor M 6E **21**
Hamilton Way BH25: New M 3E **49**
Ham La. BH21: Hamp, Lit C, Long 5D **16**
BH21: Hay 5B **16**
BH22: Long 5D **16**
Hampden La. BH6: Bour 2H **61**
HAMPRESTON 1B **24**
Hampreston Rd. BH22: Long 1C **24**
Hampshire Cl. BH23: Chri 3D **44**
Hampshire Ct. BH2: Bour 3G **5** (4H **59**)
Hampshire Hatches La. BH24: Ring 4H **13**
Hampshire Ho. BH2: Bour 3G **5**
Hampton Ct. BH2: Bour 3F **59**
Hampton Dr. BH24: Poul 2D **8**
Hampton Lodge BH4: Bour 4E **59**
Hampton Pl. BH8: Bour 6B **42**
Hamptons, The BH14: Poole 1A **70**
HAMWORTHY 4E **55**
Hamworthy Lodge BH15: Hamw 5F **55**
Hamworthy Sports Club 3F **23**
Hamworthy Station (Rail) 3D **54**
Handley Ct. BH24: Ring 4B **8**
HANGERSLEY 1G **9**
HANGERSLEY HILL .2G **9**
Hanham Rd. BH21: Cor M 6D **20**
BH21: W Min 4E **15**
Hankinson Rd. BH9: Bour 5A **42**
Hanlon Cl. BH11: Bour 1D **40**
Hannah Grange BH1: Bour 2C **60**
Hannah Way SO41: Penn 5B **34**
Hannington Gro. *BH7: Bour* *2G 61*
(off Hannington Pl.)
Hannington Pl. BH7: Bour 2G **61**
Hannington Rd. BH7: Bour 2G **61**
Hanover Grn. BH17: Poole 5D **38**
Hanover Ho. BH15: Poole 4B **56**
HAPPY BOTTOM 2F **21**
Harbeck Rd. BH8: Bour 2C **42**
Harbour Cl. BH13: S'bks 3H **69**
Harbour Ct. BH15: Poole 3B **4** (5H **55**)
BH23: Chri 1A **64**
BH25: B Sea 6E **49**
Harbour Cres. BH23: Chri 2A **64**
Harbour Ga. BH15: Poole 1C **4** (4A **56**)
Harbour Hill Cres. BH15: Poole 2C **56**
Harbour Hill Rd. BH15: Poole 3C **56**
Harbour Lights BH14: Poole 2E **57**
Harbour Pk. BH15: Poole 5B **56**
Harbour Prospect BH14: Poole 1G **69**
Harbour Rd. BH6: Bour 4E **63**
Harbour Sail BH15: Poole 3B **4** (5A **56**)
Harbour Vw. Cl. BH14: Poole 2E **57**
Harbour Vw. Ct. BH23: Chri 2F **63**
Harbour Vw. Rd. BH14: Poole 2E **57**
Harbour Watch BH14: Poole 2G **69**
Harcombe Cl. BH17: Poole 2C **38**
Harcourt *BH1: Bour* *4C 60*
(off Derby Rd.)
Harcourt Rd. BH5: Bour 2G **61**
Hardy Cl. BH22: W Moo 6D **10**
BH25: New M 2F **49**
Hardy Cres. BH21: W Min 6F **15**
Hardy Rd. BH14: Poole 3H **57**
BH22: W Moo 6D **10**
Hare La. BH25: A'ley .2B **50**
SO41: Hor 2B **50**
Hares Grn. BH7: Bour 5G **43**
Harewood Av. BH7: Bour 6F **43**
Harewood Cres. BH7: Bour 6F **43**
Harewood Gdns. BH7: Bour 6F **43**
Harewood Grn. SO41: Key 3G **67**
Harewood Pl. BH7: Bour 1H **61**
Harford Cl. SO41: Penn 4D **52**
Harford Rd. BH12: Poole 5G **39**
Harkwood Dr. BH15: Hamw 3E **55**
Harland Rd. BH6: Bour 3E **63**
Harleston Vs. BH21: W Min 5F **15**
Harley Gdns. BH1: Bour 3D **60**
Harling Ho. *BH6: Bour* *3A 62*
(off Stourwood Av.)
Harness Cl. BH21: Cole 3B **16**
Harraby Grn. BH18: Broad 2G **37**
Harrier Dr. BH21: Mer 1B **22**
Harriers Cl. BH23: Chri 5F **47**
Harrison Av. BH1: Bour 1D **60**
Harrison Cl. BH23: Burt 2G **45**
Harrison Way BH22: W Moo 4C **10**
Harris Way BH25: New M 5A **32**
Harrow Cl. BH23: Nea 4D **28**
Harrow Rd. BH23: Bock, Bran, Nea 4C **28**
Harrow Wood Farm Caravan Pk.
BH23: Bran 3E **29**
Harry Barrows Cl. BH24: Ring 5C **8**
Harry Paye Cl. BH15: Poole 3C **56**
Hart Cl. BH25: New M 1F **49**
Hartford Ct. BH1: Bour 3C **60**
Harting Rd. BH6: Bour 6B **44**
Hartmoor Gdns. BH10: Bour 4F **41**
Hartnell Ct. BH21: Cor M 6D **20**
Hartsbourne Dr. BH7: Bour 5H **43**
Hartshill Ct. BH22: Fern 5C **18**
Harts Way SO41: Ever 4H **51**
Hartwell Rd. BH17: Poole 6B **38**
Harvester Way SO41: Lymi 5F **35**
Harvey Rd. BH5: Bour 2G **61**
BH21: Mer 3C **22**
(Arrowsmith La.)
BH21: Mer 2D **22**
(Merley La.)
Harwell Rd. BH17: Poole 6B **38**
Harwood Ct. BH25: New M 2F **49**
Haskells Cl. SO43: Lyn 4E **71**
Haskells Rd. BH12: Poole 6F **39**
Haslemere Av. BH23: Highc 5H **47**
Haslemere Pl. BH23: Highc 4A **48**
Hasler Rd. BH17: Poole 3A **38**
Haslop Rd. BH21: Cole 2A **16**
Hastings Rd. BH8: Bour 3F **43**
BH17: Poole 3H **37**
Hatch Pond Rd. BH17: Poole 5A **38**
Hatfield Ct. BH25: New M 2E **49**
Hatfield Gdns. BH7: Bour 5H **43**
Hathaway Rd. BH6: Bour 3B **62**
Hatherden Av. BH14: Poole 2D **56**
Havelock Rd. BH12: Poole 2C **58**
Havelock Way BH23: Chri 3F **47**
Haven Cl. BH23: Chri 1A **64**
Haven Ct. BH13: S'bks 6F **69**
SO41: M Sea 3C **66**
Haven Gdns. BH25: New M 3H **49**
Haven Hgts. BH13: Poole 2B **70**
Haven Point SO41: Lymi 1H **53**
Haven Rd. BH13: Poole, S'bks 3H **69**
BH21: Cor M 5C **20**
Haverstock Rd. BH9: Bour 3B **42**
Haviland Ct. BH7: Bour 2F **61**
Haviland M. BH7: Bour 2F **61**
Haviland Rd. BH7: Bour 2F **61**
BH21: Stap 2G **17**
Haviland Rd. E. BH7: Bour 2F **61**
Haviland Rd. W. BH1: Bour 3F **61**
Hawden Rd. BH11: Bour 4C **40**
Hawkchurch Gdns. BH17: Poole 3C **38**
Hawk Cl. BH21: Cole .2A **16**
Hawker Cl. BH21: Mer 2D **22**
Hawkins Cl. BH24: Poul 2E **9**
Hawkins Rd. BH12: Poole 4B **40**
Hawks Lea SO41: M Sea 3D **66**
Hawkwood M. BH5: Bour 2F **61**
Hawkwood Rd. BH5: Bour 3E **61**
Haworth Cl. BH23: Chri 4E **45**
Hawthorn Cl. BH25: A'ley 1A **50**
Hawthorn Dr. BH17: Poole 4F **37**
SO41: Sway 1F **33**
Hawthorn Rd. BH9: Bour 5H **41**
BH23: Bock, Burt 5A **28**
Hawthorns, The BH23: Chri 1B **64**
Haydens Ct. SO41: Lymi 1H **53**
Haydon Rd. BH13: Poole 6D **58**
HAYES 5B **16**
Hayes Av. BH7: Bour .1E **61**
Hayes Cl. BH21: Hay .5A **16**
Hayes La. BH21: Cole, Hay 5B **16**
Hayeswood Rd. BH21: Cole 3A **16**
Haymoor Rd. BH15: Poole 6D **38**
Haynes Av. BH15: Poole 3B **56**
Haysoms Cl. BH25: New M 4H **49**
Hayward Cres. BH31: Ver 4C **6**
Haywards Farm Cl. BH31: Ver 4C **6**
Haywards La. BH21: Cor M 3C **20**
Hayward Way BH31: Ver 4B **6**
Hazel Cl. BH23: Chri .4E **47**
Hazel Ct. BH25: New M 4H **49**
Hazeldene BH18: Broad 1G **37**
Hazeldene Ct. *BH8: Bour* *6B 42*
(off Richmond Pk. Rd.)
Hazel Dr. BH22: Fern .1A **18**
Hazell Av. BH10: Bour 3D **40**
Hazel Rd. SO41: Penn 1C **52**
Hazelton Cl. BH7: Bour 5G **43**
Hazelwood Av. BH25: New M 1E **49**
Hazelwood Dr. BH31: Ver 5F **7**
Hazlebury Rd. BH17: Poole 6G **37**
Hazlemere Dr. BH24: St L 4A **12**
Headlands Adventure Cen. 2C **8**
Headlands Bus. Pk. BH24: Blas 1C **8**
Headlinglea BH13: Poole 4D **58**
Heads Farm Cl. BH10: Bour 6G **25**
Heads La. BH10: Bour 6G **25**
Headswell Av. BH10: Bour 1G **41**
Headswell Cres. BH10: Bour 1G **41**
Headswell Gdns. BH10: Bour 6G **25**
Heanor Cl. BH10: Bour 3E **41**
Hearts of Oak M. SO41: Lymi 1F **53**
Heath Av. BH15: Poole 1B **56**
Heath Cl. BH21: Cole .2B **16**
Heathcote Ct. *BH5: Bour* *3F 61*
(off Heathcote Rd.)
Heathcote Ho. BH5: Bour 4E **61**
Heathcote Rd. BH5: Bour 3F **61**
Heatherbank Rd. BH4: Bour 4E **59**
Heatherbrae La. BH16: Upt 1B **54**
Heather Cl. BH8: Bour 1D **42**
BH21: Cor M 5E **21**
BH23: Walk 3A **48**
BH24: St L 4A **12**
SO41: Hor 2E **51**
Heatherdell BH16: Upt 1B **54**
Heatherdown Rd. BH22: W Moo 6E **11**
Heatherdown Way BH22: W Moo 6E **11**
Heather Dr. BH22: Fern 2B **18**
Heather Grange BH24: Ashl H 2A **12**
Heatherlands Ri. BH12: Poole 2H **57**
Heatherlea Rd. BH6: Bour 3B **62**
Heather Lodge BH25: New M 2G **49**
Heather Rd. BH10: Bour 2F **41**
Heather Vw. Rd. BH12: Poole 6B **40**
Heather Way BH22: Fern 2B **18**
Heath Farm Cl. BH22: Fern 6A **18**
Heath Farm Rd. BH22: Fern 6A **18**
Heath Farm Way BH22: Fern 6A **18**
HEATHFIELD 2H **29**
Heathfield Av. BH12: Poole 5C **40**
Heathfield Caravan Pk. BH23: Bran 1H **29**
Heathfield Rd. BH22: W Moo 6D **10**
Heathfield Way BH22: W Moo 6D **10**
Heathlands SO41: Hor 2D **50**
Heathlands Av. BH22: W Par 1F **25**

Heathlands Cl.—Holworth Cl.

Heathlands Cl. BH23: Burt 2G 45
BH31: Ver 3E 7
Heathlands Lodge BH22: Fern 2B 18
Heath Rd. BH23: Walk 4B 48
BH24: St L 3H 11
SO41: Hor 2D 50
Heathwood Av. BH25: B Sea 5E 49
Heathwood Rd. BH9: Bour 5G 41
Heathy Cl. BH25: B Sea 5F 49
Heaton Rd. BH10: Bour 3D 40
Heavytree Rd. BH14: Poole 3F 57
Heckford La. BH15: Poole 1D 4 (4B 56)
Heckford Lodge BH15: Poole 2D 4
Heckford Rd. BH15: Poole 1D 4 (3B 56)
BH21: Cor M 6C 20
Hectors Ho. BH9: Bour 4H 41
Hedgerley BH25: B Sea 5H 49
Hedges, The BH25: A'ley 1A 50
Heights App. BH16: Upt 6C 36
Heights Rd. BH16: Upt 5C 36
Helic Ho. BH21: W Min 4E 15
Helyar Rd. BH8: Bour 3F 43
Henbest Cl. BH21: Hay 4C 16
Henbury Cl. BH17: Poole 3E 39
BH21: Cor M 5D 20
Henbury Ri. BH21: Cor M 5D 20
Henbury Vw. Rd. BH21: Cor M 5C 20
Henchard Cl. BH22: Fern 1E 25
Henderson Ct. SO41: Lymi 1H 53
Hendford Gdns. BH10: Bour 3F 41
Hendford Rd. BH10: Bour 3F 41
Hengistbury Head Nature Reserve 3G 63
Hengistbury Ho. *BH23: Chri* *1H 63*
(off Purewell)
Hengistbury Rd. BH6: Bour 3D 62
BH25: B Sea 5E 49
Hengist Pk. (Caravan Pk.) BH6: Bour 3F 63
Hengist Rd. BH1: Bour 3D 60
Henley Gdns. BH7: Bour 6G 43
Hennings Pk. Rd. BH15: Poole 2B 56
Henning Wharf *BH15: Poole* *5B 4*
(off The Quay)
Henville Rd. BH8: Bour 2C 60
Hepburn Ct. *BH23: Chri* *1D 62*
(off King's Av.)
Herbert Av. BH12: Poole 5G 39
Herbert Ct. BH12: Poole 5H 39
Herberton Rd. BH6: Bour 2A 62
Herbert Rd. BH4: Bour 5D 58
BH25: New M 2H 49
Hercules Rd. BH15: Hamw 4D 54
Hereford Ct. BH23: Chri 1D 62
Hermitage Cl. BH21: Thr C 2A 10
BH25: A'ley 1A 50
Hermitage Rd. BH14: Poole 1E 57
Herm Rd. BH12: Poole 4H 39
Heron Cl. SO41: Sway 2F 33
Heron Ct. Rd. BH3: Bour 6A 42
BH9: Bour 6A 42
Heron Dr. BH21: Cole 2A 16
Heron Ho. *BH31: Ver* *2C 6*
(off Peel Cl.)
Herons Mead BH8: Bour 6D 26
Herstone Cl. BH17: Poole 4D 38
Hesketh Cl. BH24: St I 2C 12
Hestan Cl. BH23: Chri 1B 44
Heston Way BH22: W Moo 4B 10
Hevalo Cl. BH1: Bour 2E 61
Hewitt Rd. BH15: Hamw 3E 55
Heysham Rd. BH18: Broad 2G 37
Heytesbury Rd. BH6: Bour 2B 62
Hibberd Ct. BH10: Bour 4F 41
Hibberd Way BH10: Bour 4F 41
Hibbs Cl. BH16: Upt 6C 36
Hickes Cl. BH11: Bour 1B 40
Hickory Cl. BH16: Upt 5A 36
Higham Hgts. *BH15: Poole* *5B 56*
(off Mt. Pleasant Rd.)
Highbridge Rd. BH14: Poole 4G 57
Highbury Cl. BH25: New M 2H 49
Highclere Hall *BH1: Bour* *3D 60*
(off Manor Rd.)
HIGHCLIFFE 5A 48
Highcliffe Castle 6G 47
Highcliffe Castle Golf Course 6G 47
Highcliffe Cnr. BH23: Highc 5B 48
Highcliffe Ho. BH23: Highc 5B 48
Highcliffe Rd. BH23: Chri 5C 46
Highcliffe Sailing Club 3C 64
Higher Blandford Rd. BH18: Broad 4E 21
BH21: Cor M 4E 21
Higher Merley La. BH21: Cor M 3E 21
Highfield SO41: Lymi 2F 53
Highfield Av. BH24: Ring 3C 8
SO41: Lymi 2E 53
Highfield Cl. BH21: Cor M 6E 21
SO41: Sway 1F 33
Highfield Dr. BH24: Ring 2C 8
Highfield Gdns. SO41: Sway 1F 33
Highfield Ho. BH14: Poole 3F 57
Highfield Rd. BH9: Bour 3G 41
BH21: Cor M 1E 37
BH22: W Moo 3B 10
BH24: Ring 3C 8
SO41: Lymi 1E 53
High Howe Cl. BH11: Bour 1A 40
High Howe Gdns. BH11: Bour 1A 40
High Howe La. BH11: Bour 1A 40
Highland Av. BH23: Highc 4B 48
Highland Rd. BH14: Poole 2F 57
BH21: Cole, W Min 3F 15
Highlands Cres. BH10: Bour 1E 41
Highlands Rd. BH25: B Sea 5G 49
Highland Vw. Cl.
BH21: W Min 4F 15
High Marryats BH25: B Sea 6F 49
High Mead BH22: Long 1C 24
High Mead La. BH22: Long 2C 24
Highmoor Cl. BH14: Poole 4F 57
BH21: Cor M 6D 20
Highmoor Rd. BH11: Bour 4C 40
BH14: Poole 4G 57
BH21: Cor M 6D 20
High Oaks Gdns. BH11: Bour 1A 40
High Pk. Rd. BH18: Broad 1E 37
High Pines BH23: Chri 5F 47
High Point BH14: Poole 3G 57
High Ridge Cres. BH25: A'ley 2A 50
High St. BH15: Poole 5A 4 (6H 55)
BH21: W Min 4D 14
BH23: Chri 1F 63
BH24: Ashl H 1A 12
BH24: Ring 4B 8
SO41: Lymi 2G 53
SO41: M Sea 3D 66
SO43: Lyn 3F 71
High St. Nth. BH15: Poole 2D 4 (4B 56)
HIGHTOWN 5F 9
Hightown Gdns. BH24: Ring 5D 8
Hightown Hill BH24: Hight, Pic H 5F 9
Hightown Ind. Est. BH24: Ring 5D 8
Hightown Rd. BH24: Hight, Ring 5C 8
High Trees BH13: Poole 1C 70
Hightrees SO41: Penn 4F 53
Hightrees Av. BH8: Bour 4E 43
High Trees Wlk. BH22: Fern 2B 18
Highview Cl. BH23: Chri 2C 44
Highview Ct. BH23: Highc 6A 48
Highview Gdns. BH12: Poole 6G 39
High Way BH18: Broad 2F 37
Highwood La. BH24: Highw 1H 9 & 1E 9
Highwood Rd. BH14: Poole 3A 58
SO42: Broc 4E 73
Hilary Rd. BH17: Poole 4A 38
Hilda Rd. BH12: Poole 1A 58
Hiley Rd. BH15: Poole 1A 56
Hillary Cl. SO43: Lyn 5G 71
Hillary Rd. BH23: Chri 5A 46
HILLBOURNE 3G 37
Hillbourne Rd. BH17: Poole 3G 37
Hillbrow Rd. BH6: Bour 1H 61
HILLBUTTS 3B 14
Hill Cl. BH23: Bran 3C 28
Hillcrest Av. BH22: Fern 1A 18
Hillcrest Cl. BH9: Bour 2A 42
Hillcrest Rd. BH9: Bour 2A 42
BH12: Poole 2E 57
BH21: Cor M 6C 20
Hillcroft Cl. SO41: Lymi 1G 53
Hillditch SO41: Lymi 5F 35
Hill La. BH23: Bran 3C 28
BH23: Wat 3A 46
Hillman Rd. BH14: Poole 2H 57
Hillmeadow BH31: Ver 5E 7
Hillmorton Ct. *BH8: Bour* *2A 60*
(off Wellington Rd.)
Hillside Dr. BH23: Chri 1B 44
Hillside Gdns. BH21: Cor M 1C 36
Hillside M. BH21: Cor M 1C 36
Hillside Rd. BH12: Poole 4B 40
BH21: Cor M 1C 36
BH31: Ver 2D 6
SO41: Lymi 2E 53
Hill St. BH15: Poole 4B 4 (5A 56)
Hill Ter. BH21: Mer 1E 23
Hilltop Cl. BH22: Fern 2H 17
Hilltop Rd. BH21: Cor M 6E 21
BH22: Fern 2H 17
HILL VIEW 6D 20
Hill Vw. Rd. BH10: Bour 1F 41
BH22: Fern 2A 18
Hill Way BH24: Ashl H 2B 12
Hiltom Rd. BH24: Ring 4D 8
Hilton Cl. BH15: Poole 1E 57
Hilton Grange BH1: Bour 3C 60
Hilton Rd. BH25: New M 1H 49
HINCHESLEA 5A 72
Hinchliffe Cl. BH15: Hamw 5F 55
Hinchliffe Rd. BH15: Hamw 5F 55
HINTON 2H 47
Hinton Admiral M. BH23: Hin 3G 47
Hinton Admiral Station (Rail) 3G 47
Hinton Rd. BH1: Bour 4H 5 (4H 59)
Hinton Wood BH1: Bour 5A 60
Hinton Wood Av. BH23: Chri 3G 47
Hinton Wood La. BH23: Hin 3G 47
Hive Gdns. BH13: S'bks 3H 69
Hives Way SO41: Lymi 5F 35
Hobart Rd. BH25: New M 3F 49
Hobbs Pk. BH24: St L 3B 12
Hobbs Rd. BH12: Poole 5G 39
Hoburne Caravan Pk. BH23: Chri 5E 47
Hoburne Gdns. BH23: Chri 4E 47
Hoburne La. BH23: Chri 4E 47
Hoburne Naish Holiday Pk. BH25: New M 5C 48
Hoburne Rdbt. BH23: Chri 5D 46
Hodges Cl. BH17: Poole 6C 38
Hogarth Ct. BH8: Bour 5C 42
Hogarth Way BH8: Bour 3G 43
Hogue Av. BH10: Bour 6F 25
Holbury Cl. BH8: Bour 2E 43
Holcombe Rd. BH16: Upt 1B 54
HOLDENHURST 2H 43
Holdenhurst Av. BH7: Bour 1A 62
Holdenhurst Rd. BH8: Bour 4B 60
Holdenhurst Village Rd. BH8: Bour 2F 43
Holes Bay Nth. Rdbt. BH17: Poole 1G 55
Holes Bay Pk. BH15: Poole 3H 55
Holes Bay Rd. BH15: Poole 1A 4 (1H 55)
Holes Bay Rdbt. BH15: Poole 1H 55
Holes Cl. SO41: Hor 1D 50
HOLFLEET 6A 28
Hollands Wood Dr. BH25: New M 6G 31
Holland Way BH18: Broad 6F 21
Hollenden *BH12: Poole* *3C 58*
(off Poole Rd.)
Hollies Cl. SO41: Sway 2F 33
Holloway Av. BH11: Bour 6B 24
Hollybrook BH22: W Moo 5C 10
Hollybush Ho. *BH5: Bour* *4F 61*
(off Wollstonecraft Rd.)
Holly Cl. BH16: Upt 6A 36
BH22: W Moo 5B 10
BH24: St L 3H 11
Holly Ct. BH1: Bour 1D 60
BH2: Bour 4F 59
BH5: Bour *3F 61*
(off Florence Rd.)
BH9: Bour 5H 41
BH15: Poole 3B 56
BH22: W Moo 5B 10
Holly Gdns. BH23: Burt 4H 45
SO41: M Sea 2C 66
Holly Grn. Ri. BH11: Bour 1A 40
Holly Gro. BH31: Ver 4B 6
Holly Hedge La. BH17: Poole 5A 38
Holly La. BH21: Cowg, Pamp 4A 14
BH23: Walk 3C 48
BH25: A'ley 1A 50
Holly Lodge BH13: Poole 3C 58
Hollywood La. SO41: Lymi 6F 35
Holm Cl. BH24: Poul 2E 9
Holmdene Ct. *BH2: Bour* *4F 59*
(off Cambridge Rd.)
Holme Rd. BH23: Highc 5B 48
Holmfield Av. BH7: Bour 6A 44
Holm Hill La. BH23: Hin, Oss 4B 30
Holmhurst Av. BH23: Highc 4G 47
Holm Oak Cl. BH31: Ver 2C 6
Holm Oaks SO41: Penn 3E 53
Holmsley Cl. SO41: Penn 3D 52
Holmsley Rd. BH25: Woot 1D 30
HOLMWOOD 1D 24
Holmwood Gth. BH24: Hight 5F 9
Holnest Rd. BH17: Poole 4B 38
Holt Ho. BH1: Bour 2D 60
Holt Rd. BH12: Poole 1B 58
BH21: Thr C 2A 10
Holworth Cl. BH11: Bour 2A 40

Jupiter Way—Landford Gdns.

Jupiter Way BH21: Cor M .3E 21
(not continuous)
Justin Gdns. BH10: Bour .1G 41

K

Kamptee Copse BH25: New M .5H 31
Kangaw Pl. BH15: Hamw .5D 54
Katherine Chance Cl. BH23: Burt .2G 45
Katie Cl. BH14: Poole .2G 57
Katterns Cl. BH23: Chri .3C 44
Kay Cl. BH23: Chri .6A 46
Keats Av. SO41: M Sea .2D 66
Keats Ho. BH25: New M .3G 49
Keeble Cl. BH10: Bour .5F 25
Keeble Cres. BH10: Bour .5F 25
Keeble Rd. BH10: Bour .5F 25
Keel Gdns. SO41: Lymi .1G 53
Keel Ho. BH15: Poole .2D 4
Keepers La. BH21: Stap .4E 17
Keighley Av. BH18: Broad .3F 37
Keith Rd. BH3: Bour .1E 59
Kellaway Rd. BH17: Poole .5D 38
Kelly Cl. BH17: Poole .5D 38
Kelsall Gdns. BH25: New M .2G 49
Kemp Rd. BH9: Bour .5H 41
Kempthorne Ho. SO41: Lymi .1G 53
Kenilworth Cl. BH25: New M .2H 49
Kenilworth Ct. BH13: Poole .1B 70
BH23: Chri .6E 45
Kennard Ct. BH25: New M .2F 49
Kennard Pl. *BH25: New M .2G 49*
(off Kennard Rd.)
Kennard Rd. BH25: New M .1F 49
Kennart Rd. BH17: Poole .6H 37
Kenneth Ct. BH23: Highc .6B 48
Kennington Rd. BH17: Poole .5B 38
Ken Rd. BH6: Bour .3C 62
Kensington Ct. BH1: Bour .3D 60
Kensington Dr. BH2: Bour .3F 59
Kensington Pk. SO41: M Sea .3C 66
Kent Ho. *BH4: Bour .4E 59*
(off Marlborough Rd.)
Kent Rd. BH12: Poole .1A 58
Kenyon Cl. BH15: Poole .6C 38
Kenyon Rd. BH15: Poole .6C 38
Keppel Cl. BH24: Ring .4D 8
Kerley Rd. BH2: Bour .5F 5 (5G 59)
Kernella Ct. BH4: Bour .3D 58
Kerry Cl. SO41: Penn .2E 53
Kestrel Cl. BH16: Upt .5B 36
BH22: Fern .2H 17
Kestrel Ct. BH24: Ring .3C 8
Kestrel Dr. BH23: Mude .1C 64
Keswick Ct. BH25: New M .6H 31
Keswick Rd. BH5: Bour .3F 61
BH25: New M .6H 31
Keswick Way BH31: Ver .4C 6
Keverstone Ct. BH1: Bour .4D 60
Keyes Cl. BH12: Poole .4B 40
BH23: Mude .1B 64
KEYHAVEN .3G 67
Keyhaven Marshes Nature Reserve .3H 67
Keyhaven Rd. SO41: Key, M Sea .3E 67
Key La. BH15: Poole .5A 4
Keysworth Av. BH25: B Sea .5F 49
Keysworth Rd. BH16: Hamw .3C 54
Keythorpe BH1: Bour .4C 60
Khyber Rd. BH12: Poole .2H 57
Kilbride BH13: Poole .3C 58
Kilmarnock Rd. BH9: Bour .4H 41
Kilmington Way BH23: Highc .5G 47
Kiln Cl. BH21: Cor M .1C 36
Kiln Way BH31: Ver .5G 7
Kimberley Cl. BH23: Chri .5D 44
Kimberley Rd. BH6: Bour .1A 62
BH14: Poole .4F 57
Kimber Rd. BH11: Bour .2B 40
Kimmeridge Av. BH12: Poole .5F 39
King Cl. BH24: St I .3B 12
King Ct. BH13: Poole .5D 58
Kingcup Cl. BH18: Broad .3E 37
King Edward Av. BH9: Bour .3H 41
King Edward Ct. BH9: Bour .3H 41
Kingfisher Cl. BH6: Bour .1C 62
BH22: W Moo .5D 10
Kingfisher Ct. *BH1: Bour .4C 60*
(off Christchurch Rd.)
Kingfisher Pk. BH21: W Moo .1C 10
BH24: Blas .1C 8
Kingfisher Pk. Homes BH10: Bour .1H 41
Kingfishers, The BH31: Ver .4E 7
Kingfisher Way BH23: Mude .2C 64
BH24: Poul .1D 8
King George Av. BH9: Bour .3H 41
King George Mobile Home Pk.
BH25: New M .4F 49
King John Av. BH11: Bour .5H 23
King John Cl. BH11: Bour .5H 23
Kingland Cres. BH15: Poole .3C 4 (5A 56)
Kingland Rd. BH15: Poole .3D 4 (5B 56)
King Richard Dr. BH11: Bour .6H 23
King's Arms La. BH24: Ring .4B 8
Kings Arms Row BH24: Ring .4B 8
Kings Av. BH14: Poole .5H 57
BH23: Chri .1D 62
Kingsbere Av. BH10: Bour .3D 40
Kingsbere Gdns. BH23: Highc .5A 48
Kingsbere Rd. BH15: Poole .2C 56
Kingsbridge Rd. BH14: Poole .4G 57
Kingsbrook SO41: Hor .1D 50
Kingsbury's La. BH24: Ring .4B 8
Kings Cl. BH15: Poole .2B 56
BH22: W Moo .6C 10
SO41: Lymi .1F 53
SO43: Lyn .3F 71
Kings Ct. BH6: Bour .2D 62
Kings Courtyard BH1: Bour .3C 60
Kings Cres. BH14: Poole .5A 58
SO41: Lymi .1F 53
Kings Farm La. SO41: Hor .3F 51
Kings Farm Rural Workshops SO41: Hor .2F 51
Kingsfield BH24: Ring .5C 8
SO41: Lymi .3H 53
Kingsgate BH13: Poole .4D 58
Kings Grange BH4: Bour .5F 59
Kingsholme BH8: Bour .6B 42
Kings La. SO41: Sway .4H 33
Kingsley Av. BH6: Bour .3E 63
Kingsley Cl. BH6: Bour .3E 63
Kingsley Ho. BH9: Bour .3H 41
Kingsmead Ct. BH21: W Min .4D 14
Kings M. BH4: Bour .4E 59
Kingsmill Rd. BH17: Poole .6C 38
Kings Pk. Athletics Cen. .1F 61
Kings Pk. Dr. BH7: Bour .1E 61
(Holdenhurst Rd.)
BH7: Bour .1G 61
(Petersfield Rd.)
KING'S PARK HOSPITAL .2F 61
Kings Pk. Rd. BH7: Bour .1E 61
Kings Rd. BH3: Bour .6A 42
BH25: A'ley .1A 50
SO41: Lymi .1F 53
King's Saltern Rd. SO41: Lymi .3H 53
KINGSTON .5H 13
Kingston Pk. SO41: Penn .3F 53
Kingston Rd. BH15: Poole .3B 56
King St. BH21: W Min .5D 14
Kingsway BH22: Fern .1H 17
Kingsway Cl. BH23: Chri .4D 44
Kingswell Cl. BH10: Bour .3F 41
Kingswell Gdns. BH10: Bour .2D 40
Kingswell Gro. BH10: Bour .3D 40
Kingswell Rd. BH10: Bour .3D 40
Kingswood *BH4: Bour .5E 59*
(off West Cliff Rd.)
Kingswood Pl. BH2: Bour .4F 59
Kinross Rd. BH3: Bour .1G 59
Kinsbourne Av. BH10: Bour .3F 41
KINSON .5D 24
Kinson Av. BH15: Poole .6E 39
Kinson Common Nature Reserve .6D 24
Kinson Gro. BH10: Bour .5E 25
Kinson Pk. Rd. BH10: Bour .5F 25
Kinson Pottery Ind. Est. BH14: Poole .1E 57
Kinson Rd. BH10: Bour .4C 40
Kiosks, The BH15: Poole .5B 4
Kipling Rd. BH14: Poole .2F 57
Kirby Cl. BH15: Poole .1D 56
Kirby Way BH6: Bour .3B 62
Kirkham Av. BH23: Burt .2G 45
Kirkway BH18: Broad .1H 37
Kitchener Cres. BH17: Poole .4H 37
Kitchers Cl. SO41: Sway .1F 33
Kitscroft Rd. BH10: Bour .6E 25
Kittiwake Cl. BH6: Bour .1B 62
Kittiwake Ho. *BH15: Hamw .6G 55*
(off Norton Way)
Kitwalls La. SO41: M Sea .1D 66
Kivernell Pl. SO41: M Sea .2C 66
Kivernell Rd. SO41: M Sea .3C 66
Kiwi Cl. BH15: Poole .4C 56
Knapp Cl. BH23: Chri .5E 45
Knapp Mill Av. BH23: Chri .5E 45
Knightcrest Pk. SO41: Ever .4A 52
KNIGHTON .3H 23
Knighton Caravan Pk. SO41: Ever .4A 52
Knighton Heath Cl. BH11: Bour .1A 40
Knighton Heath Golf Course .2G 39
Knighton Heath Ind. Est. BH11: Bour .2A 40
Knighton Heath Rd. BH11: Bour .1A 40
Knighton La. BH21: Mer .4H 23
Knighton Pk. BH25: B Sea .5E 49
Knightsbridge Ct. BH2: Bour .5F 5
Knights Rd. BH11: Bour .6H 23
Knightstone Gro. BH22: W Moo .5B 10
Knightwood Av. SO43: Lyn .3F 71
Knightwood Cl. BH23: Chri .5F 47
SO43: Lyn .3F 71
KNOBCROOK .3D 14
Knobcrook Rd. BH21: W Min .3D 14
Knole Ct. BH1: Bour .3D 60
Knole Gdns. BH1: Bour .3D 60
Knole Rd. BH1: Bour .2D 60
Knoll Gdns. .4G 17
Knoll Gdns. BH24: St I .3B 12
Knoll La. BH21: Cor M .3B 20
Knoll Mnr. BH2: Bour .1G 5 (2H 59)
Knowland Dr. SO41: M Sea .2D 66
Knowle Rd. SO42: Broc .2D 72
Knowles Cl. BH23: Chri .6A 46
Knowlton Gdns. BH9: Bour .1B 42
Knowlton Rd. BH17: Poole .3D 38
Knyveton Ho. *BH1: Bour .3B 60*
(off Knyveton Rd.)
Knyveton Rd. BH1: Bour .3B 60
Kyrchil La. BH21: Cole .3H 15
Kyrchil Way BH21: Cole .2H 15

L

Labrador Dr. BH15: Poole .5D 4 (6B 56)
Laburnum Cl. BH22: Fern .3H 17
BH31: Ver .4G 7
Laburnum Dr. SO41: Ever .5A 52
Laburnum Ho. BH10: Bour .1H 41
Lacey Cres. BH15: Poole .1E 57
Lacy Cl. BH21: W Min .3E 15
Lacy Dr. BH21: W Min .3E 15
Ladin Ho. *BH8: Bour .1D 60*
(off Richmond Pk. Rd.)
Ladysmith Cl. BH23: Chri .6A 46
Ladywell BH13: Poole .5D 58
LA Fitness
Poole .4E 39
Lagado Cl. BH14: Poole .1G 69
Lagland Ct. BH15: Poole .5B 4 (6A 56)
Lagland St. BH15: Poole .3C 4 (5A 56)
Lagoon Cl. BH14: Poole .1F 69
Lagoon Rd. BH14: Poole .1F 69
Laidlaw Cl. BH12: Poole .5D 40
LAKE .6D 54
Lake Av. BH15: Hamw .6D 54
Lake Cnr. *BH25: New M .1G 49*
(off Fernhill La.)
Lake Cres. BH15: Hamw .4E 55
Lake Dr. BH15: Hamw .5C 54
(not continuous)
Lake Farm Cl. BH22: Long .3D 24
Lake Gro. Rd. BH25: New M .1F 49
Lake Rd. BH11: Bour .5D 24
BH15: Hamw .6D 54
BH31: Ver .5E 7
Lakeside BH24: Hight .5E 9
Lakeside Pines BH25: New M .1H 49
Lakeside Rd. BH13: Poole .6C 58
Lake Vw. Ct. *BH15: Poole .4B 56*
(off Mt. Pleasant Rd.)
Lakeview Dr. BH24: Hight .5F 9
Lake Vw. Mnr. BH25: New M .2G 49
Lakewood Rd. BH23: Highc .4G 47
Lake Yd. BH15: Hamw .6D 54
Lambs Cl. BH17: Poole .4A 38
LAMBS GREEN .1F 21
Lambs Grn. La. BH21: Cor M .1F 21
Lampton Ct. BH9: Bour .4H 41
Lampton Gdns. BH9: Bour .4H 41
Lanark Cl. BH15: Hamw .5F 55
Lancaster Cl. BH18: Broad .6F 21
BH23: Chri .6E 47
Lancaster Dr. BH18: Broad .6E 21
BH31: Ver .3C 6
Lancaster Rd. BH21: Stap .1G 17
Lancer Cl. BH23: Chri .6D 44
Lander Cl. BH15: Poole .5D 4 (6B 56)
Landford Gdns. BH8: Bour .3D 42

Landford Way—Loewy Cres.

Landford Way BH8: Bour . . . 3D 42
Landseer Rd. BH4: Bour . . . 4E 59
Lane, The BH8: Bour . . . 2C 60
SO43: Lyn . . . 2F 71
Lanes, The BH25: New M . . . 6G 31
Langdon Ct. BH14: Poole . . . 3H 57
Langdon Rd. BH14: Poole . . . 3G 57
Langley Chase BH24: Ashl H . . . 2C 12
Langley Rd. BH14: Poole . . . 3A 58
BH23: Chri . . . 4G 47
Langside Av. BH12: Poole . . . 5C 40
Langton Cl. BH25: B Sea . . . 5H 49
Langton Dene *BH4: Bour . . . 4E 59*
(off Portarlington Rd.)
Langton Rd. BH7: Bour . . . 2F 61
Lansdell Ct. BH15: Poole . . . 4C 56
Lansdowne Ct. BH1: Bour . . . 3C 60
(Christchurch Rd.)
BH1: Bour . . . 2A 60
(off Lansdowne Rd.)
Lansdowne Cres. BH1: Bour . . . 4A 60
Lansdowne Gdns. BH1: Bour . . . 3A 60
Lansdowne M. BH1: Bour . . . 3A 60
Lansdowne Rd. BH1: Bour . . . 2A 60
Lansdown Roundabout, The BH1: Bour . . . 4A 60
Lapwing Rd. BH21: Cole . . . 2A 16
Lara Cl. BH8: Bour . . . 2D 42
Larch Cl. BH17: Poole . . . 4E 37
BH24: St I . . . 3C 12
SO41: Hor . . . 2D 50
Larch Way BH22: Fern . . . 1A 18
Lark Rd. BH23: Mude . . . 1C 64
Larks Cl. BH22: Fern . . . 2H 17
Larksfield Av. BH9: Bour . . . 2C 42
Larkshill Cl. BH25: New M . . . 1H 49
Larks Ri. BH22: Fern . . . 2H 17
Lascelles Ct. BH7: Bour . . . 1H 61
Lascelles Rd. BH7: Bour . . . 1H 61
Laser Quest
Bournemouth . . . 3H 5 (4A 60)
Latch Farm Av. BH23: Chri . . . 5E 45
LATCHMOOR . . . 6D 72
Latchmoor Ct. SO42: Broc . . . 3F 73
Latimer Ct. BH9: Bour . . . 5H 41
BH13: Poole . . . 5D 58
Latimer M. BH9: Bour . . . 5H 41
Latimer Rd. BH9: Bour . . . 5H 41
Latimers Cl. BH23: Highc . . . 4H 47
Laundry La. SO41: M Sea . . . 3E 67
Laurel Cl. BH21: Cor M . . . 5D 20
BH23: Chri . . . 4F 47
BH24: St L . . . 3A 12
SO41: Hor . . . 1C 50
Laurel Dr. BH18: Broad . . . 1H 37
Laurel Gdns. BH18: Broad . . . 1A 38
Laurel La. BH24: St L . . . 4A 12
Laurels, The BH22: Fern . . . 2A 18
SO42: Broc . . . 4E 73
Lavender Cl. BH31: Ver . . . 4G 7
Lavender Gdns. SO41: Hor . . . 2C 50
Lavender Ho. BH8: Bour . . . 2B 60
Lavender Knot BH14: Poole . . . 3E 57
Lavender La. BH23: Chri . . . 5C 44
Lavender Rd. BH8: Bour . . . 1D 42
SO41: Hor . . . 2C 50
Lavender Vs. *BH23: Highc . . . 5B 48*
(off Waterford Rd.)
Lavender Wlk. BH8: Bour . . . 1D 42
BH25: B Sea . . . 5G 49
(off Highlands Rd.)
Lavender Way BH18: Broad . . . 2D 36
Laverstock Ct. BH6: Bour . . . 4B 62
Lavinia Rd. BH12: Poole . . . 6G 39
Lawford Ri. BH9: Bour . . . 2A 42
Lawford Rd. BH9: Bour . . . 1A 42
Lawn Cl. SO41: M Sea . . . 3E 67
Lawn Ct. BH2: Bour . . . 3F 59
Lawn Rd. SO41: M Sea . . . 3E 67
SO41: Penn . . . 2D 52
Lawns, The BH23: Highc . . . 5B 48
Lawns Cl. BH21: Cole . . . 3C 16
Lawns Rd. BH21: Cole . . . 3B 16
Lawn Vw. BH25: Bash . . . 6D 30
Lawrence Ct. BH8: Bour . . . 1C 60
Lawrence Dr. BH13: Poole . . . 6A 58
Lawrence Rd. BH24: Poul . . . 1E 9
Lawson Rd. BH12: Poole . . . 1F 57
Layard Dr. BH21: Mer . . . 2B 22
Layard Theatre . . . 1F 23
Laymoor La. BH21: Lit C . . . 4D 16
Layton Ct. BH12: Poole . . . 2H 57
Layton Rd. BH12: Poole . . . 2H 57
Lea, The BH31: Ver . . . 4E 7
LEAGREEN . . . 5F 51
Lea Green Farm SO41: Down . . . 5F 51
Leamington Rd. BH9: Bour . . . 6A 42
Leaphill Rd. BH7: Bour . . . 1G 61
Learning La. BH10: Bour . . . 2E 41
Learoyd Rd. BH17: Poole . . . 6B 38
Leat Pk. BH23: Bran . . . 4C 28
Lea Way BH11: Bour . . . 5A 24
Lechlade Gdns. BH7: Bour . . . 5G 43
Ledbury Rd. BH23: Chri . . . 2B 64
Ledgard Cl. BH14: Poole . . . 3F 57
Lee Ct. BH22: Fern . . . 4B 18
Leedam Rd. BH10: Bour . . . 1F 41
Leelands SO41: Penn . . . 4F 53
Lees Cl. BH23: Chri . . . 1B 44
Leeson Dr. BH22: Fern . . . 2H 17
Leeson Rd. BH7: Bour . . . 6E 43
Legg La. BH21: W Min . . . 5F 15
Legion Cl. BH15: Hamw . . . 5E 55
Legion Rd. BH15: Hamw . . . 5E 55
Leicester Rd. BH13: Poole . . . 3A 58
LEIGH . . . 5H 15
Leigham Va. Rd. BH6: Bour . . . 3B 62
Leigh Cl. BH21: W Min . . . 5G 15
Leigh Comn. BH21: W Min . . . 4G 15
Leigh Common Nature Reserve . . . 4H 15
Leigh Gdns. BH21: W Min . . . 5F 15
Leigh La. BH21: Cole . . . 4G 15
LEIGH PARK . . . 6G 15
Leigh Pk. SO41: Lymi . . . 1E 53
Leigh Rd. BH21: W Min . . . 5E 15
BH25: New M . . . 2G 49
Leighton Lodge BH2: Bour . . . 3F 59
Lentham Cl. BH17: Poole . . . 4B 38
Lentune Way SO41: Lymi . . . 3F 53
Leonard Hackett Ct. BH2: Bour . . . 2H 59
Le Patourel Cl. BH23: Chri . . . 6H 45
Leslie Rd. BH9: Bour . . . 5H 41
BH14: Poole . . . 4E 57
Leven Av. BH4: Bour . . . 2F 59
Leven Cl. BH4: Bour . . . 3F 59
Levet's La. BH15: Poole . . . 4A 4 (5H 55)
Lewens Cl. BH21: W Min . . . 5E 15
Lewens La. BH21: W Min . . . 5E 15
Lewesdon Dr. BH18: Broad . . . 1F 37
Lewis Ct. BH6: Bour . . . 3D 62
Lewis Gdns. BH10: Bour . . . 2E 41
LEWIS MANNING HOSPICE . . . 2G 69
Leybourne Av. BH10: Bour . . . 6E 25
(not continuous)
Leybourne Cl. BH10: Bour . . . 6E 25
LEYBROOK COMMON . . . 5F 13
Leydene Av. BH8: Bour . . . 4F 43
Leydene Cl. BH8: Bour . . . 4F 43
Leyland Rd. BH12: Poole . . . 3A 40
Leyside BH23: Chri . . . 1B 64
Liberty Cl. BH21: Wool . . . 1F 11
Liberty Ct. *BH1: Bour . . . 4C 60*
(off Christchurch Rd.)
BH23: Chri . . . 6D 44
Liberty's Owl, Raptor and Reptile Cen. . . . 6E 9
Liberty Way BH15: Poole . . . 4D 4 (5B 56)
Library M. BH12: Poole . . . 2H 57
Library Rd. BH9: Bour . . . 4H 41
BH12: Poole . . . 2A 58
BH22: Fern . . . 4B 18
Liederbach Dr. BH31: Ver . . . 5G 7
Lifeboat Quay BH15: Poole . . . 2A 4 (4H 55)
Lighthouse, The *BH2: Bour . . . 5F 59*
(off Chine Cres. Rd.)
BH6: Bour . . . 3A 62
Lighthouse (Poole's Cen. for the Arts)
. . . 2D 4 (5B 56)
Lights Cl. BH23: Chri . . . 6F 45
Lilac Cl. BH24: Ring . . . 3D 8
LILLIPUT . . . 1G 69
Lilliput Ct. BH14: Poole . . . 4F 57
Lilliput Rd. BH14: Poole . . . 1G 69
Lilliput Sailing Club . . . 6F 57
Lime Cl. BH15: Poole . . . 1D 56
Lime Gro. SO41: Ever . . . 5H 51
Limes, The BH2: Bour . . . 2E 5
Lime Tree Ho. SO41: Lymi . . . 1G 53
Limited Rd. BH9: Bour . . . 4A 42
Linbrook Almshouses BH24: Rock . . . 1E 9
Linbrook Ct. BH24: Ring . . . 2C 8
Lin Brook Dr. BH24: Poul . . . 1E 9
Linbrook Vw. BH24: Linf . . . 1H 9
Lincoln Av. BH1: Bour . . . 1D 60
BH23: Chri . . . 3D 44
Lincoln Rd. BH12: Poole . . . 6H 39
Lindberg Rd. BH21: Stap . . . 1G 17
Linden Cl. BH22: W Par . . . 2F 25
Linden Ct. *BH1: Bour . . . 2A 60*
(off Lansdowne Rd.)
BH8: Bour . . . 6C 42
(off Richmond Pk. Rd.)
BH24: Ring . . . 3B 8
Linden Gdns. BH24: Ring . . . 3B 8
Linden Rd. BH9: Bour . . . 2A 42
BH12: Poole . . . 1G 57
BH22: W Par . . . 2F 25
Lindens, The BH23: Burt . . . 2H 45
Linden Way SO41: Lymi . . . 1E 53
Lindsay Ct. BH13: Poole . . . 3C 58
Lindsay Gdns. BH13: Poole . . . 3C 58
Lindsay Mnr. BH13: Poole . . . 3C 58
Lindsay Pk. BH13: Poole . . . 3C 58
Lindsay Rd. BH13: Poole . . . 3B 58
Lindsey Ct. BH22: Fern . . . 6A 18
Lindurn Ct. BH12: Poole . . . 3C 58
Lineside BH23: Burt . . . 5G 45
LINFORD . . . 1H 9
Linford Cl. BH25: New M . . . 1G 49
Linford Rd. BH24: Hang, Poul . . . 2E 9
Lingdale Rd. BH6: Bour . . . 1B 62
Lingfield Ct. BH22: Fern . . . 5C 18
Lingfield Grange BH13: Poole . . . 4D 58
Ling Rd. BH12: Poole . . . 5E 39
Lingwood Av. BH23: Mude . . . 1A 64
Linhorns La. BH25: New M . . . 5G 31
Link Mall *BH15: Poole . . . 3D 4*
(off High St.)
Link Ri. BH21: Cor M . . . 5E 21
Link Rd. BH24: Poul . . . 2E 9
Links Dr. BH23: Chri . . . 4B 44
Linkside Av. BH8: Bour . . . 5E 43
Links Rd. BH14: Poole . . . 5H 57
Links Vw. Av. BH14: Poole . . . 5A 58
Linmead Dr. BH11: Bour . . . 5C 24
Linnet Cl. BH24: Hight . . . 5E 9
Linnet Ct. BH25: New M . . . 3F 49
Linnet Rd. BH17: Poole . . . 5F 37
Linnies La. SO41: Sway . . . 4E 33
Linthorpe Rd. BH15: Poole . . . 3C 56
Linton Lawns BH22: Fern . . . 6C 18
Linwood Rd. BH9: Bour . . . 6B 42
Lionheart Cl. BH11: Bour . . . 6H 23
Lions Cl. BH15: Poole . . . 3B 56
LIONS HILL . . . 2G 11
Lions Hill Way BH24: Ashl H . . . 2G 11
Lions La. BH24: Ashl H . . . 2H 11
Lions Wood BH24: St L . . . 3A 12
Lisle Cl. SO41: Lymi . . . 2F 53
Lissenden BH13: Poole . . . 4C 58
Litchford Rd. BH25: A'ley . . . 1A 50
Lit. Barrs Dr. BH25: New M . . . 1H 49
Little Burn SO41: Sway . . . 1F 33
LITTLE CANFORD . . . 5D 16
Little Ct. BH13: Poole . . . 1B 70
BH14: Poole . . . 2G 69
Littlecroft Av. BH9: Bour . . . 2B 42
Littlecroft Rd. BH12: Poole . . . 1F 57
Lit. Dene Copse SO41: Penn . . . 3D 52
Little Dewlands BH31: Ver . . . 3B 6
LITTLEDOWN . . . 5G 43
Littledown Av. BH7: Bour . . . 6E 43
Littledown Cen. . . . 5G 43
Littledown Ct. BH1: Bour . . . 3A 60
Littledown Dr. BH7: Bour . . . 6E 43
Lit. Forest Mans. BH1: Bour . . . 4A 60
Lit. Forest Rd. BH4: Bour . . . 2F 59
Little Fosters BH13: S'bks . . . 3A 70
Little Lonnen BH21: Cole . . . 1H 15
Littlemead Cl. BH17: Poole . . . 6G 37
Littlemoor Av. BH11: Bour . . . 1H 39
LITTLE PAMPHILL . . . 4A 14
Litzo, The BH5: Bour . . . 4E 61
Livingstone Rd. BH5: Bour . . . 3H 61
BH12: Poole . . . 1F 57
BH21: W Min . . . 5G 15
BH23: Chri . . . 6H 45
Llewellin Cl. BH16: Upt . . . 5C 36
Llewellin Ct. BH16: Upt . . . 6C 36
Loader Cl. BH9: Bour . . . 5A 42
Loch Rd. BH14: Poole . . . 2A 58
Lockerley Cl. SO41: Lymi . . . 3G 53
Locksley Dr. BH22: Fern . . . 6A 18
Lockyers Dr. BH22: Fern . . . 3D 18
Lockyers Rd. BH21: Cor M . . . 3E 21
Loders Cl. BH17: Poole . . . 2B 38
Lodge Cl. BH14: Poole . . . 3A 58
Lodge Ct. BH14: Poole . . . 3A 58
Lodge Rd. BH23: Chri . . . 5C 44
SO41: Penn . . . 2D 52
Loewy Cres. BH12: Poole . . . 3H 39

92 A-Z Bournemouth

Lombard Av.—Marine Dr. E.

Lombard Av. BH6: Bour .2B 62
Lombardy Cl. BH31: Ver .4F 7
Londesborough Pl. SO41: Lymi .3F 53
London Tavern Caravan Park, The
BH24: Poul .2E 9
Lone Pine Dr. BH22: W Par .6C 18
Lone Pine Mobile Homes Pk.
BH22: Fern .6D 18
Lone Pine Way BH22: W Par .1H 25
Longacre Dr. BH22: Fern .5A 18
Longbarrow Cl. BH8: Bour .4F 43
Long Cl. SO41: Penn .2C 52
Longespee Rd. BH21: Mer .3C 22
Longfield Dr. BH11: Bour .5C 24
BH22: W Par .3G 25
Longfield Rd. SO41: Hor .3F 51
LONGFLEET .1D 4 (3B 56)
Longfleet Dr. BH17: Poole .4B 38
Longfleet Rd. BH15: Poole .2D 4 (4B 56)
Longford Pl. SO41: Penn .4F 53
LONGHAM .2C 24
Longham Bus. Cen.
BH22: Long .1D 24
Longham Farm Cl. BH22: Long .3D 24
Long La. BH21: Cole .2F 15
BH24: Crow .6D 8
Longleat Gdns. BH25: New M .2E 49
Longmeadow La. BH17: Poole .6E 37
Long Rd. BH10: Bour .1E 41
Lonnen Rd. BH21: Cole .2H 15
Lonnen Wood Cl. BH21: Cole .1A 16
Lonsdale Rd. BH3: Bour .6H 41
Loraine Av. BH23: Highc .5C 48
Lord Cl. BH17: Poole .6D 38
Loring Rd. BH23: Chri .5D 44
Lorne Pk. Rd. BH1: Bour .4A 60
Louise Ct. BH21: Cor M .5D 20
Love La. SO41: M Sea .3D 66
Lwr. Ashley Rd.
BH25: A'ley, New M .2B 50
Lwr. Blandford Rd. BH18: Broad .2H 37
LOWER BUCKLAND .6G 35
Lwr. Buckland Rd. SO41: Lymi .6F 35
Lwr. Golf Links Rd. BH18: Broad .6H 21
LOWER HAMWORTHY .6F 55
LOWER KINGSTON .6H 13
Lwr. Mead End Rd. SO41: Sway .2D 32
LOWER PARKSTONE .3E 57
LOWER PENNINGTON .5F 53
Lwr. Pennington La. SO41: Penn .3F 53
Lower Woodside SO41: Lymi .5G 53
Lowther Gdns. BH8: Bour .2C 60
Lowther Rd. BH8: Bour .1A 60
Lucas Rd. BH12: Poole .1G 57
BH15: Hamw .6A 4 (6H 55)
Lucerne Av. BH6: Bour .2B 62
Lucerne Rd. SO41: M Sea .3D 66
Luckham Cl. BH9: Bour .3B 42
Luckham Gdns. BH9: Bour .3C 42
Luckham Pl. BH9: Bour .3B 42
Luckham Rd. BH9: Bour .3B 42
Luckham Rd. E. BH9: Bour .3B 42
Lucky La. SO41: Pil .2H 35
Lukas Ct. *BH8: Bour .1C 60*
(off Richmond Pk. Rd.)
BH8: Bour .2B 60
(Ascham Rd.)
Lulworth Av. BH15: Hamw .6E 55
Lulworth Cl. BH15: Hamw .6E 55
Lulworth Ct. BH15: Hamw .5E 55
Lulworth Cres. BH15: Hamw .6E 55
Lumby Dr. BH24: Poul .3D 8
Lumby Dr. Mobile Home Pk.
BH24: Poul .3D 8
Luscombe Rd. BH14: Poole .5G 57
Luscombe Valley Nature Reserve .2H 69
Luther Rd. BH9: Bour .5H 41
Lych Ga. Ct. BH24: Hight .5E 9
Lydford Gdns. BH11: Bour .3C 40
Lydford Rd. BH11: Bour .3C 40
Lydgate SO41: M Sea .2A 66
Lydlinch Cl. BH22: W Par .2F 25
Lydwell Cl. BH11: Bour .6B 24
Lyell Rd. BH12: Poole .1G 57
Lyme Cres. BH23: Highc .5H 47
Lymefields SO41: M Sea .1E 67
LYMINGTON .2G 53
Lymington Ent. Cen. SO41: Bold .5G 35
Lymington Health and Leisure Cen. .3E 53
Lymington-Keyhaven Nature Reserve .6H 53
LYMINGTON NEW FOREST HOSPITAL .5G 35
Lymington Pier Station (Rail) .1H 53
Lymington Reedbeds Nature Reserve .5G 35
Lymington Rd. BH23: Chri, Highc .6E 47
BH25: New M .4G 49
(not continuous)
SO41: Down, Ever .4C 50
SO41: Ever, M Sea .5A 52
SO42: Broc .6F 73
Lymington Town Station (Rail) .1H 53
LYMORE .6A 52
Lymore La. SO41: Key, Lymo .5A 52
Lymore Valley SO41: Lymo .6A 52
Lyndale Cl. SO41: M Sea .2E 67
LYNDHURST .3G 71
Lyndhurst Rd. BH23: Bock, Bran, Wat .1B 46
BH23: Chri .5C 46
SO42: Broc .3F 73
Lyndon Gate *BH2: Bour .5F 59*
(off Chine Cres. Rd.)
Lynes Ct. BH24: Ring .4B 8
Lyne's La. BH24: Ring .4B 8
Lynn Rd. BH17: Poole .5D 38
Lynric Cl. BH25: B Sea .6G 49
Lynton Cres. BH23: Chri .2B 44
Lynwood Cl. BH22: Fern .2B 18
Lynwood Ct. SO41: Lymi .2F 53
Lynwood Dr. BH21: Mer .3C 22
Lyon Av. BH25: New M .2H 49
Lyon Rd. BH12: Poole .3A 40
Lyric Pl. SO41: Lymi .1G 53
Lysander Cl. BH23: Chri .6E 47
Lystra Rd. BH9: Bour .2A 42
Lytchett Dr. BH18: Broad .3F 37
Lytchett Minster & Upton By-Pass
BH16: Upt .5A 36
BH17: Upt .6D 36
Lytchett Way BH16: Upt .1B 54
Lyteltane Rd. SO41: Lymi .3F 53
Lytham Rd. BH18: Broad .2G 37
Lytton Rd. BH1: Bour .2C 60

M

Mabey Av. BH10: Bour .3F 41
Macandrew Rd. BH13: Poole .2B 70
Macaulay Rd. BH18: Broad .1G 37
McIntyre Rd. BH23: Bour A .3F 27
McKinley Rd. BH4: Bour .5E 59
Maclaren Rd. BH9: Bour .2H 41
Maclean Rd. BH11: Bour .2B 40
Macpennys Woodland Garden .2E 29
McWilliam Cl. BH12: Poole .5E 41
McWilliam Rd. BH9: Bour .3A 42
Madeira Ct. BH1: Bour .3A 60
Madeira Rd. BH1: Bour .3H 5 (3A 60)
BH14: Poole .2H 57
Madeira Wlk. SO41: Lymi .2H 53
Madeline Cl. BH12: Poole .6F 39
Madeline Cres. BH12: Poole .6F 39
Madison Av. BH1: Bour .1D 60
Madrisa Ct. SO41: Lymi .1G 53
Magdalen La. BH23: Chri .1E 63
Magistrates' Court
Bournemouth .3A 60
Poole .4D 56
Magna Cl. BH11: Bour .5B 24
Magna Gdns. BH11: Bour .5B 24
Magna Rd. BH11: Bour .3E 23
BH21: Mer .3E 23
Magnolia Cl. BH6: Bour .2E 63
BH31: Ver .5G 7
Magnolia Ct. BH4: Bour .4F 59
BH25: New M .2H 49
Magnolia Ho. BH10: Bour .1H 41
Magpie Cl. BH8: Bour .2C 42
Magpie Gro. BH25: New M .3F 49
Mag's Barrow BH22: W Par .1G 25
Maiden La. SO41: Lymi .4G 53
Maidment Cl. BH11: Bour .1A 40
Main Rd. SO41: Portm, Wal .5H 35
Maitland Ct. SO41: Lymi .2F 53
Maitlands, The BH4: Bour .5F 59
Majorca Mans. BH2: Bour .3E 5 (4G 59)
Malan Ct. BH17: Poole .5C 38
Malcomb Cl. BH6: Bour .4E 63
Mallard Cl. BH8: Bour .4C 42
BH23: Mude .1C 64
SO41: Hor .2E 51
Mallard Rd. BH8: Bour .4D 42
BH21: Cole .2A 16
Mallard Rd. Retail Pk. BH8: Bour .4D 42
Mallory Cl. BH23: Chri .5B 46
Mallow Cl. BH18: Broad .2E 37
BH23: Chri .5E 47
Mallows, The BH25: A'ley .1B 50
Malmesbury Cl. BH23: Chri .2E 63
Malmesbury Ct. BH8: Bour .1C 60
Malmesbury Mews *BH8: Bour .2C 60*
(off Malmesbury Pk. Pl.)
Malmesbury Pk. Pl. BH8: Bour .2C 60
Malmesbury Pk. Rd. BH8: Bour .1A 60
Malmesbury Rd. BH24: St L .4A 12
Maloren Way BH22: W Moo .6E 11
Malthouse BH15: Poole .4B 4 (5A 56)
Maltings, The BH15: Poole .4C 56
Malvern Cl. BH9: Bour .2A 42
Malvern Ct. *BH9: Bour .3A 42*
(off Malvern Rd.)
BH23: Chri .5B 46
(off Dorset Rd.)
Malvern Rd. BH9: Bour .2A 42
Manchester Rd. SO41: Sway .1F 33
Mandalay Cl. BH31: Ver .4C 6
Mandale Cl. BH11: Bour .1C 40
Mandale Rd. BH11: Bour .2B 40
Manderley SO41: M Sea .4E 67
Manning Av. BH23: Chri .4E 47
Mannings Heath Retail Pk. BH12: Poole .5E 39
Mannings Heath Rd. BH12: Poole .3F 39
Mannings Heath Rdbt. BH17: Poole .2F 39
Mannington Hall *BH4: Bour .5E 59*
(off Portarlington Rd.)
Mannington Pl. BH2: Bour .4E 5
Mannington Way BH22: W Moo .5B 10
Manor, The *BH1: Bour .4C 60*
(off Derby Rd.)
Manor Av. BH12: Poole .5G 39
Manor Cl. BH22: Fern .4C 18
SO41: M Sea .1D 66
Manor Ct. BH24: Ring .3B 8
Mnr. Farm Cl. BH25: New M .4F 49
Mnr. Farm Rd. BH10: Bour .5D 24
Manor Farmyard BH8: Bour .2H 43
Manor Gdns. BH24: Ring .3B 8
BH25: New M .2H 49
BH31: Ver .3D 6
Manorhurst *BH4: Bour .3E 59*
(off Snowdon Rd.)
Manor La. BH31: Ver .4D 6
Manor Pk. BH15: Poole .2H 55
Manor Rd. BH1: Bour .4B 60
BH23: Chri .1E 63
BH24: Ring .4C 8
BH25: A'ley, New M .2G 49
BH31: Ver .3D 6
SO41: M Sea .1D 66
Manor Way BH31: Ver .2D 6
Mansel Cl. BH12: Poole .6E 41
Mansfield Av. BH14: Poole .3G 57
Mansfield Cl. BH14: Poole .3G 57
BH22: W Par .1F 25
Mansfield Ct. *BH4: Bour .5E 59*
(off Portarlington Rd.)
Mansfield Rd. BH9: Bour .4G 41
BH14: Poole .3G 57
BH24: Ring .4B 8
(not continuous)
Manton Cl. BH15: Hamw .4E 55
Manton Rd. BH15: Hamw .4E 55
(not continuous)
Maple Bus. Pk. BH21: Stap .2F 17
Maple Cl. BH23: Highc .6H 47
BH25: B Sea .6H 49
Maple Dr. BH22: Fern .1A 18
Maple Lodge BH16: Upt .6C 36
Maple Rd. BH9: Bour .5H 41
BH15: Poole .1D 4 (4B 56)
Mapperton Cl. BH17: Poole .3D 38
Marabout Cl. BH23: Chri .6H 45
Marchwood BH1: Bour .4C 60
Marchwood Rd. BH10: Bour .2E 41
Marden Paddock SO42: Broc .3E 73
Margards La. BH31: Ver .4B 6
Marian Cl. BH21: Cor M .1C 36
Mariann Ct. BH6: Bour .3B 62
Marianne Rd. BH12: Poole .5E 41
BH21: Cole .2A 16
Marian Rd. BH21: Cor M .1C 36
Marie Cl. BH12: Poole .6H 39
Marina, The BH5: Bour .4E 61
Marina Ct. BH5: Bour .4E 61
Marina Dr. BH14: Poole .6F 57
Marina Towers BH5: Bour .4E 61
Marina Vw. BH23: Chri .2D 62
Marine Ct. BH25: B Sea .6D 48
Marine Dr. BH25: B Sea .6E 49
Marine Dr. E. BH25: B Sea .6F 49

A-Z Bournemouth 93

Marine Dr. W. BH25: B Sea 6D 48
Marine Point BH25: B Sea 6F 49
Marine Prospect BH25: B Sea 6F 49
Marine Rd. BH6: Bour 4B 62
Mariners Ct. BH23: Mude 1C 64
　SO41: Lymi 3H 53
Mariners Reach BH25: B Sea 6G 49
Market Cl. BH15: Poole 4B 4 (5A 56)
Market Pl. BH24: Ring 4B 8
Market St. BH15: Poole 5A 4 (6H 55)
Market Way BH21: W Min 5F 15
Markham Av. BH10: Bour 5F 25
Markham Cl. BH10: Bour 4F 25
Markham Rd. BH9: Bour 5A 42
Mark's La. BH25: Bash 5G 31
Marks Rd. BH9: Bour 2H 41
Marlborough Ct. BH4: Bour 4E 59
　(off Marlborough Rd.)
　BH12: Poole 3D 58
　(off Princess Rd.)
　BH21: W Min 4E 15
Marlborough Mans. BH7: Bour 1H 61
　(off Christchurch Rd.)
Marlborough Pines BH4: Bour 4E 59
　(off Marlborough Rd.)
Marlborough Pl. BH21: W Min 4F 15
　SO41: Lymi 6F 35
Marlborough Rd. BH4: Bour 4E 59
　BH14: Poole 3G 57
Marley Av. BH25: New M 1E 49
Marley Cl. BH25: New M 2F 49
Marley Mt. SO41: Sway 2C 32
Marline Rd. BH12: Poole 1H 57
Marlott Rd. BH15: Poole 2A 56
Marlow Dr. BH23: Chri 2B 44
Marlpit Dr. BH23: Walk 3A 48
Marlpit La. BH25: Bash 3G 31
Marmion Grn. BH23: Chri 6B 46
Marnhull Rd. BH15: Poole 3B 56
Marpet Cl. BH11: Bour 5B 24
Marquis Way BH11: Bour 6G 23
Marram Cl. SO41: Lymi 5G 35
Marryat Ct. BH23: Highc 6B 48
　BH25: New M 2F 49
Marryat Rd. BH25: New M 2F 49
Marshal Rd. BH17: Poole 4H 37
Marsh Ct. BH6: Bour 4B 62
　(off Clifton Rd.)
Marshes End (Park & Ride) 6G 37
Marshfield BH21: Cole 2H 15
Marshlands Cl. BH23: Chri 1H 63
Marsh La. BH16: Upt 6A 36
　BH23: Chri 1H 63
　(Purewell)
　BH23: Chri 3D 44
　(St Catherine's Hill La.)
　SO41: Lymi 5F 35
Marshwood Av. BH17: Poole 3D 38
Marston Cl. BH25: New M 6H 31
Marston Gro. BH23: Chri 4H 45
Marston Rd. BH15: Poole 4A 4 (5H 55)
　BH25: New M 6H 31
Martello Ho. BH13: Poole 2B 70
Martello Pk. BH13: Poole 2B 70
Martello Rd. BH13: Poole 6A 58
Martello Rd. Sth. BH13: Poole 1B 70
Martello Towers BH13: Poole 2B 70
Martells, The BH25: B Sea 6H 49
Martha Ct. BH12: Poole 6A 40
Martin Cl. BH17: Poole 6F 37
Martindale Av. BH21: Hay 4B 16
　(not continuous)
Martingale Cl. BH16: Upt 6D 36
Martins Cl. BH22: Fern 2C 18
Martins Dr. BH22: Fern 1C 18
Martin's Hill Cl. BH23: Burt 4G 45
Martins Hill La. BH23: Burt 4G 45
Martin's Rd. SO42: Broc 2F 73
Martins Way BH22: Fern 2C 18
Marwell Cl. BH7: Bour 6G 43
Maryland Cl. SO41: M Sea 3B 66
Maryland Gdns. SO41: M Sea 3B 66
Maryland Rd. BH16: Hamw 3C 54
Mary La. BH22: W Moo 5B 10
Mary Mitchell Cl. BH24: Ring 4B 8
　(off Lyne's La.)
Mary Mitchell Ct. BH23: Chri 1D 62
　(off King's Av.)
Masters Ct. BH2: Bour 4F 59
Masterson Cl. BH23: Chri 6H 45
Matchams La. BH23: Hurn 4H 27
Matlock Rd. BH22: Fern 6A 18
Matthew Ct. BH6: Bour 3B 62

Maturin Cl. SO41: Lymi 2G 53
Maundeville Cres. BH23: Chri 5B 44
Maundeville Rd. BH23: Chri 5C 44
Maureen Cl. BH12: Poole 6F 39
Maurice Rd. BH8: Bour 5D 42
Mavis Rd. BH9: Bour 4B 42
Maxwell Cl. BH11: Bour 5A 24
Maxwell Rd. BH9: Bour 5A 42
　BH13: Poole 2B 70
　BH18: Broad 2D 36
May Av. SO41: Lymi 6F 35
May Ct. BH9: Bour 5G 41
Mayfair BH4: Bour 5E 59
Mayfair Gdns. BH11: Bour 1C 40
Mayfield Av. BH14: Poole 4A 58
Mayfield Cl. BH22: Fern 3A 18
Mayfield Dr. BH22: Fern 3A 18
Mayfield Rd. BH9: Bour 3H 41
Mayfield Way BH22: Fern 3A 18
Mayflower Cl. SO41: Lymi 2H 53
Mayford Rd. BH17: Poole 1D 58
May Gdns. BH11: Bour 2A 40
　BH23: Walk 3B 48
May La. SO41: Pil 2H 35
Maylyn Rd. BH16: Bea H 3A 36
Mazion BH12: Poole 5F 39
　(off Ringwood Rd.)
Mead Cl. BH18: Broad 4G 37
MEAD END 2D 32
Mead End Rd. SO41: Sway 2D 32
Meadow, The BH25: New M 5C 48
Meadowbank BH16: Upt 5C 36
Meadow Cl. BH22: W Par 2F 25
　BH23: Bran 3C 28
　BH24: Ring 2D 8
Meadow Ct. BH9: Bour 2A 42
　BH21: W Min 5F 15
　BH31: Ver 5E 7
Meadow Ct. Cl. BH9: Bour 2A 42
Meadow Crest Wood SO42: Broc 2C 72
Meadow Farm La. BH21: Cor M 3D 20
Meadow Gro. BH31: Ver 4F 7
Meadowland BH23: Chri 1A 64
Meadowlands BH24: Ring 6C 8
　SO41: Lymi 1D 52
Meadow La. BH23: Burt 3G 45
Meadow Point BH21: W Min 6E 15
Meadow Rise BH18: Broad 6F 21
Meadow Rd. BH24: Ring 3D 8
　BH25: New M 1H 49
　SO41: Penn 3E 53
Meadows, The BH25: New M 4F 49
　SO43: Lyn 4F 71
Meadows Cl. BH16: Upt 5C 36
Meadows Dr. BH16: Upt 6C 36
Meadowsweet Rd. BH17: Poole 5E 37
Meadow Vw. Rd. BH11: Bour 1A 40
Meadow Way BH24: Ring 3D 8
　BH25: B Sea 6G 49
　BH31: Ver 4E 7
Mead Rd. SO41: Penn 3D 52
Meadway, The BH23: Chri 3F 47
Medina Way BH23: Fri C 1E 65
Medlar Cl. BH23: Burt 4H 45
Medway Rd. BH22: Fern 3E 19
Meerut Rd. SO42: Broc 2E 73
Meeting Ho. La. BH24: Ring 4B 8
Melbourne Ct. BH5: Bour 2H 61
　(off Seabourne Rd.)
Melbourne Rd. BH8: Bour 1C 60
　BH23: Chri 4C 44
Melbury Av. BH12: Poole 6H 39
Melbury Cl. BH22: Fern 5B 18
　BH23: Chri 2F 53
Melford Ct. BH1: Bour 4A 60
Melgate Cl. BH9: Bour 4H 41
Mellstock Rd. BH15: Poole 1H 55
Melrose Cl. BH25: A'ley 2A 50
Melton Ct. BH13: Poole 3C 58
Melverley Gdns. BH21: W Min 4F 15
Melville Gdns. BH9: Bour 5H 41
Melville Rd. BH9: Bour 5G 41
Mendip Cl. BH25: New M 3A 50
　BH31: Ver 4D 6
Mendip Ct. BH23: Chri 5B 46
　(off Dorset Rd.)
Mendip Rd. BH31: Ver 3D 6
Mentone Rd. BH14: Poole 4E 57
Meon Rd. BH7: Bour 1H 61
Meredith Cl. BH23: Chri 6A 46
Meriden Cl. BH13: Poole 2B 70
Meridians, The BH23: Chri 1D 62
Meridiens BH15: Poole 3C 56

Merino Way BH22: W Moo 6D 10
Meriton Ct. BH1: Bour 2A 60
　(off Lansdowne Rd.)
Merlewood Cl. BH2: Bour 1G 5 (3H 59)
MERLEY 2C 22
Merley Ct. Touring Pk. BH21: Mer ...2A 22
Merley Dr. BH23: Highc 5A 48
Merley Gdns. BH21: Mer 2B 22
Merley Ho. Holiday Pk. BH21: Mer ...2H 21
Merley Ho. La. BH21: Mer 2H 21
Merley La. BH21: Mer 2B 22
Merley Pk. Rd. BH21: A'ton 3F 21
Merley Ways BH21: Mer 1A 22
Merlin Cl. BH24: Hight 5E 9
Merlin Way BH25: Mude 2C 64
Mermaid Ct. BH5: Bour 4E 61
Merriefield Av. BH18: Broad 6H 21
Merriefield Cl. BH18: Broad 5H 21
Merriefield Dr. BH18: Broad 5H 21
Merrifield BH21: Cole 1G 15
MERRITOWN 4E 27
Merritown La. BH23: Hurn 4D 26
Merrivale Av. BH6: Bour 2C 62
Merrow Av. BH12: Poole 6D 40
Merrow Chase BH13: Poole 2B 70
　(off Haven Rd.)
Merryfield Cl. BH23: Bran 3C 28
　BH31: Ver 3D 6
MERRY FIELD HILL 1G 15
Merryfield La. BH10: Bour 1E 41
Merryweather Est. BH24: Poul 3E 9
Merton Ct. BH23: Highc 6A 48
Merton Gro. BH24: Ring 3B 8
Methuen Cl. BH8: Bour 2C 60
Methuen Rd. BH8: Bour 2B 60
　BH17: Poole 3H 37
Mews, The BH2: Bour 4F 59
　BH31: Ver 5E 7
Meybury Cl. BH23: Bran 4C 28
Meyrick Cl. BH23: Bran 4C 28
Meyrick Ct. BH2: Bour 2H 59
Meyrick Gate BH2: Bour 1H 5
Meyrick Pk. Cres. BH3: Bour 1H 59
Meyrick Park Golf Course 1F 5 (3G 59)
Meyrick Pk. Mans. BH2: Bour ...2G 5 (3H 59)
Meyrick Rd. BH1: Bour 4B 60
Michelgrove Rd. BH5: Bour 4E 61
Michelmersh Grn. BH8: Bour 3D 42
Mickleham Cl. BH12: Poole 5D 40
Middlebere Cres. BH16: Hamw 3C 54
MIDDLE BOCKHAMPTON 5A 28
Middle Comn. Rd. SO41: Penn 2C 52
Middlehill Dr. BH21: Cole 3B 16
Middlehill Rd. BH21: Cole 2H 15
Middle La. BH24: Ring 4C 8
Middle Rd. BH10: Bour 6E 25
　BH15: Poole 1C 56
　SO41: Lymi 2F 53
　SO41: Sway 1F 33
　SO41: Tip 3B 32
Middleton Gdns. BH7: Bour 1F 61
Middleton M. BH25: New M 4F 49
Middleton Rd. BH9: Bour 3G 41
　BH24: Ring 3C 8
Midland Rd. BH9: Bour 4H 41
Midway Path BH13: S'bks 6G 69
Midwood Av. BH8: Bour 4F 43
Milborne Cres. BH12: Poole 6A 40
Milborne Ct. BH22: Fern 3A 18
Milbourne Rd. BH22: Fern 3A 18
Milburn Cl. BH4: Bour 3E 59
Milburn Rd. BH4: Bour 3D 58
Mildenhall BH4: Bour 5F 59
Milestone Rd. BH15: Poole 1B 56
Milford Cl. BH22: W Moo 5D 10
Milford Cres. SO41: M Sea 3E 67
Milford Cres. SO41: M Sea 2E 67
Milford Dr. BH11: Bour 6B 24
MILFORD ON SEA 3E 67
MILFORD ON SEA WAR MEMORIAL HOSPITAL
　..................................3E 67
Milford Pl. SO41: M Sea 3E 67
Milford Rd. BH25: New M 4H 49
　SO41: Ever, Lymi, Penn 5A 52
Milford Trad. Est. SO41: M Sea 3E 67
Milky Down BH24: Hight, Poul 4F 9
Millbank Ho. BH21: W Min 4E 15
Millbank Rd. BH25: A'ley 1A 50
Miller Cl. BH25: A'ley 1A 50
Miller Ct. BH12: Poole 5F 39
　BH23: Chri 1D 62
Miller Gdns. BH6: Bour 2H 61
Miller Rd. BH23: Chri 6H 45
Millfield BH17: Poole 6G 37

Millhams Cl. BH10: Bour 5D 24	Monument La. SO41: Wal 6H 35	Mude Gdns. BH23: Mude 2C 64
Millhams Dr. BH10: Bour 5D 24	Moonrakers Way BH23: Chri ...4G 47	Mude Valley Nature Reserve 1C 64
Millhams Mead Nature Reserve 5C 24	Moorcroft Av. BH23: Burt 2G 45	Mulberry Gro. SO41: Ever 5H 51
Millhams Rd. BH10: Bour 4C 24	MOORDOWN 3H 41	Mulberry M. BH6: Bour 2B 62
Millhams St. BH23: Chri 1F 63	Moordown Cl. BH9: Bour 2A 42	Mullins Cl. BH12: Poole 5E 41
Millhams St. Nth. BH23: Chri ...1F 63	Moore Av. BH11: Bour 1C 40	Munster Rd. BH12: Poole 4H 57
Mill La. BH14: Poole 5F 57	Moore Cl. BH25: New M 4F 49	Murley Rd. BH9: Bour 5A 42
BH21: W Min 4D 14	Moorfield Gro. BH9: Bour 3H 41	Murre Ho. BH15: Hamw 6F 55
BH23: Highc 5B 48	Moorfields Rd. BH13: Poole 1B 70	MUSCLIFF 1B 42
BH23: Hurn 5H 27	Moorhills BH21: W Min 5F 15	Muscliffe La. BH9: Bour 1A 42
SO41: Lymi 1H 53	Moorings, The BH3: Bour 5F 41	Muscliffe Rd. BH9: Bour 4H 41
SO41: Penn, Sway ...4H 33	BH23: Chri 2D 62	Museum of Electricity 6F 45
SO42: Broc 3F 73	Moorings Cl. BH15: Hamw 6F 55	Myrtle Cl. SO41: Hor 1D 50
Mill Mdw. SO41: M Sea 2C 66	Moorland Av. BH25: B Sea 5F 49	Myrtle Rd. BH8: Bour 1C 60
Mill Rd. BH23: Chri 5E 45	Moorland Cres. BH16: Upt 6B 36	
Mill Rd. Nth. BH8: Bour 2D 42	Moorland Ga. BH24: Ring 6C 8	
Mill Rd. Sth. BH8: Bour 3D 42	Moorland Pde. BH16: Upt 6B 36	
Mills, The BH12: Poole 1A 58	Moorland Rd. BH11: Bour 3D 60	
Millstream Cl. BH17: Poole 6G 37	Moorlands Cl. SO42: Broc 3C 72	**N**
BH21: W Min 5E 15	Moorlands Ri. BH22: W Moo 4D 10	
Millstream Ct. BH24: Ring 4B 8	Moorlands Rd. BH22: W Moo ...5B 10	Nada Rd. BH23: Chri 4F 47
Millstream Trad. Est. BH24: Ring ...6C 8	BH31: Ver 2D 6	Nairn Ct. BH3: Bour 6G 41
Mill St. BH21: Cor M 6B 14	Moorland Way BH16: Upt 1B 54	Nairn Rd. BH3: Bour 1G 59
BH21: Cor M, Stu M ...1A 20	Moorlea BH8: Bour 2B 60	BH13: Poole 2A 70
Millyford Cl. BH25: New M 5D 48	Moor Rd. BH18: Broad 6H 21	Naish M. BH25: B Sea 6G 49
Milne Rd. BH17: Poole 4H 37	Moors Cl. BH23: Hurn 4H 27	Naish Rd. BH25: B Sea 6D 48
Milner Rd. BH4: Bour 5E 59	Moorside BH11: Bour 2D 40	Namu Rd. BH9: Bour 4G 41
Milton Bus. Cen. BH25: New M ...3E 49	Moorside Gdns. BH11: Bour 2D 40	Nansen Av. BH15: Poole 2B 56
Milton Cl. BH14: Poole 4H 57	Moorside Rd. BH11: Bour 2C 40	Napier Rd. BH15: Hamw 4B 54
Milton Ct. BH22: Fern 4B 18	BH21: Cor M 6D 20	Narrow La. BH24: Poul 3F 9
Milton Gate *BH25: New M* 4F 49	BH22: W Moo 5C 10	Naseby Rd. BH9: Bour 4A 42
(off Old Milton Rd.)	MOORTOWN 6C 8	Natasha Gdns. BH12: Poole 6G 39
Milton Gro. BH25: New M 3H 49	Moortown Dr. BH21: Mer 3F 23	Nathan Gdns. BH15: Hamw 4D 54
Milton Mead BH25: New M 3E 49	Moortown La. BH24: Crow, Ring ...6C 8	Navarac Ct. BH14: Bour 4G 57
Milton Rd. BH8: Bour 2A 60	Moorvale Rd. BH9: Bour 3A 42	Navier Ct. BH15: Poole ...2D 4 (4B 56)
BH14: Poole 4H 57	Moor Vw. Rd. BH15: Poole 1C 56	Nea Cl. BH23: Chri 5F 47
BH21: W Min 3E 15	Morant Arms *SO42: Broc* 3F 73	NEACROFT 5D 28
Milverton Cl. BH23: Highc 4G 47	*(off Brookley Rd.)*	Neacroft Cl. BH25: New M 5D 48
Mimosa Av. BH21: Mer 3B 22	Morant Ct. BH25: New M 2H 49	Nea Meadow Nature Reserve 5G 47
Minstead Rd. BH10: Bour 2E 41	Morant Rd. BH24: Poul 2D 8	Nea Rd. BH23: Chri 5G 47
Minster Ct. *BH12: Poole* 3C 58	Moray Ct. BH21: W Min 4D 14	Needles Cl. SO41: M Sea 3C 66
(off Princess Rd.)	Morden Av. BH22: Fern 5A 10	Needles Point BH1: Bour 4C 60
Minster Pk. BH21: W Moo 2C 10	Morden Rd. BH9: Bour 4G 41	SO41: M Sea 3D 66
Minster Vw. BH21: W Min 4E 15	Moreton Rd. BH9: Bour 1B 42	Needles Vw. BH6: Bour 4C 62
Minster Way BH16: Upt 5B 36	Morgan Ct. BH2: Bour 2F 5	Neighbourhood Cen. BH17: Poole ...3C 38
Minterne Grange BH12: Poole ...2G 69	Moriconium Quay BH15: Hamw ...6D 54	Nelson Cl. BH25: New M 2F 49
Minterne Rd. BH9: Bour 3A 42	Morley Cl. BH5: Bour 2G 61	Nelson Cl. BH15: Poole 4C 4 (5A 56)
BH14: Poole 2G 69	BH23: Burt 2G 45	BH23: Chri 1D 62
BH23: Chri 1A 64	Morley Rd. BH5: Bour 2G 61	Nelson Dr. BH23: Mude 1B 64
Minton M. BH2: Bour 4H 5	Mornish Rd. BH13: Poole 5B 58	Nelson Pl. SO41: Lymi 2H 53
Mirage BH13: S'bks 4H 69	Morrison Av. BH12: Poole 6B 40	Nelson Rd. BH4: Bour 3C 58
Mission La. BH18: Broad 3G 37	Morris Rd. BH17: Poole 5B 38	BH12: Poole 3C 58
Mission Rd. BH18: Broad 3G 37	Mortimer Cl. BH23: Mude 1C 64	Netherhall Gdns. BH4: Bour 4E 59
Mitchell Cl. BH25: B Sea 6G 49	Mortimer Rd. BH8: Bour 4B 42	Netherwood Pl. BH21: Cowg 4C 14
Mitchell Rd. *BH17: Poole* 6D 38	Mosbach Pl. SO41: Lymi 1G 53	Netley Cl. BH15: Poole 6E 39
BH21: Stap 2G 17	Moser Gro. SO41: Sway 1E 33	Nettleton Cl. BH7: Bour 6C 38
Mitre Ct. BH23: Chri 6E 45	Mossley Av. BH12: Poole 4B 40	New Borough Rd. BH21: W Min ...6F 15
Moat Ct. BH4: Bour 2D 58	Motcombe Rd. BH13: Poole 5C 58	Newbridge Way SO41: Penn 4E 53
Moat La. BH25: B Sea 4F 49	Mount, The BH24: Poul 3E 9	Newbury Dr. BH10: Bour 4F 41
Model Town at Wimborne Minster 5D 14	Mount Av. BH25: New M 4G 49	Newcombe Rd. BH6: Bour 1C 62
Moffat Rd. BH23: Chri 6H 45	Mountbatten Cl. BH23: Mude ...2C 64	BH22: W Moo 5B 10
Molefields SO41: M Sea 2E 67	Mountbatten Cl. BH25: New M ...2F 49	New Ct. BH24: Ring 4A 8
Molyneaux Rd. BH25: A'ley 2B 50	Mountbatten Dr. BH22: Fern 4A 18	Newcroft Gdns. BH23: Chri 5E 45
Monarch Ct. *BH4: Bour* 4E 59	Mountbatten Gdns. BH8: Bour ...3F 43	Newenham Rd. SO41: Lymi 3G 53
(off Marlborough Rd.)	Mountbatten Rd. BH4: Bour 6D 58	New Flds. Bus. Pk. BH17: Poole ...5B 38
Moneyfly Rd. BH31: Ver 4F 7	BH13: Poole 6D 58	New Forest Rd. SO42: Broc 2C 72
Monks Cl. BH22: W Moo 1E 19	Mountclere *BH4: Bour* 6E 59	New Forest Golf Course 2H 71
Monks Ct. SO41: Lymi 3H 53	*(off Alumhurst Rd.)*	New Forest Mus. 3G 71
Monkshood BH23: Chri 4D 46	Mount Cl. BH25: New M 4G 49	New Forest National Pk. ...3F 29 & 5D 72
Monks Way BH11: Bour 6G 23	Mt. Grace Dr. BH14: Poole 2G 69	Newfoundland Dr. Rdbt. BH15: Poole ...5D 4
Monkswell Grn. BH23: Chri 1H 63	Mt. Heatherbank BH1: Bour 3G 5	Newgate M. *BH2: Bour* 4G 59
Monkton Cl. BH22: Fern 2B 18	Mountjoy Cl. BH21: Mer 1D 22	*(off Norwich Av.)*
Monkton Ct. BH4: Bour 3E 59	MOUNT PLEASANT	New Harbour Rd. BH15: Hamw ...6A 4 (6H 55)
Monkton Cres. BH12: Poole 5A 40	BH21 .....4E 21	New Harbour Rd. Sth. BH15: Hamw ...6H 55
Monkton Hgts. *BH5: Bour* 3D 60	SO41 .....3B 34	New Harbour Rd. W. BH15: Hamw ...6G 55
(off Boscombe Spa Rd.)	Mt. Pleasant BH24: Ring 4C 8	Newlands Mnr. SO41: Ever 6H 51
Monkworthy Cl. BH24: Ashl H ...2B 12	Mt. Pleasant Camping Pk. BH23: Hurn ...2H 27	Newlands Rd. BH7: Bour 1G 61
Monkworthy Dr. BH24: Ashl H ...2B 12	Mt. Pleasant Dr. BH8: Bour 4F 43	BH23: Chri 6B 46
Monmouth Cl. BH24: Ring 5C 8	BH23: Bran 2E 29	BH25: New M 4H 49
BH31: Ver 5F 7	Mt. Pleasant La. SO41: Lymi 3B 34	Newlands Way BH18: Broad 2D 36
Monmouth Ct. BH24: Ring 4B 8	Mt. Pleasant Rd. BH15: Poole ...5B 56	New La. BH25: Bash 5F 31
Monmouth Dr. BH31: Ver 5F 7	Mount Rd. BH11: Bour 1D 40	SO41: M Sea 3F 67
Monsal Av. BH22: Fern 6A 18	BH14: Poole 2F 57	Newlyn Way BH12: Poole 6A 40
Montacute Way BH21: Mer 3C 22	Mount Zion BH1: Bour 4A 60	Newmans Cl. BH21: W Min 6F 15
Montague Rd. BH5: Bour 3H 61	MUDEFORD 2C 64	BH22: W Moo 2C 10
Montagu Pk. BH23: Highc 6A 48	Mudeford BH23: Mude 2B 64	Newman's La. BH22: W Moo 3A 10
Montagu Rd. BH23: Highc 6B 48	Mudeford Grn. Cl. BH23: Mude ...2B 64	New Merrifield BH21: Cole 2G 15
Monteray Dr. SO41: Hor 1D 50	Mudeford La. BH23: Chri, Mude ...1A 64	*(not continuous)*
Montgomery Av. BH11: Bour 2D 40	*(not continuous)*	NEW MILTON 3G 49
Montrose Cl. BH31: Ver 3D 6	Mudeford Lifeboat Station 3C 64	New Milton Health & Leisure Cen. 3F 49
Montrose Dr. BH10: Bour 3D 40	Mudeford Quay BH23: Mude 3C 64	New Milton Indoor Bowls Club 2G 49
BH31: Ver 3D 6	Mudeford Sailing Club 3A 64	New Milton Station (Rail) 2G 49
		Newmorton Rd. BH9: Bour 1A 42
		New Orchard BH15: Poole ...4A 4 (5H 55)

New Pde.—Orchard Av.

New Pde. BH10: Bour 2G **41**
New Pk. Rd. BH6: Bour 3A **62**
New Quay Rd. BH15: Hamw 6A **4** (6H **55**)
New Rd. BH10: Bour 5G **25**
BH12: Poole 1H **57**
BH22: Fern, W Par 4B **18**
BH24: Ring 3H **13**
SO41: Key 3G **67**
Newstead Rd. BH6: Bour 3B **62**
New St. BH15: Poole 5A **4** (6H **55**)
BH24: Ring 5C **8**
SO41: Lymi 1G **53**
New St. M. SO41: Lymi 1G **53**
Newton Morrell BH14: Poole 4H **57**
Newton Rd. BH13: Poole 1A **70**
BH25: B Sea 5H **49**
NEWTOWN
BH12 6F **39**
BH21 4D **20**
Newtown Bus. Pk. BH12: Poole 6F **39**
Newtown La. BH21: Cor M 4D **20**
BH31: Ver 4D **6**
Newtown Rd. BH31: Ver 3E **7**
(not continuous)
New Valley Rd. SO41: M Sea 3C **66**
NHS WALK-IN CENTRE (BOSCOMBE) 2E **61**
Nichola Ct. BH12: Poole 6F **39**
Nicholas Cl. BH23: Walk 3B **48**
Nicholas Gdns. BH10: Bour 3E **41**
Nicholson Cl. BH17: Poole 5C **38**
Nightingale Cl. BH31: Ver 4E **7**
Nightingale Ho. BH15: Poole 2D **4**
Nightingale La. BH15: Poole 3B **4** (5A **56**)
Nightjar Cl. BH17: Poole 5F **37**
Nimrod Way BH21: Stap 2F **17**
Noble Cl. BH11: Bour 4B **40**
Noel Cl. SO42: Broc 3F **73**
Noel Rd. BH10: Bour 4D **40**
Noon Gdns. BH31: Ver 3F **7**
Noon Hill Dr. BH31: Ver 3F **7**
Noon Hill Rd. BH31: Ver 3F **7**
Norcliffe Cl. BH11: Bour 2D **40**
Norfolk Av. BH23: Chri 3D **44**
Norleywood BH23: Highc 5H **47**
Norman Av. BH12: Poole 1B **58**
NORMANDY 4H **53**
Normandy Cl. SO41: Sway 1E **33**
Normandy Dr. BH23: Chri 6H **45**
Normandy Farm Nature Reserve 4H **53**
Normandy La. SO41: Lymi 3H **53**
Normandy Way BH15: Hamw 5D **54**
Norman Gdns. BH12: Poole 1C **58**
Normanhurst Av. BH8: Bour 4D **42**
Normans Way BH25: A'ley 2A **50**
Normanton Cl. BH23: Chri 4D **44**
Norris Cl. BH24: Ashl H 3A **12**
Norris Gdns. BH25: New M 4G **49**
Norrish Rd. BH12: Poole 2G **57**
North Av. BH10: Bour 5F **25**
NORTH BOCKHAMPTON 4B **28**
NORTHBOURNE 6F **25**
Northbourne Av. BH10: Bour 6F **25**
Northbourne Gdns. BH10: Bour 6G **25**
Northbourne M. BH10: Bour 5F **25**
Northbourne Pl. BH10: Bour 6F **25**
Northbourne Rdbt. BH10: Bour 5G **25**
Northbrook Rd. BH18: Broad 3G **37**
North Cl. SO41: Lymi 1G **53**
North Comn. La. SO41: Lymi 4B **34**
Northcote Rd. BH1: Bour 3B **60**
North Dr. BH24: St L 1F **19**
BH25: Oss 4D **30**
North E. Sector BH23: Bour A 2E **27**
Northerwood Av. SO43: Lyn 3E **71**
Northey Rd. BH6: Bour 1C **62**
Northfield Rd. BH24: Poul, Ring 2C **8**
SO41: M Sea 3F **67**
North Greenlands SO41: Penn 3E **53**
North Haven Yacht Club 5G **69**
North Head SO41: M Sea 2A **66**
Northleigh La. BH21: Cole 3G **15**
Nth. Lodge Rd. BH14: Poole 3A **58**
Northmead Dr. BH17: Poole 5F **37**
Northmere Dr. BH12: Poole 6B **40**
Northmere Rd. BH12: Poole 1A **58**
Northover Cl. BH3: Bour 6F **41**
Northover La. SO41: Tip 4C **32**
Northover Rd. SO41: Penn 1C **52**
NORTH POULNER 1E **9**
Nth. Poulner Rd. BH24: Poul 2D **8**
North Rd. BH7: Bour 2E **61**
BH14: Poole 3D **56**
SO42: Broc 3F **73**
Northshore BH13: S'bks 5G **69**
North St. BH15: Poole 3C **4** (5A **56**)
SO41: Penn 3E **53**
Northumberland Ct. BH24: Ring 4B **8**
NORTH WEIRS 3C **72**
North Weirs SO42: Broc 2B **72**
North West Ind. Area BH23: Bour A 2D **26**
North Wood Ho. *BH4: Bour* *4E **59***
(off Poole Rd.)
Nortoft Rd. BH8: Bour 1B **60**
Norton Cl. BH23: Chri 6H **45**
Norton Gdns. BH9: Bour 4G **41**
Norton Rd. BH9: Bour 5G **41**
Norton Way BH15: Hamw 6G **55**
Norway Cl. BH9: Bour 4H **41**
Norwich Av. BH2: Bour 3E **5** (4F **59**)
Norwich Av. W. BH2: Bour 4F **59**
Norwich Ct. BH2: Bour 4E **5**
Norwich Mans. BH2: Bour 4F **59**
Norwich Rd. BH2: Bour 4E **5** (4G **59**)
Norwood Pl. BH5: Bour 2H **61**
Nouale La. BH24: Poul 4F **9**
Noyce Gdns. BH8: Bour 3H **43**
NUFFIELD HEALTH BOURNEMOUTH 2A **60**
Nuffield Ind. Est. BH17: Poole 5B **38**
(not continuous)
Nuffield Rd. BH17: Poole 6A **38**
Nugent Rd. BH6: Bour 3D **62**
Nursery Rd. BH9: Bour 2A **42**
BH24: Ring 5C **8**
Nursling Grn. BH8: Bour 3D **42**
Nuthatch Cl. BH17: Poole 6F **37**
BH22: Fern 1H **17**
Nutley Cl. BH11: Bour 1B **40**
Nutley Way BH11: Bour 2B **40**

O

Oak Av. BH23: Chri 5B **44**
Oak Cl. BH21: Cor M 6C **20**
BH22: W Par 2G **25**
SO43: Lyn 4F **71**
OAKDALE 1C **56**
Oakdale Rd. BH15: Poole 1C **56**
Oakdene Cl. BH21: W Min 4F **15**
Oakdene Holiday Pk. BH24: St L 2G **19**
Oak Dr. BH15: Poole 5B **56**
Oakenbrow SO41: Sway 1E **33**
Oakfield SO41: Lymi 2G **53**
Oakfield Rd. BH15: Poole 1A **56**
Oakford Ct. BH8: Bour 2D **42**
Oak Gdns. BH11: Bour 4D **40**
SO41: Ever 5H **51**
Oakham Grange BH22: Fern 3C **18**
OAKHAVEN HOSPICE 4F **53**
Oak Ho. SO41: Lymi 5F **35**
Oakhurst BH13: Poole 4D **58**
BH23: Chri *6B **46***
(off Newlands Rd.)
Oakhurst Cl. BH22: W Moo 5D **10**
Oakhurst La. BH22: W Moo 5D **10**
Oakhurst Rd. BH22: W Moo 6D **10**
Oaklands SO41: Lymi 3H **53**
Oaklands Cl. BH31: Ver 3C **6**
Oakland Wlk. BH22: W Par 2H **25**
Oak La. BH24: Ring 3D **8**
Oakleigh Way BH23: Highc 6H **47**
OAKLEY 1B **22**
Oakley Gdns. BH16: Upt 6A **36**
Oakley Hgts. BH2: Bour 2F **5** (3G **59**)
Oakley Hill BH21: Mer 6F **15**
Oakley La. BH21: Mer 1B **22**
Oakley Rd. BH21: Mer 1B **22**
Oakley Shop. Cen. BH21: Mer 2C **22**
Oakley Straight BH21: Mer 2C **22**
Oakmead Gdns. BH11: Bour 1A **40**
Oakmead Rd. BH17: Poole 5F **37**
Oakmead Sports Cen. 1B **40**
Oak Rd. BH8: Bour 1C **60**
BH16: Upt 1C **54**
BH25: A'ley 2A **50**
Oaks, The BH31: Ver 2C **6**
Oaks Dr. BH24: St L 4H **11**
Oaks Mead BH31: Ver 3E **7**
Oaktree Ct. SO41: M Sea 3C **66**
Oak Tree Pde. *BH23: Bran* *3D **28***
(off Ringwood Rd.)
Oaktree Pde. BH23: Bran 2D **28**
Oak Tree Pk. (Caravan Pk.)
BH24: St L 1F **19**
Oakwood BH3: Bour 6G **41**
Oakwood Av. BH25: New M 1H **49**
Oakwood Cl. BH9: Bour 3B **42**
BH24: Ashl H 2B **12**
Oakwood Rd. BH9: Bour 3A **42**
BH23: Highc 4G **47**
Oakwoood Ct. BH25: New M 2H **49**
Oasis, The BH13: Poole 3C **58**
Oasis M. BH16: Upt 6A **36**
Oates Rd. BH9: Bour 4G **41**
Oban Rd. BH3: Bour 6G **41**
Oberfield Rd. SO42: Broc 2C **72**
Ober Rd. SO42: Broc 2D **72**
Oceanarium 6H **5** (5H **59**)
Ocean Breeze BH4: Bour 6E **59**
Ocean Hgts. BH5: Bour 4F **61**
Odeon ABC Cinema
Bournemouth 4H **5** (4H **59**)
Odeon Cinema
Bournemouth 4H **5** (4H **59**)
Okeford Ho. BH9: Bour 6H **41**
Okeford Rd. BH18: Broad 3A **38**
Old Barn Cl. BH23: Chri 3B **44**
BH24: Ring 4E **9**
Old Barn Farm Rd. BH21: Wool 2E **11**
Old Barn La. BH23: Chri 3B **44**
Old Barn Rd. BH23: Chri 3B **44**
Old Boat Yard, The BH23: Chri 5C **44**
Old Bound Rd. BH16: Upt 1C **54**
Old Brewery, The BH15: Poole 4B **4**
Old Bridge Rd. BH6: Bour 5B **44**
Old Christchurch La. BH1: Bour 3H **5** (4H **59**)
Old Christchurch Rd. BH1: Bour 4G **5** (4H **59**)
SO41: Ever 4H **51**
Old Coach M. BH14: Poole 3E **57**
Old Coastguard Rd. BH13: S'bks 5F **69**
Old Courthouse, The
BH14: Poole 2G **57**
Old Dairy Cl. BH15: Poole 6B **38**
Old Farm Cl. BH24: Poul 1E **9**
Old Farmhouse M. *SO41: Lymi* *6G **35***
(off Lwr. Buckland Rd.)
Old Farm Rd. BH15: Poole 1C **56**
Old Farm Wlk. SO41: Lymi 2F **53**
Old Forge Cl. BH24: Poul 2E **9**
Old Forge Rd. BH21: Stap 3F **17**
Old Ham La. BH21: Lit C 4C **16**
Old Highways M. BH21: W Min 5G **15**
Old Kiln Rd. BH16: Upt 6D **36**
Old Lifeboat House
Poole 5C **4** (6A **56**)
Old Maltings, The SO41: Lymi 1F **53**
Old Manor Cl. BH21: W Min 5G **15**
Old Market Rd. BH21: Cor M 3A **20**
Old Mill Ho. BH24: Ring 5B **8**
OLD MILTON 4F **49**
Old Milton Grn. BH25: New M 4F **49**
Old Milton Grn. Pde. BH25: New M 4F **49**
Old Milton Rd. BH25: New M 4F **49**
Old Mulberry Cl. BH10: Bour 4C **40**
Old Orchard BH15: Poole 5B **4** (6A **56**)
(not continuous)
Old Orchards SO41: Lymi 3H **53**
Old Pines Cl. BH22: Fern 5C **18**
Old Priory Rd. BH6: Bour 3D **62**
Old Rectory Cl. BH21: Cor M 3D **20**
Old Rectory M. BH15: Hamw 5F **55**
Old Rd. BH21: W Min 5D **14**
Old Rope Walk, The BH15: Hamw 6F **55**
Old St John's M. BH9: Bour 2H **41**
Old Sandpit La. BH16: Bea H 3A **36**
Old Sawmill Cl. BH31: Ver 2B **6**
Old School Cl. BH14: Poole 3E **57**
BH22: Fern 4A **18**
Old Stacks Gdns. BH24: Ring 5E **9**
OLD TOWN 4B **4** (5A **56**)
Old Town Mkt. BH15: Poole 4B **4** (5A **56**)
Old Town M. BH15: Poole 4B **4**
Old Vicarage Cl. BH10: Bour 5G **25**
Old Vicarage La. SO41: Sway 2G **33**
Old Wareham Rd. BH12: Poole 6E **39**
BH16: Bea H 3A **36**
BH21: Cor M 3A **36**
Oliver Rd. SO41: Penn 2E **53**
Olivers Rd. BH21: Cole 3A **16**
Olivers Way BH21: Cole 3A **16**
Olivia Cl. BH16: Upt 2D **54**
Onslow Gdns. BH21: W Min 3F **15**
Ophir Gdns. BH8: Bour 2B **60**
Ophir Rd. BH8: Bour 2B **60**
Oratory Gdns. BH13: Poole 1B **70**
Orchard, The BH11: Bour 5H **23**
BH23: Bran 3E **29**
SO41: M Sea 3D **66**
Orchard Av. BH14: Poole 5D **56**

96 A-Z Bournemouth

Pennywell Gdns. BH25: A'ley	Pines, The BH1: Bour 3A 60	Poplar Cl. BH15: Poole 5A 4
...........................1B 50	(Benjamin Ct.)	BH21: W Min 4F 15
Penrhyn BH1: Bour 3D 60	BH1: Bour 3C 60	BH23: Bran 3E 29
Penrith Cl. BH31: Ver 4C 6	(Knyveton Rd.)	BH23: Highc 5B 48
Penrith Rd. BH5: Bour 3G 61	BH13: Poole 5C 58	Poplar Cres. BH24: Ring 4D 8
Penrose Rd. BH22: Fern 3B 18	Pineside BH9: Bour 5A 42	Poplar La. BH23: Bran 2E 29
Peppercorn SO41: Sway 1G 33	Pinesprings Dr. BH18: Broad 2E 37	Poplar Rd. BH25: A'ley 1B 50
Peppercorn Cl. BH23: Chri 5A 46	Pine Springs Nature Reserve 3E 37	Poplar Way BH24: Ring 4D 8
Percy Rd. BH5: Bour 3E 61	Pinetops Cl. SO41: Penn 2D 52	Poppy Cl. BH16: Upt 6A 36
Peregrine Rd. BH23: Mude 1C 64	Pine Tree Cl. BH21: Cole 4F 15	BH23: Chri 5D 46
Pergin Cres. BH17: Poole 6H 37	Pine Tree Glen BH4: Bour 4E 59	Poppy Ct. BH6: Bour 3B 62
Pergin Way BH17: Poole 6H 37	Pine Tree Wlk. BH17: Poole 5F 37	Portadene BH4: Bour 5F 59
Perrin Lock Ct. BH23: Chri 1D 62	Pine Va. Cres. BH10: Bour 2G 41	Portarlington Cl. BH4: Bour 5F 59
(off King's Av.)	Pine Vw. Cl. BH16: Upt 1C 54	Portarlington Ct. BH4: Bour 4E 59
Perryfield Gdns. BH7: Bour 5H 61	BH31: Ver 2B 6	(off Portarlington Rd.)
Perry Gdns. BH15: Poole 5C 4 (6A 56)	Pine Vw. Gdns. BH10: Bour 1H 41	Portarlington Rd. BH4: Bour 4E 59
(not continuous)	Pine Vw. Rd. BH31: Ver 2B 6	Portchester Ct. BH8: Bour 2B 60
Persley Rd. BH10: Bour 1F 41	BH31: Ver 4F 7	Portchester Pl. BH8: Bour 2B 60
Perth Cl. BH23: Chri 4C 44	Pine Wlk. BH22: W Moo 4C 10	Portchester Rd. BH8: Bour 1A 60
Peter Grant Way BH22: Fern 4A 18	BH31: Ver 4F 7	Portelet Cl. BH12: Poole 4H 39
Peters Cl. BH16: Upt 1C 54	Pinewood Av. BH10: Bour 6F 25	Porter Rd. BH17: Poole 6H 37
Petersfield Pl. BH7: Bour 6H 43	Pinewood Cl. BH10: Bour 6F 25	Porters La. BH21: Cole 3C 16
Petersfield Rd. BH7: Bour 1G 61	BH16: Upt 6A 36	Portesham Gdns. BH9: Bour 1B 42
Petersham Rd. BH17: Poole 5F 37	BH23: Walk 3A 48	Portesham Way BH17: Poole 2C 38
Peterson's Tower 5G 33	Pinewood Ct. BH22: W Moo 5B 10	Portfield Cl. BH23: Chri 5E 45
Peters Rd. BH22: Fern 6D 18	Pinewood Gdns. BH22: Fern 2B 18	Portfield Rd. BH23: Chri 6D 44
Petit Rd. BH9: Bour 2A 42	Pinewood Rd. BH13: Poole 6D 58	Portland Pl. BH2: Bour 1G 5 (3H 59)
Petwyn Cl. BH22: Fern 3E 19	BH16: Upt 6A 36	Portland Rd. BH9: Bour 4A 42
Peverell Rd. BH16: Hamw 3B 54	BH22: Fern 1A 18	Portman Cres. BH5: Bour 3H 61
Peveril Cl. BH24: Ashl H 1B 12	BH23: Highc 4H 47	Portman M. BH7: Bour 2F 61
Phelipps Rd. BH21: Cor M 4D 20	BH24: St I 3B 12	Portman Rd. BH7: Bour 2F 61
Phippard Way BH15: Poole 5B 56	SO41: Hor 2C 50	Portman Ter. BH5: Bour 3H 61
Phoenix BH14: Poole 3F 57	Pinkney La. SO43: Lyn 6E 71	Portmore Cl. BH18: Broad 5A 22
Phyldon Cl. BH12: Poole 2G 57	Pinnacle, The BH1: Bour 4H 5	Port St James BH15: Poole 5A 4
Phyldon Rd. BH12: Poole 1F 57	Pipers Ash BH24: Poul 3E 9	Portswood Dr. BH10: Bour 1A 42
Piazza, The BH1: Bour 3E 61	Pipers Dr. BH23: Chri 6C 46	Port Vw. Caravan Pk. BH23: Hurn .1H 27
(off Palmerston Rd.)	Pippin Cl. BH23: Chri 3C 44	Post Office La. BH15: Poole 3C 4
Pickard Rd. BH22: Fern 2D 18	SO41: Lymi 3G 53	BH24: St I 2C 12
Pickering Cl. BH18: Broad 3G 37	Pitmore La.	Post Office Rd. BH1: Bour ...4G 5 (4H 59)
PICKET HILL 3H 9	SO41: Penn, Sway 1G 33	**Potterne Hill Nature Reserve** 5E 7
Pickford Rd. BH9: Bour 4G 41	Pittmore Rd. BH23: Burt 3G 45	Potterne Way BH21: Thr C 5E 7
Pier App. BH2: Bour 5H 5 (5H 59)	Pitts Pl. BH25: A'ley 3B 50	Potterne Wood Cl. BH31: Ver 5G 7
Pier Theatre, The 6H 5 (5H 59)	Pitwines Cl. BH15: Poole 3C 4 (5A 56)	Potters Way BH14: Poole 5G 57
Pig Shoot La.	**Place Watermill** 2F 63	Pottery Junc. BH12: Poole 2A 58
BH23: Hurn 1F 43	Plantagenet Cres. BH11: Bour 6H 23	Pottery Rd. BH14: Poole 4E 57
PIKESHILL 2E 71	Plantation SO41: Ever 5A 52	**POULNER** 2E 9
Pikes Hill SO43: Lyn 2E 71	Plantation Ct. BH17: Poole 4A 38	Poulner Pk. BH24: Poul 2E 9
Pikes Hill Av. SO43: Lyn 2E 71	SO41: Lymi 1F 53	Pound Cl. BH15: Poole 2D 56
PILFORD 1B 16	Plantation Dr. BH23: Walk 3A 48	BH24: Ring 3C 8
Pilford Heath Rd. BH21: Cole 1A 16	Plantation Rd. BH17: Poole 4A 38	Pound La. BH15: Poole 2C 56
Pilford La. BH21: Cole 1A 16	Plant Pk. Rd. BH24: Match 4E 13	BH23: Chri 1F 63
Pilgrim Pk. (Caravan Pk.)	Plassey Cres. BH10: Bour 6E 25	(off High St.)
BH24: Poul 3E 9	Platoff Rd. SO41: Lymi 5G 53	Pound Rd. SO41: Penn 2D 52
Pilgrim Pl. SO41: Lymi 1A 58	Playfields Dr. BH17: Poole 1A 58	Powell Rd. BH14: Poole 4F 57
Pilgrim's Cl. BH25: A'ley 1A 50	Pleasance Way BH25: New M 2F 49	Powerscourt BH2: Bour 5F 59
Pilgrims Way BH17: Poole 6G 37	Plecy Cl. BH22: W Par 6B 18	(off Chine Cres. Rd.)
PILLEY 2H 35	Plemont Cl. BH12: Poole 4A 40	Powerscourt Rd. BH25: B Sea 6D 48
PILLEY BAILEY 2H 35	Pless Rd. SO41: M Sea 2A 66	Powis Cl. BH25: New M 2H 49
Pilley Hill SO41: Pil 2H 35	Plover Cl. SO41: M Sea 3F 67	Powlett Rd. SO41: Lymi 2G 53
Pilley St. SO41: Pil 2H 35	Plover Ho. BH15: Hamw 6G 55	Preston Cl. BH16: Upt 6C 36
Pilot Hight Rd. BH11: Bour 1C 40	(off Broomhill Way)	Preston La. BH23: Burt 3H 45
Pilsdon Dr. BH17: Poole 3C 38	Plumer Rd. BH17: Poole 4G 37	Preston Rd. BH15: Poole 1A 56
Pimpern Cl. BH17: Poole 3C 38	Point, The BH5: Bour 4E 61	Preston Way BH23: Chri 5F 47
Pine Av. BH6: Bour 3A 62	**POKESDOWN** 2G 61	Prestwood Cl. BH25: B Sea 4F 49
BH12: Poole 6B 40	**Pokesdown Station (Rail)** 2G 61	Priestlands La. SO41: Lymi 2E 53
Pinebeach Ct. BH13: Poole 1C 70	Poles La. SO41: Lymi 4G 53	Priestlands Pl. SO41: Lymi 2F 53
Pinecliffe Av. BH6: Bour 3A 62	Policemans La. BH16: Upt 6A 36	Priestlands Rd. SO41: Penn 2E 53
Pinecliffe Rd. BH25: New M 6C 48	Pomona Cl. BH22: Fern 3B 18	Priestley Rd. BH10: Bour 4D 40
Pinecliff Rd. BH13: Poole 1C 70	Pompey's La. BH21: Fern 5G 17	**Priest's House Mus. & Garden** 4E 15
Pine Cl. BH22: Fern 2A 18	BH22: Long 1D 24	Primrose Cl. BH1: Bour 2D 60
BH25: B Sea 5E 49	Pond Cl. BH25: New M 2G 49	Primrose Gdns. BH17: Poole 4F 37
Pine Ct. Bus. Cen.	Ponsonby Rd. BH14: Poole 3H 57	Primrose Way BH21: Cor M 4E 21
BH1: Bour 4A 60	Pony Dr. BH16: Upt 6D 36	BH23: Chri 4D 46
Pine Cres. BH23: Highc 6G 47	**POOLE** 2C 4 (5A 56)	Prince of Wales Rd. BH4: Bour 3D 58
Pine Dr. BH13: Poole 6G 57	Poole Commerce Cen.	Princes Ct. BH5: Bour 3E 61
BH24: St I 3B 12	BH12: Poole 2B 58	BH12: Poole 3C 58
Pine Dr. E. BH13: Poole 5C 58	Poole Crematorium BH17: Mer 6B 22	BH21: Fern 3B 18
Pine End BH22: Fern 6D 18	**POOLE GENERAL HOSPITAL** 4B 56	Princes Cres. SO43: Lyn 3H 71
Pine Glen Av. BH22: Fern 1A 18	Poole Harbour Yacht Club 6G 55	Princes Pl. BH25: A'ley 1A 50
Pine Grange BH1: Bour 4A 60	Poole Hill BH2: Bour 4E 5 (4G 59)	Princes Rd. BH22: Fern 4B 18
Pine Gro. BH22: W Moo 5C 10	Poole La. BH11: Bour 1B 40	Princess Av. BH23: Chri 1F 63
Pineholt Cl. BH24: St I 2C 12	Poole La. Rdbt. BH11: Bour 1A 40	Princess Ga. BH12: Poole 3C 58
Pine Ho. BH25: New M 2G 49	**Poole Mus.** 5A 4 (6H 55)	Princess M. BH12: Poole 3C 58
Pinehurst SO41: M Sea 3C 66	**Poole Pottery** 5B 4 (6A 56)	Princess Rd. BH4: Bour 3D 58
Pinehurst Av. BH23: Mude 2B 64	Poole Rd. BH2: Bour 4F 59	BH12: Poole 3C 58
Pinehurst Pk. (Caravan Site)	BH4: Bour 3D 58	Princess Royal Cl. SO41: Lymi 1F 53
BH22: W Moo 5D 10	BH12: Poole 3B 58	Pringles Cl. BH22: Fern 4C 18
Pinehurst Rd. BH22: W Moo 6C 10	BH16: Upt 6C 36	Pringles Dr. BH22: Fern 4C 18
Pinelands BH1: Bour 3D 60	BH21: W Min 5E 15	Prior Cl. BH7: Bour 2F 61
Pinelands Ct. BH8: Bour 6C 42	**Poole Stadium** 1C 4 (4A 56)	Priors Cl. BH23: Fri C 6E 47
Pine Mnr. Rd. BH24: Ashl H 1B 12	**Poole Station (Rail)** 2C 4 (4A 56)	Priors Rd. BH17: Poole 5F 37
Pine Pk. Mans. BH13: Poole 3C 58	Poole Trade Pk. BH12: Poole 5E 39	Priors Wlk. BH21: W Min 4D 14
Pine Rd. BH9: Bour 4H 41	Popes Rd. BH15: Poole 1B 56	Priory Ct. BH6: Bour 2A 62
BH21: Cor M 2F 21		

Priory Gdns.—Ringwood Rd.

Priory Gdns. BH22: W Moo .1E 19
Priory Ind. Pk. BH23: Chri .6D 46
Priory M. BH23: Chri .1F 63
Priory Quay BH23: Chri .2G 63
Priory Rd. BH2: Bour .5F 5 (5G 59)
BH22: W Moo .1E 19
Priory Vw. Pl. BH9: Bour .2A 42
Priory Vw. Rd. BH9: Bour .2A 42
BH23: Burt .2G 45
Private Rd. SO41: Lymi .6G 35
Privet Rd. BH9: Bour .5G 41
Promenade
BH13: Poole, S'bks .5H 69
(not continuous)
BH14: Poole .5D 56
BH15: Hamw .6F 55
BH15: Poole .6C 56
(Catalina Dr.)
BH15: Poole .1A 4 (3H 55)
(Sterte Av. W.)
BH23: Fri C .2D 64
Prosperous St. BH15: Poole .5B 4 (6A 56)
Prunus Cl. BH22: Fern .2H 17
Prunus Dr. BH22: Fern .2H 17
Puddletown Cres. BH17: Poole .3D 38
Puffin Ho. *BH15: Hamw .6G 55*
(off Stone Cl.)
Pullman Ct. BH22: W Moo .5B 10
Pullman Way BH24: Ring .5C 8
Purbeck Av. BH15: Hamw .6E 55
Purbeck Cl. BH16: Upt .6B 36
Purbeck Ct. BH5: Bour .4H 61
BH23: Chri .5B 46
(off Dorset Rd.)
Purbeck Dr. BH31: Ver .4D 6
Purbeck Gdns. BH14: Poole .2D 56
Purbeck Hgts. BH14: Poole .2F 57
Purbeck Ho. BH8: Bour .3B 60
Purbeck Rd. BH2: Bour .4E 5 (4G 59)
BH25: B Sea .6D 48
Purbeck Vs. BH14: Poole .4F 57
Purchase Rd. BH12: Poole .6D 40
PUREWELL .1H 63
Purewell BH23: Chri .1H 63
Purewell Cl. BH23: Chri .1A 64
Purewell Ct. BH23: Chri .6A 46
Purewell Cross BH23: Chri .1A 64
Purewell Cross Rd. BH23: Chri .6G 45
Purewell Gate BH23: Chri .1G 63
Purewell Mews BH23: Chri .1G 63
Pussex La. BH23: Hurn .3G 27
Pye Cl. BH21: Cor M .4D 20
Pye Cnr. BH21: W Min .5D 14
Pye La. BH21: W Min .5D 14
Pyrford Gdns. SO41: Lymi .3G 53
Pyrford M. SO41: Lymi .3G 53

Q

Quaker Ct. BH24: Ring .5B 8
Quantock Ct. *BH23: Chri .5B 46*
(off Hunt Rd.)
Quarry Chase BH4: Bour .4E 59
Quarry Cl. BH21: Cole .2B 16
Quarry Dr. BH21: Cole .2B 16
Quarry Rd. BH21: Cole .2B 16
Quarterdeck, The BH5: Bour .4F 61
Quay, The BH15: Poole .5A 4 (6H 55)
BH23: Chri .2G 63
Quay Ct. BH23: Chri .5D 44
Quay Hill SO41: Lymi .1H 53
Quayle Dr. BH11: Bour .5B 24
Quay Point BH15: Poole .5B 4 (6A 56)
Quay Rd. BH23: Chri .1F 63
SO41: Lymi .1H 53
Quay St. SO41: Lymi .1H 53
Queen Anne Dr. BH21: Mer .3B 22
Queen Elizabeth Av. SO41: Lymi .1F 53
Queen Elizabeth Ct. BH21: W Min .5D 14
Queen Elizabeth Leisure Cen. .3B 14
Queen Katherine Rd. SO41: Lymi .2H 53
Queen Mary Av. BH9: Bour .3H 41
Queens Av. BH23: Chri .2F 63
Queensbury Mans. BH1: Bour .4A 60
Queens Cl. BH22: W Moo .6B 10
Queens Ct. *BH4: Bour .3F 59*
(off Wharfdale Rd.)
BH8: Bour .5B 42
BH25: A'ley .2B 50
Queens Gdns. BH2: Bour .3F 59
Queens Gro. BH25: A'ley .1A 50
Queensland Rd. BH5: Bour .2G 61
Queensmead *BH21: W Min .4E 15*
(off Allenview Rd.)
Queensmount BH8: Bour .6C 42
Queen's Pde. SO43: Lyn .3F 71
Queen's Pk. Av. BH8: Bour .5B 42
Queens Pk. Gdns. BH8: Bour .6C 42
Queen's Park Golf Course .6D 42
Queens Pk. Rd. BH8: Bour .6D 42
Queens Pk. Sth. Dr. BH8: Bour .6D 42
Queens Pk. West Dr. BH8: Bour .6C 42
Queens Rd. BH2: Bour .4F 59
BH14: Poole .3H 57
BH21: Cor M .6D 20
BH22: Fern .2B 18
BH23: Chri .1A 64
SO43: Lyn .3G 71
Queen St. SO41: Lymi .2F 53
Queens Way BH24: Ring .4D 8
Queensway BH25: New M .2E 49
Queenswood Av. BH8: Bour .4E 43
Queenswood Dr. BH22: Fern .2B 18
Quest Ho. BH8: Bour .1A 60
Quince La. BH21: Cole .4G 15
Quintin Cl. BH23: Highc .5H 47
Quomp BH24: Ring .4C 8

R

Racecourse Vw. SO43: Lyn .2F 71
Rachael Cl. BH12: Poole .6G 39
Radar Way BH23: Chri .6D 46
Radipole Rd. BH17: Poole .3E 39
Raglan Gdns. BH11: Bour .3C 40
Railway Ter. BH23: Hin .3G 47
Raleigh Cl. BH23: Mude .2B 64
BH24: Poul .3E 9
BH25: New M .2F 49
Raleigh Rd. BH12: Poole .3A 40
Ralph Jessop Ct. BH12: Poole .6A 40
Ralph Rd. BH21: Cor M .4E 21
Ramley Rd. SO41: Penn .5B 34
Rampart, The SO41: Lymi .6F 35
Ramsey Ct. BH23: Chri .1D 62
BH25: New M .2F 49
Randalls Hill BH16: Bea H, Lyt M .4A 36
Randolph Rd. BH1: Bour .3E 61
BH14: Poole .2G 57
Ranelagh Rd. BH23: Highc .6H 47
Rashley M. SO41: Lymi .1G 53
Ravana Ct. *BH8: Bour .2A 60*
(off Wellington Rd.)
Ravenscourt Rd. BH6: Bour .2A 62
SO41: Lymi .2F 53
Ravensdale Cl. BH12: Poole .1G 57
Ravenshall BH4: Bour .5F 59
Ravens Way SO41: M Sea .3D 66
Ravenswood Pk. Caravan Site BH24: Crow .6H 9
Raven Way BH23: Mude .2C 64
Ravine Ct. BH13: Poole .2B 70
Ravine Rd. BH5: Bour .3H 61
BH13: Poole .1B 70
Raymond Cl. BH31: Ver .3F 7
Rayners Dr. BH12: Poole .2H 57
Rayscliff *BH4: Bour .5E 59*
(off West Cliff Rd.)
Rebbeck Rd. BH7: Bour .1G 61
Recreation Rd. BH12: Poole .1H 57
Rectory Av. BH21: Cor M .2D 20
Rectory Rd. BH15: Poole .1A 56
Redan Cl. BH23: Highc .6H 47
Redbreast Rd. BH9: Bour .2A 42
Redbreast Rd. Nth. BH9: Bour .2A 42
Redcliffe Cl. BH23: Burt .3G 45
Redcliffe Ct. *BH1: Bour .4C 60*
(off Manor Rd.)
Redcotts BH21: W Min .4D 14
Redcotts La. BH21: W Min .4D 14
Redcotts Rd. BH21: W Min .4D 14
RED HILL .1H 41
Redhill Av. BH9: Bour .3G 41
Redhill Cl. BH10: Bour .2G 41
Redhill Ct. BH10: Bour .1H 41
Redhill Cres. BH9: Bour .2H 41
Redhill Dr. BH10: Bour .3G 41
Redhill Pk. Homes BH10: Bour .6H 25
Redhill Rdbt. BH10: Bour .1H 41
Redhoave Rd. BH17: Poole .4C 38
Redhorn Cl. BH16: Hamw .3C 54
Red House Mus. & Garden .1F 63
Redlands BH12: Poole .2B 58
Redlands Ct. *BH6: Bour .3D 62*
(off Foxholes Rd.)
Red La. BH21: Cor M .3A 20
Redmans Vw. BH31: Ver .3C 6
Red Oaks Cl. BH22: Fern .2H 17
Red Roofs BH22: Fern .6C 18
Redshank Cl. BH17: Poole .4F 37
Redvers Cl. SO41: Lymi .2G 53
Redvers Rd. BH23: Chri .6A 46
Redwood Cl. BH24: Ring .4D 8
SO41: Lymi .6E 35
Redwood Dr. BH22: Fern .1A 18
Redwood Rd. BH16: Upt .5A 36
Reef, The BH5: Bour .4E 61
Reefside *BH5: Bour .3E 61*
(off Florence Rd.)
Regency Ct. BH1: Bour .3C 60
Regency Cres. BH23: Chri .5D 44
Regency Ho. *BH1: Bour .3A 60*
(off Lorne Pk. Rd.)
Regency Pl. BH24: Ring .3C 8
Regent Centre, The
Christchurch .1F 63
Regent Dr. BH7: Bour .5F 43
Regents Ct. BH13: Poole .4C 58
Regent Way BH23: Chri .1F 63
Reginald Noble Ct. BH4: Bour .3D 58
Reid St. BH23: Chri .6E 45
Rempstone Rd. BH21: Mer .2B 22
Renault Dr. BH18: Broad .4G 37
Renouf Cl. SO41: Penn .2E 53
Rest A While Pk. BH24: St L .4A 12
Restharrow BH1: Bour .3A 60
Retreat, The BH23: Chri .1H 63
Retreat Rd. BH21: W Min .5F 15
Reuben Dr. BH15: Hamw .5D 54
Reynard Ct. BH15: Poole .4D 56
Rhinefield Cl. SO42: Broc .2D 72
Rhinefield Rd. BH25: Woot .1E 31
SO42: Broc .2A 72
Rhiners Cl. SO41: Sway .1F 33
Ribble Cl. BH18: Broad .3G 37
Ribbonwood Hgts. BH14: Poole .3F 57
Ricardo Cres. BH23: Mude .1C 64
Ricardo Way SO41: Bold .4F 35
Rice Gdns. BH16: Hamw .3D 54
Rice Ter. BH16: Hamw .3D 54
Richard Cl. BH16: Upt .5B 36
Richards Cl. BH10: Bour .3F 41
Richmond Ct. BH8: Bour .6C 42
BH25: New M .2G 49
SO41: M Sea .3C 66
Richmond Dene BH2: Bour .1H 5
Richmond Gdns. BH1: Bour .3H 5 (4H 59)
Richmond Gdns. Shopping Cen.
BH1: Bour .3H 5 (4H 59)
Richmond Hgts. BH1: Bour .2H 5
Richmond Hill BH2: Bour .4G 5 (4H 59)
Richmond Hill Dr. BH2: Bour .3G 5 (4H 59)
Richmond Hill Ga.
BH2: Bour .3G 5
Richmond Ho. BH2: Bour .3G 5 (4H 59)
Richmond Pk. Av. BH8: Bour .6B 42
Richmond Pk. Cl. BH8: Bour .1D 60
Richmond Pk. Cres. BH8: Bour .6C 42
Richmond Pk. Lodge *BH8: Bour .1C 60*
(off Richmond Pk. Rd.)
Richmond Pk. Rd. BH8: Bour .6B 42
Richmond Rd. BH14: Poole .2G 57
BH21: W Min .5F 15
Richmond Wood Rd. BH8: Bour .6B 42
Ridgefield Gdns. BH23: Chri .5F 47
Ridgemount Gdns.
BH15: Hamw .4E 55
Ridgeway BH18: Broad .1H 37
BH21: Cor M .3D 20
BH22: W Par .3G 25
Ridgeway La. SO41: Lymi .3F 53
Ridley Rd. BH9: Bour .5H 41
Ridout Cl. BH10: Bour .4D 40
Riggs Gdns. BH11: Bour .3B 40
Rigler Rd. BH15: Hamw .6G 55
Rimbury Way BH23: Chri .5E 45
Ringbury SO41: Lymi .5F 35
RINGWOOD .4B 8
Ringwood Brewery .5B 8
Ringwood Health & Leisure Cen. .4C 8
Ringwood Rd. BH10: Bour .5B 24
BH11: Bour .3H 39
BH12: Poole .5F 39
BH14: Poole .3D 56
BH21: Thr C, Wool .2A 10 & 1E 11
BH22: Fern, Long, W Moo .1D 24
BH23: Bran, Hin, Walk .2C 28
(not continuous)

Ringwood Rd. BH24: St I, St L 1E 19	Roscrea Dr. BH6: Bour 3F 63	Russell Gdns. BH16: Hamw 3C 54
(not continuous)	Rosebery Cl. BH31: Ver 4G 7	BH24: St I 2D 12
BH31: Ver 2D 6	Rosebery Rd. BH5: Bour 2G 61	Russell Mt. BH4: Bour 3E 59
Ringwood Rd. Retail Pk. BH11: Bour 2A 40	Rosebud Av. BH9: Bour 3A 42	Russel Rd. BH10: Bour 5E 25
Ringwood Town & Country Experience **2B 8**	Rosecrae Cl. BH25: New M 1F 49	Russet Cl. BH22: Fern 3B 18
Ringwood Trad. Est. BH24: Ring 5C 8	Rose Cres. BH15: Poole 1D 56	Russett Cl. SO41: Lymi 3H 53
Ripon Rd. BH9: Bour 5A 42	Rosedale Cl. BH23: Chri 1A 64	Rutland Mnr. BH13: Poole 3C 58
Rise, The SO42: Broc 3E 73	Rosedene Lodge BH12: Poole 2D 58	Rutland Rd. BH9: Bour 5B 42
Ritchie Pl. BH22: W Moo 3B 10	Rose Farm Cl. BH2: Fern 6H 17	BH23: Chri 4D 44
Ritchie Rd. BH11: Bour 1D 40	Rose Gdns. BH9: Bour 3H 41	Ryall Rd. BH17: Poole 4B 38
River Cl. BH21: W Min 3E 15	Rosehill Cl. BH23: Bran 2D 28	Ryan Cl. BH22: Fern 2A 18
River Ct. BH23: Bour A 3G 27	Rosehill Dr. BH23: Bran 2C 28	Ryan Gdns. BH11: Bour 5D 24
SO41: Lymi 1H 53	Roselands BH1: Bour 2A 60	BH22: Fern 2A 18
Riverdale La. BH23: Chri 1E 63	(off Lansdowne Rd.)	Rydal Cl. BH23: Chri 1B 44
River Gdns. SO41: M Sea 3E 67	Rosemary Ct. BH23: Highc 6B 48	Rydal Ho. BH4: Bour 5E 59
River Glade BH23: Chri 2B 44	Rosemary Gdns. BH12: Poole 6F 39	(off Portarlington Rd.)
Riverlea Rd. BH23: Chri 1E 63	Rosemary Rd. BH12: Poole 6F 39	Ryecroft Av. BH11: Bour 6A 24
Rivermead Gdns. BH23: Chri 3C 44	Rosemount Rd. BH4: Bour 5D 58	
Riversdale BH21: W Min 5E 15	Rosewood Gdns. BH25: New M 1F 49	
Riversdale Rd. BH6: Bour 3E 63	Roslin Gdns. BH3: Bour 6F 41	
Riverside BH10: Bour 1H 41	Roslin Hall BH1: Bour 4C 60	
BH24: Ring 5B 8	Roslin Rd. BH3: Bour 6G 41	
Riverside Av. BH7: Bour 3H 43	Roslin Rd. Sth. BH3: Bour 6F 41	Saddle Cl. BH21: Cole 3C 16
Riverside Bus. Pk. SO41: Lymi 1H 53	(not continuous)	Safety Dr. BH17: Poole 1G 55
Riverside Ct. BH22: W Moo 4B 10	Ross Gdns. BH11: Bour 6G 23	Saffron Ct. BH11: Bour 2H 39
Riverside La. BH6: Bour 2D 62	Ross Glades BH3: Bour 1G 59	(off Saffron Way)
Riverside Pk. BH23: Chri 2E 63	Rossiters Quay BH23: Chri 1G 63	Saffron Dr. BH23: Chri 5D 46
Riverside Pk. Ind. Est. BH21: W Min 6F 15	Rossley Cl. BH23: Chri 3G 47	Saffron Way BH11: Bour 2H 39
Riverside Rd. BH6: Bour 2D 62	**ROSSMORE** **6B 40**	St Albans Av. BH8: Bour 6B 42
BH22: W Moo 5A 10	Rossmore Pde. BH12: Poole 5F 39	St Albans Cres. BH8: Bour 5B 42
Riverslea Mews BH23: Chri 1H 63	Rossmore Rd. BH12: Poole 5G 39	St Albans Rd. BH8: Bour 6B 42
Rivers Reach SO41: Lymi 2H 53	Ross Rd. BH24: Poul 1E 9	St Aldhelms BH14: Poole 3B 58
River Way BH23: Chri 4B 44	Rotary Cl. BH21: Cole 2H 15	St Aldhelm's Cl. BH13: Poole 4B 58
Riviera BH1: Bour 4B 60	Rothbury Pk. BH25: New M 3H 49	St Aldhelm's Pl. BH13: Poole 3B 58
Riviera Ct. BH2: Bour 4F 59	Rotherfield Rd. BH5: Bour 4H 61	St Aldhelm's Rd. BH13: Poole 3B 58
BH13: Poole 2B 70	BH23: Highc 4A 48	St Andrews BH23: Chri 1D 62
R L Stevenson Av. BH4: Bour 4D 58	Rothesay Dr. BH23: Highc 6G 47	St Andrews Rd. BH18: Broad 6G 21
Roberts Cl. SO41: Ever 4A 52	Rothesay Rd. BH4: Bour 1E 59	St Anne's Av. BH6: Bour 2C 62
Robertshaw Ho. SO43: Lyn 2F 71	Rotterdam Dr. BH23: Chri 6H 45	St Annes Gdns. SO41: Lymi 2F 53
Roberts La. BH17: Poole 6F 37	Roumelia La. BH5: Bour 3E 61	St Anne's Rd. BH16: Upt 6B 36
Roberts Rd. BH7: Bour 1G 61	Roundhaye Gdns. BH11: Bour 5B 24	St Ann's Ct. BH1: Bour 2E 61
BH17: Poole 4H 37	Roundhaye Rd. BH11: Bour 6B 24	**ST ANN'S HOSPITAL** **3A 70**
Roberts Way BH16: Upt 6A 36	Roundhouse Ct. SO41: Lymi 2F 53	St Anthony's Rd. BH2: Bour 2H 59
Robin Cres. BH25: Bash 6D 30	(off Queen St.)	St Antony's BH4: Bour 5F 59
Robin Gdns. BH23: Chri 5E 45	Roundways BH11: Bour 2A 40	St Aubyn's Ct. BH15: Poole 4A 4 (5H 55)
Robin Gro. BH25: New M 3F 49	Rowan Cl. BH23: Chri 5F 47	St Aubyns La. BH24: Hang 2G 9
Robins Way BH23: Mude 2D 64	BH24: St L 3H 11	St Augustin's Rd. BH2: Bour 2H 59
Robinswood Dr. BH22: Fern 1B 18	SO41: Sway 2F 33	**St Barbe Mus.** **1G 53**
Robsall Cl. BH12: Poole 6A 40	Rowan Dr. BH17: Poole 4E 37	St Boniface Gdns. BH10: Bour 2F 41
Rochester Rd. BH11: Bour 1D 40	BH23: Chri 5F 47	St Brelades BH14: Poole 6G 57
Rockbourne Gdns. BH25: New M 5D 48	BH31: Ver 5F 7	St Brelades Av. BH12: Poole 3H 39
Rockford Cl. BH6: Bour 4D 62	Rowans Pk. SO41: Lymi 2F 53	St Catherines BH21: W Min 5E 15
Rockley Caravan Pk. BH15: Hamw 3C 54	Rowbarrow Cl. BH17: Poole 3C 38	St Catherines Ct. BH1: Bour 4C 60
Rockley Cruising Club **4A 54**	Rowe Gdns. BH12: Poole 6B 40	**ST CATHERINE'S HILL** **2C 44**
Rockley M. BH15: Hamw 5E 55	Rowena Rd. BH6: Bour 2D 62	St Catherine's Hill La. BH23: Chri 3D 44
Rockley Rd. BH15: Hamw 5E 55	Rowland Av. BH15: Poole 1C 56	**St Catherine's Hill Nature Reserve** **2C 44**
ROCKLEY SANDS **4B 54**	**ROWLANDS** **4E 15**	St Catherine's Pde. BH23: Chri 4D 44
Rodbourne Cl. SO41: Ever 5H 51	Rowlands Hill BH21: W Min 4E 15	St Catherine's Path BH6: Bour 4C 62
Rodlease La. SO41: Bold 1G 35	Rownhams Rd. BH8: Bour 2C 42	St Catherine's Rd. BH6: Bour 3D 62
Rodney Cl. BH12: Poole 6A 40	Roxborough BH4: Bour 4E 59	St Catherine's Ter. BH6: Bour 4C 62
Rodney Ct. BH15: Poole 5C 4 (6A 56)	(off Portarlington Rd.)	St Catherine's Way BH23: Chri 2B 44
Rodney Dr. BH23: Mude 1B 64	Royal Arc. BH1: Bour 3E 61	St Clair Rd. BH13: Poole 3A 70
Rodway BH21: W Min 5E 15	**ROYAL BOURNEMOUTH HOSPITAL** **4H 43**	St Cleeve Way BH22: Fern 6A 18
Rodways Cnr. BH21: W Min 5E 15	Royal Cl. BH23: Chri 5D 44	St Clements Gdns. BH1: Bour 2D 60
Rodwell Cl. BH10: Bour 5E 25	**Royal Motor Yacht Club** **5F 69**	St Clements Gdns. BH1: Bour 2D 60
Roebuck Cl. BH25: New M 2H 49	Royal Oak Rd. BH10: Bour 6E 25	St Clements La. BH15: Poole 5A 4 (6H 55)
Roeshot Cres. BH23: Chri 4G 47	Royal Victoria M. BH4: Bour 4F 59	St Clements Rd. BH1: Bour 2D 60
Roeshot Hill BH23: Chri 4E 47	Royden La. SO41: Bold 1F 35	BH12: Poole 6E 39
Roi-Mar Home Pk. BH8: Bour 1D 42	Roysdean Mnr. BH1: Bour 3C 60	BH15: Poole 6E 39
Rolls Dr. BH6: Bour 3F 63	(off Derby Rd.)	St David's Ct. BH1: Bour 2E 61
Roman Hgts. BH21: Cor M 3E 21	Royster Cl. BH17: Poole 4A 38	St David's Rd. BH16: Upt 5B 36
Roman Rd. BH17: Poole 3E 37	Royston Dr. BH21: W Min 4F 15	St Denys BH25: New M 4G 49
BH18: Broad 1E 37	Royston Pl. BH25: B Sea 5H 49	St George's Almshouses BH15: Poole 5A 4
(not continuous)	Rozelle Rd. BH14: Poole 3G 57	St Georges Av. BH8: Bour 5C 42
BH21: Cor M 3E 21	Rozel Mnr. BH13: Poole 5D 58	BH12: Poole 5F 39
ROMFORD **2A 6**	Rubens Cl. BH25: New M 2B 50	St Georges Cl. BH8: Bour 5C 42
Romney Cl. BH10: Bour 2G 41	Rufford Gdns. BH6: Bour 2C 62	BH23: Chri 6F 47
Romney Ct. BH4: Bour 4E 59	Rufus Ct. SO43: Lyn 3G 71	St Georges Ct. BH1: Bour 2E 61
(off Portarlington Rd.)	Rugby Rd. BH17: Poole 4G 37	BH22: Fern 4C 18
Romney Rd. BH10: Bour 1G 41	Runnymede Av. BH11: Bour 5H 23	St Georges Dr. BH11: Bour 2H 39
Romsey Rd. SO43: Lyn 3G 71	Runton Rd. BH12: Poole 2B 58	BH22: Fern 5A 18
Rookcliff SO41: M Sea 3C 66	Runway, The BH23: Chri 6D 46	BH23: Bran 3D 28
Rookcliff Way SO41: M Sea 3C 66	Rushall La. SO41: Bold 1A 36	St Georges Gate BH2: Bour 4F 59
Rooker Ct. BH14: Poole 1E 57	**RUSHCOMBE BOTTOM** **4F 21**	(off Norwich Av. W.)
Rookes La. SO41: Lymi 3F 53	Rushcombe Way BH21: Cor M 5E 21	St Helier Rd. BH12: Poole 4H 39
Rook Hill Rd. BH23: Fri C 1D 64	Rushford Warren BH23: Mude 2B 64	**ST IVES** **2C 12**
Rookwood SO41: M Sea 3C 66	Rushmere Rd. BH6: Bour 6A 44	St Ives End La. BH24: St I 3C 12
Roosevelt Cres. BH11: Bour 5D 24	Rushton Cres. BH3: Bour 1H 59	St Ives Gdns. BH2: Bour 2H 59
Rope Hill SO41: Bold 2E 35	Ruskin Av. BH9: Bour 2B 42	St Ives Pk. BH24: Ashl H 2C 12
Ropers La. BH16: Upt 6D 36	**Russell-Cotes Art Gallery & Museum** **5A 60**	St Ives Wood BH24: St I 2D 12
Ropley Rd. BH7: Bour 6A 44	Russell Cotes Rd. BH1: Bour 5A 60	St James BH5: Bour 4E 61
Rosamund Av. BH21: Mer 2C 22	Russell Ct. BH25: New M 2G 49	St James Cl. BH15: Poole 5A 4 (6H 55)
Roscrea Dr. BH6: Bour 3F 63	Russell Dr. BH23: Chri 1H 63	St James Ct. BH1: Bour 2C 60
		BH13: Poole 4C 58

Shackleton Sq.—Sovereign Cen.

Shackleton Sq. BH23: Bran 2D **28**
Shaftesbury Cl. BH22: W Moo 5D **10**
Shaftesbury Ct. *BH3: Bour* *1H* ***59***
(off Wimborne Rd.)
Shaftesbury Rd. BH8: Bour 1C **60**
BH15: Poole 1D **4** (4B **56**)
BH22: W Moo 6D **10**
Shaggs Mdw. SO43: Lyn 3F **71**
Shakespeare Rd. BH6: Bour 6B **44**
BH21: W Min 3E **15**
Shallows La. SO41: Bold, Pil 3F **35**
Shamrock Ct. BH21: W Min 5E **15**
Shapland Av. BH11: Bour 6A **24**
Shapwick Rd. BH15: Hamw 6G **55**
Shard Cl. BH31: Ver 3E **7**
Sharlands Cl. BH18: Broad 2H **37**
Sharp Rd. BH12: Poole 6C **40**
Sharvells Rd. SO41: M Sea 2C **66**
Shaves La. BH25: New M 6G **31**
Shawford Gdns. BH8: Bour 3D **42**
Shawford Rd. BH8: Bour 2D **42**
Shaw Rd. BH24: Poul 1E **9**
Shears Brook Cl. BH23: Bran 2D **28**
Shearwater Ho. *BH15: Hamw* *6G* ***55***
(off Norton Way)
Shelbourne Cl. BH8: Bour 1C **60**
Shelbourne Rd. BH8: Bour 1B **60**
Sheldrake Gdns. SO41: Hor 2F **51**
Sheldrake Rd. BH23: Mude 2C **64**
Shelley Cl. BH1: Bour 2E **61**
BH23: Chri 6E **47**
BH24: Ashl H 2H **11**
Shelley Ct. BH22: Fern 4B **18**
Shelley Gdns. BH1: Bour 2E **61**
Shelley Hamlets BH23: Chri 6F **47**
Shelley Hill BH23: Chri 6F **47**
Shelley Ho. BH25: New M 3G **49**
Shelley Mnr. *BH5: Bour* *3F* ***61***
(off Beechwood Av.)
Shelley Rd. BH1: Bour 2E **61**
BH12: Poole 2H **57**
Shelley Rd. E. BH7: Bour 2E **61**
Shelley Way SO41: M Sea 2D **66**
Shelton Rd. BH6: Bour 1A **62**
Shenstone Ct. BH25: New M 4G **49**
Shepherd Cl. BH23: Highc 4H **47**
Shepherds Way BH7: Bour 6G **43**
SO41: Ever 4H **51**
Sheppards Fld. BH21: W Min 3D **14**
Sherborn Cres. BH17: Poole 3E **39**
Sherborne Dr. BH22: Fern 5B **18**
Sherfield Cl. BH8: Bour 3D **42**
Sheringham Rd. BH12: Poole 2B **58**
Sherlock Homes SO41: Lymi 2F **53**
Sherrin Cl. BH15: Poole 2B **56**
Sherwood Av. BH14: Poole 5D **56**
BH22: Fern 6A **18**
Sherwood Cl. BH23: Chri 6D **44**
Sherwood Dr. BH31: Ver 3F **7**
Shetland Vw. BH31: Ver 3E **7**
Shillingstone Dr. BH9: Bour 1B **42**
Shillingstone Gdns. BH12: Poole 6B **40**
Shillito Rd. BH12: Poole 2H **57**
Shingle Bank Dr. SO41: M Sea 3D **66**
Shipstal Cl. BH16: Hamw 3C **54**
Shipwrights Wlk. SO41: Key 4G **67**
Shires Cl. BH24: Ring 6C **8**
Shires Copse BH6: Bour 4D **62**
Shires Mead BH31: Ver 3E **7**
SHIRLEY 1B **28**
Shirley Cl. BH22: W Moo 5C **10**
BH23: Bran 2D **28**
Shirley Holms SO41: Bold, Lymi 2A **34**
Shirley Rd. BH9: Bour 4A **42**
BH12: Poole 1F **57**
BH16: Upt *6C* ***36***
(off Douglas Cl.)
SHOBLEY 2H **9**
Shoreacres BH13: S'bks 6F **69**
Shore Av. BH16: Upt 1C **54**
Shore Cl. BH16: Upt 1C **54**
SO41: M Sea 3D **66**
Shorefield Caravan Pk. SO41: Down 6E **51**
Shorefield Cres. SO41: M Sea 2C **66**
Shorefield Rd. SO41: Down 6D **50**
Shorefield Way SO41: M Sea 2C **66**
Shore Gdns. BH16: Upt 1B **54**
Shore La. BH16: Upt 2B **54**
Shore Rd. BH13: S'bks 3H **69**
Short Cl. BH12: Poole 5C **40**
Shortcut Way BH25: New M 4F **49**
Shorts Cl. BH23: Burt 4G **45**
Shottsford Rd. BH15: Poole 2A **56**
Showboat BH13: S'bks 6F **69**
Shrubb's Av. SO41: Lymi 1G **53**
Shrubbs Hill Gdns. SO43: Lyn 4F **71**
Shrubbs Hill Rd. SO43: Lyn 3F **71**
Sidney Gdns. BH9: Bour 1B **42**
Sidney Smith Ct. BH17: Poole 3C **38**
Sidney St. SO41: Hor 3E **51**
Sienna Ho. *BH1: Bour* *2E* ***61***
(off Palmerston Rd.)
Silchester Cl. BH2: Bour 1G **5** (2H **59**)
Silver Birch Cl. BH12: Poole 3C **58**
Silver Bus. Pk. BH23: Chri 6B **46**
Silverdale BH25: B Sea 5H **49**
Silverdale Cl. BH18: Broad 1E **37**
Silver Jubilee Ct. BH11: Bour 3C **40**
Silver Springs *BH4: Bour* *3E* ***59***
(off Surrey Rd.)
Silver St. BH23: Chri 1F **63**
SO41: Hor, Sway 1D **50**
Silver Way BH23: Highc 5G **47**
Silverways BH23: Highc 5G **47**
Silverwood Cl. BH21: Mer 1B **22**
Silverwood Ct. BH8: Bour 2A **60**
Simmonds Cl. BH15: Poole 2B **56**
Singleton Dr. BH10: Bour 3E **41**
Sir David English Sports Cen. 4C **42**
Sir Peter Thompson Ho. BH15: Poole 4B **4**
Siskin Cl. BH22: Fern 2H **17**
Sixpenny Cl. BH12: Poole 6B **40**
Skinner St. BH15: Poole 5B **4** (6A **56**)
Skipton Cl. BH18: Broad 3G **37**
Sky End La. SO41: Hor 3E **51**
Slade Cl. SO41: Hor 2E **51**
Slader Bus. Pk. BH17: Poole 4C **38**
Slades Farm Rd. BH10: Bour 4E **41**
Slade's La. BH10: Bour 5E **41**
Sleepbrook Cl. BH31: Ver 3C **6**
SLEIGHT 2C **20**
Sleight La. BH21: Cor M 2C **20**
Slepe Cres. BH12: Poole 5B **40**
Slinn Rd. BH23: Chri 6A **46**
Slip Way BH15: Poole 3A **4** (5H **55**)
Slop Bog Nature Reserve 1B **18**
Slough La. BH16: Upt 1A **54**
Smithfield Pl. BH9: Bour 4H **41**
Smithson Cl. BH12: Poole 5E **41**
Smithy La. BH25: Bash 5F **31**
Smugglers La. BH21: Cole, W Min 1F **15**
Smugglers La. Nth. BH23: Chri 3F **47**
Smugglers La. Sth. BH23: Chri 5F **47**
Smugglers Reach BH23: Mude 2C **64**
Smugglers Vw. BH25: New M 6C **48**
Smugglers Way SO41: M Sea 3E **67**
Smugglers Wood Rd. BH23: Chri 4F **47**
Smythe Gdns. SO41: Sway 2F **33**
Snail's La. BH24: Blas, Rock 1C **8**
Snowdon Rd. BH4: Bour 3E **59**
Snowdrop Gdns. BH23: Chri 4D **46**
Soberton Rd. BH8: Bour 6D **42**
Solar Ct. BH13: Poole 4C **58**
Solent Av. SO41: Lymi 2H **53**
Solent Cl. SO41: Lymi 2H **53**
Solent Ct. SO41: M Sea 3B **66**
Solent Dr. BH25: B Sea 6G **49**
Solent Flats SO41: M Sea 3E **67**
Solent Lodge BH25: New M 4F **49**
Solent Mead SO41: Lymi 2G **53**
Solent Meads Golf Course 3F **63**
Solent Pines BH1: Bour 4C **60**
SO41: M Sea 3B **66**
Solent Rd. BH6: Bour 4E **63**
BH23: Walk 3B **48**
BH25: New M 6D **48**
Solent Vw. BH6: Bour 4E **63**
Solent Vw. Ct. SO41: Penn 3E **53**
Solent Way SO41: M Sea 3F **67**
Solly Cl. BH12: Poole 6A **40**
Solomon Way BH15: Hamw 5D **54**
Somerby Rd. BH15: Poole 1B **56**
SOMERFORD 5B **46**
Somerford Av. BH23: Chri 5D **46**
Somerford Bus. Pk. BH23: Chri 6C **46**
Somerford Rd. BH23: Chri 1A **64**
Somerford Rdbt. BH23: Chri 5C **46**
Somerford Way BH23: Chri 6A **46**
Somerley Rd. BH9: Bour 6A **42**
Somerley Vw. BH24: Ring 3C **8**
Somerset Rd. BH7: Bour 2F **61**
BH23: Chri 6C **44**
Somerton Cl. BH25: A'ley 2B **50**
Somerville Ct. BH25: New M 2F **49**
Somerville Rd. BH2: Bour 4F **59**
BH24: Poul 3E **9**
Sonning Way BH8: Bour 3B **42**
Sopers La. BH17: Poole 4G **37**
BH23: Chri 1E **63**
(not continuous)
Sopley Cl. BH25: New M 5D **48**
Sopley Common (Nature Reserve) 3H **27**
Sopwith Cl. BH23: Mude 1D **64**
Sopwith Cres. BH21: Mer 2C **22**
Sorrel Gdns. BH18: Broad 3F **37**
Sorrell Ct. BH23: Chri 5D **46**
Sorrell Way BH23: Chri 5D **46**
Southampton Rd. BH24: Poul, Ring 4B **8**
SO41: Bold, Lymi 1D **34**
SO43: Lyn 3G **71**
South Av. BH25: New M 3H **49**
SOUTH BOCKHAMPTON 1A **46**
SOUTHBOURNE 4C **62**
Southbourne Cliff Dr. BH6: Bour 4D **62**
Southbourne Coast Rd. BH6: Bour 4C **62**
Southbourne Gro. BH6: Bour 3A **62**
Southbourne La. Central *BH6: Bour* *3A* ***62***
(off Chestnut Av.)
Southbourne La. E. *BH6: Bour* *3A* ***62***
(off Grand Av.)
Southbourne La. W. *BH6: Bour* *3H* ***61***
(off Fishermans Av.)
Southbourne Overcliff Dr. BH6: Bour 4A **62**
Southbourne Prom. BH6: Bour 4A **62**
Southbourne Rd. BH6: Bour 1H **61**
SO41: Lymi 2E **53**
Southbourne Sands BH6: Bour 4B **62**
Southbrook Cl. BH17: Poole 3E **39**
Southcliff Ct. BH6: Bour 4D **62**
Southcliffe Rd. BH23: Fri C 1D **64**
BH25: New M 6D **48**
South Cliff Rd. BH2: Bour 6G **5** (5H **59**)
Southcote Ho. *BH1: Bour* *3C* ***60***
(off Vale Rd.)
Southcote Rd. BH1: Bour 3B **60**
South Ct. SO41: M Sea 3D **66**
Southdown Ct. *BH23: Chri* *5B* ***46***
(off Dorset Rd.)
Southdown Way BH22: W Moo 6D **10**
South Dr. BH24: St L 2F **19**
BH25: Bash, Oss 5D **30**
South E. Sector BH23: Bour A 3G **27**
Southern Av. BH22: W Moo 6E **11**
Southern Cl. BH22: W Moo 1E **19**
Southernhay Ct. SO41: M Sea 3D **66**
Southernhay Rd. BH31: Ver 3F **7**
Southern La. BH25: New M 5F **49**
Southern Oaks BH25: New M 4F **49**
Southern Rd. BH6: Bour 3A **62**
SO41: Lymi 2F **53**
Southey Rd. BH23: Chri 5B **46**
Southfield BH24: Ring 5C **8**
Southfield M. BH24: Ring 5C **8**
South Gro. SO41: Lymi 2H **53**
Sth. Haven Cl. BH16: Hamw 4B **54**
Southill Av. BH12: Poole 1G **57**
Southill Gdns. BH9: Bour 4A **42**
Southill Rd. BH9: Bour 4A **42**
BH12: Poole 1G **57**
Sth. Kinson Dr. BH11: Bour 1C **40**
Southlands SO41: Penn 3E **53**
Southlands Av. BH6: Bour 3D **62**
BH21: Cor M 5D **20**
Southlands Cl. BH21: Cor M 5D **20**
Southlands Ct. BH18: Broad 2G **37**
Southlawns Wlk. BH25: B Sea 4F **49**
Southlea Av. BH6: Bour 2D **62**
South Pk. Rd. BH12: Poole 5C **40**
South Rd. BH1: Bour 2E **61**
BH15: Poole 4C **4** (5A **56**)
BH21: Cor M 4D **20**
South St. SO41: Penn 3E **53**
SOUTH SWAY 5H **33**
Sth. Sway La. SO41: Sway 3G **33**
South Vw. BH2: Bour 1G **5** (2H **59**)
South Vw. Pl. BH2: Bour 5E **5** (5G **59**)
South Vw. Rd. BH23: Chri 1E **63**
Southville Rd. BH5: Bour 2H **61**
SOUTH WEIRS 4C **72**
South Weirs SO42: Broc 4C **72**
Sth. Western Cres. BH14: Poole 5F **57**
Southwick Pl. BH6: Bour 6A **44**
Southwick Rd. BH6: Bour 1A **62**
Southwood Av. BH6: Bour 3A **62**
BH23: Walk 4A **48**
Southwood Cl. BH22: Fern 3A **18**
BH23: Walk 4A **48**
Sovereign Bus. Pk. BH15: Poole 1H **55**
Sovereign Cen. BH1: Bour 2E **61**

Sovereign Cl.—Summerhill

Sovereign Cl. BH7: Bour 5F 43
Sovereign Sq. *BH1: Bour* *3E 61*
(off Christchurch Rd.)
Sparkford Cl. BH7: Bour 5H 43
Sparky's Pl. BH1: Bour 2D 60
Spartina Dr. SO41: Lymi 5G 35
Speedwell Dr. BH23: Chri 5D 46
Spellers Way BH23: Chri 1A 64
Spencer Ct. BH25: New M 3G 49
Spencer Rd. BH1: Bour 3C 60
BH13: Poole 1A 70
BH25: New M 2G 49
Spetisbury Cl. BH9: Bour 2B 42
Spicer Ct. BH2: Bour 4E 5 (4G 59)
Spicer La. BH11: Bour 6A 24
Spinacre BH25: B Sea 5H 49
Spindle Cl. BH18: Broad 3F 37
Spindlewood Cl. BH25: B Sea 4G 49
Spinners Cl. BH22: W Moo 6C 10
Spinners Garden 3G 35
Spinney, The BH12: Poole 1C 58
BH24: Ashl H 1B 12
Spinney Cl. BH24: St L 3H 11
Spinneys La. BH22: Fern 4B 18
Spinney Way BH25: New M 5G 31
Spitfire BH15: Poole 1B 56
Spittlefields BH24: Ring 4D 8
Splashdown Waterpark 4E 39
Springbank Rd. BH7: Bour 5F 43
SPRINGBOURNE 1C 60
Springbourne Ct. BH1: Bour 2D 60
Spring Cl. BH31: Ver 4D 6
Springdale Av. BH18: Broad 6F 21
Springdale Gro. BH21: Cor M 1D 36
Springdale Rd. BH18: Broad 1D 36
BH21: Cor M 1D 36
Springfield Av. BH6: Bour 3E 63
BH23: Chri 3B 44
Springfield Cl. BH31: Ver 4D 6
SO41: Lymi 2H 53
Springfield Cres. BH14: Poole 3F 57
Springfield Gdns. BH25: A'ley 3B 50
Springfield Rd. BH14: Poole 2E 57
BH31: Ver 4D 6
Springfield Touring Pk. BH21: Cor M 1E 21
Spring Gdns. BH12: Poole 2H 57
Spring La. BH25: A'ley 3B 50
Springmead SO41: Lymi 2H 53
Spring Rd. BH1: Bour 2C 60
SO41: Lymi 2H 53
Springvale Av. BH7: Bour 5F 43
Spring Wlk. BH1: Bour 2D 60
Springwater Cl. BH11: Bour 2C 40
Springwater Dr. BH23: Chri 1H 63
Springwater Rd. BH11: Bour 2C 40
Spruce Cl. BH17: Poole 4E 37
Spur Cl. BH21: Cole 3C 16
Spurgeon Rd. BH7: Bour 1H 61
Spur Hill Av. BH14: Poole 4H 57
Spur Rd. BH14: Poole 4H 57
Square, The BH1: Bour 4G 5 (4H 59)
BH21: W Min 4D 14
BH24: St L 1F 19
SO41: Penn 2E 53
Square Cl. BH21: Lit C 6E 17
Squirrels, The BH13: Poole 4C 58
Squirrels Cl. BH23: Chri 3B 44
Squirrel Wlk. BH31: Ver 4D 6
Stables, The BH1: Bour 3E 61
BH23: Chri 6D 44
Stacey Cl. BH12: Poole 6G 39
Stacey Gdns. BH8: Bour 3F 43
Stadium Way BH15: Poole 1C 4 (4A 56)
Stafford Rd. BH1: Bour 4A 60
Stag Bus. Pk. BH24: Ring 6C 8
Stag Cl. BH25: New M 1E 49
Stagswood BH31: Ver 3B 6
Stalbridge Dr. BH22: Fern 5B 18
Stalbridge Rd. BH17: Poole 6G 37
Stalham Rd. BH12: Poole 1B 58
Stallards La. BH24: Ring 4B 8
Stamford Rd. BH6: Bour 2A 62
Stanfield Cl. BH12: Poole 6H 39
Stanfield Rd. BH9: Bour 5G 41
BH12: Poole 6H 39
BH22: Fern 3A 18
Stanford Gdns. SO41: Lymi 3F 53
Stanford Hill SO41: Lymi 2F 53
Stanford Ri. SO41: Sway 1F 33
Stanford Rd. SO41: Lymi 2F 53
Staniforth Ct. BH23: Chri 1H 63
Stanley Cl. BH31: Ver 4E 7
STANLEY GREEN 1A 56
Stanley Grn. Cres. BH15: Poole 2A 56
Stanley Grn. Ind. Est. BH15: Poole 2H 55
Stanley Grn. Rd. BH15: Poole 2A 56
Stanley Holiday Cen.
BH25: New M 5A 32
Stanley Pearce Ho. BH17: Poole 4A 38
Stanley Rd. BH1: Bour 2C 60
BH15: Poole 5C 4 (6B 56)
BH23: Highc 5A 48
SO41: Lymi 3H 53
Stannington Cl. BH25: New M 3H 49
STANPIT 1A 64
Stanpit BH23: Chri 1A 64
Stanpit Marsh Nature Reserve 2H 63
Stanton Rd. BH10: Bour 3E 41
STAPEHILL 4E 17
Stapehill Cres. BH21: Hay 4C 16
Stapehill Rd. BH21: Lit C, Stap 4E 17
Staple Cl. La. BH15: Poole 1A 56
Staplecross La. BH23: Burt 5H 45
Stapleford Av. BH22: Fern 3D 18
Star La. BH24: Ring 4B 8
Starlight Farm Cl. BH31: Ver 2E 7
Station App. BH18: Broad 1G 37
BH25: New M 2G 49
SO42: Broc 3F 73
Station Rd. BH14: Poole 3F 57
BH15: Hamw 6G 55
BH21: W Min 6F 15
BH22: W Moo 3B 10
BH23: Chri 6E 45
BH23: Hin 2G 47
BH25: New M 2G 49
BH31: Ver 2B 6
SO41: Sway 1F 33
Station St. SO41: Lymi 1H 53
Station Ter. BH21: W Min 5F 15
Staunton BH2: Bour 5H 5
Steamer Point Local Nature Reserve 6G 47
Steamer Point Vis. Cen. 1F 65
Stedman Rd. BH5: Bour 2H 61
Steepdene BH14: Poole 4F 57
Steeple Cl. BH17: Poole 2B 38
Steepleton Rd. BH18: Broad 3A 38
Stella Ct. BH23: Highc 6B 48
Stem La. BH25: Bash, New M 6E 31
Stem La. Ind. Est. BH25: New M 2E 49
Stem La. Trad. Est. BH25: New M 2E 49
Stenhurst Rd. BH15: Poole 1C 56
Stephanie Ct. *BH16: Upt* *6D 36*
(off Poole Rd.)
Stephen Langton Dr. BH11: Bour 6H 23
Stephen's Castle Nature Reserve 1E 7
Stephen's Wlk. *BH24: Ring* *4B 8*
(off Lyne's La.)
Stepnell Reach BH16: Hamw 2C 54
STERTE 1A 4 (3H 55)
Sterte Av. BH15: Poole 3H 55
Sterte Av. W. BH15: Poole 3H 55
Sterte Cl. BH15: Poole 3H 55
Sterte Ct. BH15: Poole 1B 4 (3A 56)
Sterte Esplanade BH15: Poole 1B 4 (4A 56)
Sterte Ind. Est. BH15: Poole 3H 55
Sterte Rd. BH15: Poole 1B 4 (4A 56)
Stevenson Cres. BH14: Poole 4H 57
Stevenson Lodge BH4: Bour 4E 59
Stevenson Rd. BH6: Bour 4E 63
Stevensons Cl. BH21: W Min 5E 15
Stewart Cl. BH8: Bour 2C 60
Stewart Mews *BH8: Bour* *2C 60*
(off Stewart Cl.)
Stewart Rd. BH8: Bour 1A 60
Stewarts Way BH22: Fern 2C 18
Stibbs Way BH23: Bran 2D 28
Stillmore Rd. BH11: Bour 2H 39
Stillwater Pk. BH24: Poul 1E 9
Stinsford Cl. BH9: Bour 1B 42
Stinsford Rd. BH17: Poole 4B 38
Stirling Bus. Pk. BH21: Stap 2F 17
Stirling Cl. BH25: New M 2H 49
Stirling Ct. *BH1: Bour* *4D 60*
(off Manor Rd.)
BH4: Bour *5E 59*
(off Portarlington Rd.)
BH8: Bour 6B 42
BH25: New M 2H 49
Stirling Rd. BH3: Bour 6G 41
Stirling Way BH23: Mude 1D 64
Stirrup Cl. BH16: Upt 6D 36
BH21: Cole 3C 16
Stoborough Dr. BH18: Broad 3F 37
Stockbridge Cl. BH17: Poole 3F 39
Stocks Farm Rd. BH22: W Par 2H 25
Stockwood Ct. *BH2: Bour* *2H 59*
(off St Winifred's Rd.)
Stoke Prior *BH4: Bour* *4E 59*
(off Poole Rd.)
Stokes Av. BH15: Poole 3A 56
Stokewood Leisure Cen. 6A 42
Stokewood Rd. BH3: Bour 1H 59
STONE 3C 14
Stonechat Cl. BH22: Fern 1H 17
Stonechat Ct. BH23: Chri 6B 46
Stone Cl. BH15: Hamw 6G 55
Stonecrop Cl. BH18: Broad 3E 37
Stone Gdns. BH8: Bour 3G 43
Stone La. BH21: W Min 3C 14
Stone La. Ind. Est. BH21: W Min 3C 14
Stoneleigh BH13: Poole 1B 70
Stoneleigh Av. SO41: Hor 1D 50
Stony La. BH23: Burt, Chri 2F 45
Stony La. Sth. BH23: Chri 1G 63
Stopples La. SO41: Hor 1D 50
Story La. BH18: Broad 1H 37
Stourbank Rd. BH23: Chri 1E 63
Stourcliffe Av. BH6: Bour 3A 62
Stour Cl. BH21: Lit C 5D 16
Stour Ct. *BH12: Poole* *3C 58*
(off Princess Rd.)
Stourcroft Dr. BH23: Chri 3B 44
Stourfield Rd. BH5: Bour 3H 61
Stour Gdns. BH10: Bour 1G 41
Stourpaine Rd. BH17: Poole 3B 38
Stour Pk. BH10: Bour 5G 25
Stour Rd. BH8: Bour 1C 60
BH23: Chri 2D 62
Stourton *BH4: Bour* *4E 59*
(off Marlborough Rd.)
Stourvale Av. BH23: Chri 5B 44
Stourvale M. BH6: Bour 1A 62
Stourvale Pl. BH5: Bour 2H 61
Stourvale Rd. BH5: Bour 2H 61
BH6: Bour 2H 61
Stour Valley Nature Reserve 6H 25
Stourview Ct. BH6: Bour 2A 62
Stour Vw. Gdns. BH21: Cor M 2E 21
Stour Wlk. BH8: Bour 1D 42
BH21: W Min 6F 15
Stour Way BH23: Chri 3B 44
Stourwood Av. BH6: Bour 4A 62
Stourwood Lodge BH6: Bour 3A 62
Stourwood Rd. BH6: Bour 3B 62
Stouts La. BH23: Bran 2D 28
Strand St. BH15: Poole 5A 4 (6H 55)
Stratfield Pl. BH25: New M 2E 49
Stratford Pl. SO41: Lymi 6F 35
Strathmore Dr. BH31: Ver 3E 7
Strathmore Rd. BH9: Bour 1A 42
Stratton Rd. BH9: Bour 1C 42
Strete Mt. BH23: Chri 6A 46
Stretton Ct. BH14: Poole 3F 57
Strides La. BH24: Ring 4B 8
Strode Gdns. BH24: St I 2D 12
Stroud Cl. BH21: Cole 3A 16
STROUDEN 4E 43
Strouden Av. BH8: Bour 4B 42
Strouden Rd. BH9: Bour 4A 42
Stroud Gdns. BH23: Chri 1A 64
Stroud La. BH23: Chri 1A 64
Stroud Pk. Av. BH23: Chri 1A 64
Struan Cl. BH24: Ashl H 1B 12
Struan Ct. BH24: Ashl H 1C 12
Struan Dr. BH24: Ashl H 1C 12
Struan Gdns. BH24: Ashl H 1B 12
Stuart Cl. BH16: Upt 6B 36
Stuart Rd. BH23: Highc 5B 48
Stubbings Mdw. (Caravan Pk.) BH24: Ring 4A 8
Studland Dene *BH4: Bour* *6E 59*
(off Studland Rd.)
Studland Dr. SO41: M Sea 2C 66
Studland Rd. BH4: Bour 6E 59
Studley Cl. BH23: Highc 5C 48
Studley Ct. BH25: New M 5D 48
Sturminster Rd. BH9: Bour 1D 42
Sturt La. BH8: Bour 2H 43
Suffolk Av. BH23: Chri 4D 44
Suffolk Cl. BH21: Cole 3C 16
Suffolk Rd. BH2: Bour 3E 5 (4F 59)
(not continuous)
Suffolk Rd. Sth. BH2: Bour 3F 59
Summercroft Way BH22: W Moo 4C 10
Summerfield Cl. BH21: Hay 5B 16
BH23: Burt 3G 45
Summer Flds. BH31: Ver 5D 6
Summerfields BH7: Bour 6F 43
Summerhill BH13: S'bks 6G 69

Summers Av.—Tresillian Way

Summers Av. BH11: Bour .5D 24
Summer's La. BH23: Burt .4H 45
Summertrees Ct. BH25: A'ley .1B 50
Sunbury Cl. BH11: Bour .5C 24
Sunbury Ct. BH2: Bour .3F 5
BH4: Bour .4E 59
(off Marlborough Rd.)
Sunderland Dr. BH23: Chri .6D 46
Sundew Cl. BH23: Chri .4E 47
BH25: A'ley .1B 50
Sundew Rd. BH18: Broad .3E 37
Sunningdale BH4: Bour .4E 59
(off Portarlington Rd.)
BH15: Poole .4C 56
BH23: Chri .1D 62
Sunningdale Cres. BH10: Bour .1E 41
Sunningdale Gdns. BH18: Broad .6G 21
Sunnybank Dr. BH21: Cole .3B 16
Sunnybank Rd. BH21: Cole .3B 16
Sunnybank Way BH21: Cole .3B 16
Sunnyfield Rd. BH25: B Sea .5G 49
Sunny Hill Ct. BH12: Poole .2H 57
Sunnyhill Rd. BH6: Bour .2H 61
BH12: Poole .2H 57
Sunnylands Av. BH6: Bour .3D 62
Sunnyleigh M. BH8: Bour .2C 60
Sunnymoor Rd. BH11: Bour .4C 40
Sunnyside Pk. (Caravan Site) BH24: St I .2E 13
Sunnyside Rd. BH12: Poole .6H 39
Sunridge Cl. BH12: Poole .1C 58
Sunridge Shades BH14: Poole .4G 57
Sunrise Ct. BH22: Fern .4B 18
Sunset Lodge BH13: Poole .5C 58
Surrey Cl. BH23: Chri .3D 44
Surrey Ct. BH4: Bour .3E 59
Surrey Gdns. BH4: Bour .3E 59
Surrey Glade BH4: Bour .3E 59
(off Surrey Rd.)
Surrey Ho. BH2: Bour .3F 59
Surrey Lodge BH4: Bour .3F 59
Surrey Rd. BH2: Bour .3F 59
BH4: Bour .3E 59
BH12: Poole .2C 58
Surrey Rd. Sth. BH4: Bour .3E 59
Sussex Cl. BH9: Bour .1B 42
Sutherland Av. BH18: Broad .6E 21
Sutton Cl. BH17: Poole .3F 39
Sutton Pl. SO42: Broc .3F 73
Sutton Rd. BH9: Bour .4B 42
Swallow Cl. BH17: Poole .5F 37
Swallow Dr. SO41: M Sea .3E 67
Swallow Way BH21: Cole .2A 16
Swan Mead BH24: Hight .5E 9
Swanmore Cl. BH7: Bour .6H 43
Swanmore Rd. BH7: Bour .1H 61
Swansbury Dr. BH8: Bour .3H 43
SWAY .2F 33
Sway Ct. SO41: Sway .3G 33
Sway Gdns. BH8: Bour .3D 42
Sway Pk. Ind. Est. SO41: Sway .2F 33
Sway Rd. BH25: Bash, New M .5G 31
SO41: Lymi, Penn .6A 34
SO41: Tip .5G 31
SO42: Broc .6E 73
Sway Station (Rail) .2F 33
Sweep, The BH24: Ring .4B 8
Swift Cl. BH17: Poole .5F 37
Swordfish Dr. BH23: Chri .6D 46
Sycamore Cl. BH17: Poole .4F 37
BH23: Chri .5B 44
SO41: M Sea .2C 66
Sycamore Ct. BH24: Poul .1E 9
Sycamore Pl. BH21: Stap .4D 16
Sycamore Rd. SO41: Hor .1D 50
Sycamores, The BH4: Bour .3F 59
(off Surrey Rd.)
Sydling Cl. BH17: Poole .3F 39
Sydney Rd. BH18: Broad .2G 37
BH23: Chri .4C 44
Sylmor Gdns. BH9: Bour .3A 42
Sylvan Cl. BH24: St L .3H 11
SO41: Hor .3F 51
Sylvan Rd. BH12: Poole .1F 57
Sylvan Wood BH23: Highc .6G 47
Symes Rd. BH15: Hamw .3E 55

T

TADDEN .2A 14
Tadden Wlk. BH18: Broad .3F 37
Tait Cl. BH17: Poole .6C 38
Talbot Av. BH3: Bour .5F 41
Talbot Ct. BH3: Bour .5F 41
(off Talbot Av.)
BH9: Bour .4H 41
Talbot Dr. BH12: Poole .5D 40
BH23: Chri .3H 47
TALBOT HEATH .6E 41
Talbot Hill Rd. BH9: Bour .5F 41
Talbot Mdws. BH12: Poole .5D 40
Talbot M. BH10: Bour .4D 40
Talbot Ri. BH10: Bour .3E 41
Talbot Rd. BH9: Bour .5F 41
Talbot Rdbt. BH3: Bour .6F 41
TALBOT VILLAGE .4E 41
TALBOT WOODS .6F 41
Tamar Cl. BH22: Fern .4E 19
Tamlyn's Farm Mews BH23: Chri .1H 63
(off Purewell)
Tammy Ct. BH8: Bour .2B 60
(off Ascham Rd.)
Tamworth Rd. BH7: Bour .2F 61
Tanglewood Ct. BH25: New M .2H 49
Tanglewood Lodge BH17: Poole .5F 37
Tangmere Cl. BH23: Mude .1D 64
Tangmere Pl. BH17: Poole .6C 38
Tan Howse Cl. BH7: Bour .5H 43
Tapper Ct. BH21: W Min .5G 15
Tarn Dr. BH17: Poole .4F 37
Tarrant Cl. BH17: Poole .3C 38
Tarrant Rd. BH9: Bour .2B 42
Tarrants, The BH2: Bour .3F 59
Tasman Cl. BH23: Chri .5D 44
Tatnam Cres. BH15: Poole .3B 56
Tatnam Rd. BH15: Poole .3A 56
Tattenham Rd. SO42: Broc .4E 73
Tattersalls BH1: Bour .4C 60
Taverner Cl. BH15: Poole .5B 56
Taylor Dr. BH8: Bour .1D 42
Taylor's Bldgs. BH15: Poole .5B 4 (6A 56)
Taylor Way BH31: Ver .3E 7
Teasel Way BH22: W Moo .6C 10
Tebourba Cotts. SO41: Sway .2F 33
Technology Rd. BH17: Poole .5G 37
Tedder Cl. BH11: Bour .2D 40
Tedder Gdns. BH11: Bour .2D 40
Tedder Rd. BH11: Bour .2D 40
Telford Pl. SO41: M Sea .3E 67
Telford Rd. BH21: Stap .1G 17
Temple M. BH1: Bour .1D 60
Templer Cl. BH11: Bour .4B 40
Temple Trees BH4: Bour .4E 59
(off Portarlington Rd.)
Tennyson Rd. BH9: Bour .3H 41
BH14: Poole .4E 57
BH21: W Min .3E 15
Tensing Rd. BH23: Chri .5A 46
Terence Av. BH17: Poole .4A 38
Terence Rd. BH21: Cor M .6C 20
Tern Ct. BH6: Bour .1B 62
Tern Ho. BH15: Hamw .6G 55
(off Norton Way)
Terrace Rd. BH2: Bour .4F 5 (4G 59)
Terrace Vista BH2: Bour .4G 5
Terrington Av. BH23: Chri .4G 47
Thames All. BH15: Poole .5A 4
Thames Cl. BH22: Fern .3E 19
Thames M. BH15: Poole .5A 4 (6H 55)
Thames St. BH15: Poole .5A 4 (6H 55)
Thatched Cott. Pk. SO43: Lyn .2H 71
Thatchers La. BH23: Shir .1B 28
The ....
Names prefixed with 'The' for example 'The Acorns' are indexed under the main name such as 'Acorns, The'
Theobold Rd. BH23: Bour A .3G 27
Thetchers Cl. BH25: New M .6H 31
Thetford Rd. BH12: Poole .2B 58
Thistlebarrow Rd. BH7: Bour .1E 61
Thistle Cl. BH23: Chri .5E 47
Thomas Lockyer Cl. BH31: Ver .4E 7
Thoresby Ct. BH25: New M .2E 49
Thornbury BH4: Bour .4E 59
(off Marlborough Rd.)
Thornbury Rd. BH6: Bour .3E 63
Thorncombe Cl. BH9: Bour .1B 42
BH17: Poole .4C 38
Thorne Cl. BH31: Ver .3C 6
Thorne Way BH21: Wool .1F 11
Thornfield Dr. BH23: Highc .4H 47
Thornham Rd. BH25: A'ley .2B 50
Thornley Rd. BH10: Bour .1F 41
Thorn Rd. BH17: Poole .2B 38
Thornton Cl. BH21: Cor M .6C 20
Three Acre Cl. BH25: B Sea .5E 49
Three Acre Dr. BH25: B Sea .5F 49
Three Cross Rd. BH21: W Moo .1C 10
BH22: W Moo .2C 10
THREE LEGGED CROSS .2A 10
Three Lions Cl. BH21: W Min .4D 14
THROOP .1D 42
Throop Cl. BH8: Bour .3G 43
Throop Rd. BH8: Bour .6D 26
Throopside Av. BH9: Bour .1D 42
Thrush Rd. BH12: Poole .4G 39
Thursby Rd. BH23: Highc .4H 47
Thwaite Rd. BH12: Poole .2D 58
Tidemill Cl. BH23: Chri .5E 45
Tiffany Cl. SO41: Hor .1D 50
Tilburg Rd. BH23: Chri .6H 45
Tilebarn La. SO42: Broc .6E 73
Tiller Gdns. BH11: Bour .6C 24
Tillingbourne Ct. BH12: Poole .3C 58
(off Princess Rd.)
Timothy Cl. BH10: Bour .6F 25
Tincleton Gdns. BH9: Bour .1B 42
Tins, The SO41: Lymi .1F 53
Tin Yd. La. BH23: Bock .6A 28
TIPTOE .3B 32
Tiptoe Rd. BH25: Woot .2G 31
Tithe Barn SO41: Lymi .6G 35
Tiverton Ct. BH4: Bour .4E 59
(off Marlborough Rd.)
Tivoli Theatre .4D 14
Todber Cl. BH11: Bour .2H 39
Toft Mans. BH1: Bour .4C 60
Tollard Cl. BH12: Poole .5A 40
Tollard Ct. BH2: Bour .6F 5
Tollerford Rd. BH17: Poole .2B 38
Tolpuddle Gdns. BH9: Bour .1B 42
Tolstoi Rd. BH14: Poole .1E 57
Tonge Rd. BH11: Bour .5D 24
Topiary, The BH14: Poole .2D 56
Top La. BH24: Ring .4C 8
Torbay Rd. BH14: Poole .4G 57
Torvaine Pk. BH14: Poole .3E 57
Totland Ct. SO41: M Sea .3C 66
Totmel Rd. BH17: Poole .3E 39
Tourist Info. Cen.
Bournemouth .4H 5 (4H 59)
Christchurch .1F 63
Lymington .1G 53
Lyndhurst .3G 71
Poole .5B 4 (6H 55)
Ringwood .4B 8
Wimborne Minster .5E 15
Tourney Rd. BH11: Bour .5A 24
Towans, The BH13: S'bks .5G 69
Tower Ct. BH1: Bour .1H 5 (3H 59)
BH2: Bour .6E 5 (5G 59)
Tower La. BH21: Cole .3F 15
Tower Pk. BH12: Poole .4F 39
Tower Pk. Leisure Complex .4E 39
Tower Pk. Rdbt. BH17: Poole .6D 38
Tower Rd. BH1: Bour .2E 61
BH13: Poole .5D 58
Tower Rd. W. BH13: Poole .6C 58
Towers Farm BH21: Cor M .4D 20
Towers Way BH21: Cor M .4D 20
Towngate Bri. BH15: Poole .3B 4 (5A 56)
Towngate Ho. BH15: Poole .2D 4
Towngate M. BH24: Ring .5C 8
Towngate Shop. Cen. BH15: Poole .3C 4
TOWNSEND .3G 43
Townsend Cl. BH11: Bour .5D 24
Townsville Rd. BH9: Bour .3B 42
Tozer Cl. BH11: Bour .3B 40
Trafalgar Ct. BH23: Mude .2B 64
Trafalgar Pl. SO41: Lymi .1H 53
Trafalgar Rd. BH9: Bour .6H 41
Tranmere Cl. SO41: Lymi .3H 53
Treebys Cl. BH23: Burt .4H 45
Tree Hamlets BH16: Upt .2C 54
Treeside BH23: Chri .3E 47
Treetops BH4: Bour .3E 59
(off Surrey Rd.)
Trefoil Way BH23: Chri .5E 47
Tregonwell Cl. BH2: Bour .4F 5
Tregonwell Ct. BH2: Bour .4E 5
Tregonwell Rd. BH2: Bour .4F 5 (4G 59)
Trelawney Ct. BH8: Bour .2A 60
Treloen Ct. BH8: Bour .2A 60
(off Wellington Rd.)
Trentham Av. BH7: Bour .5H 43
Trentham Cl. BH7: Bour .5H 43
Trent Way BH22: Fern .3E 19
Tresillian Cl. BH23: Walk .3B 48
Tresillian Way BH23: Walk .3B 48

104 A-Z Bournemouth

SAFETY CAMERA INFORMATION

PocketGPSWorld.com's CamerAlert is a self-contained speed and red light camera warning system for SatNavs and Android or Apple iOS smartphones/tablets. Visit www.cameralert.co.uk to download.

Safety camera locations are publicised by the Safer Roads Partnership which operates them in order to encourage drivers to comply with speed limits at these sites. It is the driver's absolute responsibility to be aware of and to adhere to speed limits at all times.

By showing this safety camera information it is the intention of Geographers' A-Z Map Company Ltd., to encourage safe driving and greater awareness of speed limits and vehicle speed. Data accurate at time of printing.